# Museums *of the* Northwest

Discover the
Best Collections
in Washington,
Oregon, and Lower
British Columbia

## Harriet Baskas

SASQUATCH BOOKS
SEATTLE

Printed in the United States
Distributed in Canada by Raincoast Books Ltd.

02 01 00 99                    5 4 3 2 1

Library of Congress Cataloging in Publication Data

Baskas, Harriet.
    Museums of the Northwest : discover the best collections in Washington, Oregon, and Lower British Columbia / Harriet Baskas.
        p.      cm.
Includes index.
ISBN: 1-57061-152-1
1. Museums—Northwest, Pacific—Guidebooks. 2. Northwest, Pacific—Guidebooks. I. Title.
AM12.N67B37  1999
069'.09795—dc21                    98-51573

Cover photograph: Morton Beebe-S.F. /Corbis
Cover design: Karen Schober
Interior design and composition: Virginia Hand Design
Indexer: Miriam Bulmer
Map: John Zilly

Cover notes: Sculpture pictured on front cover is *Hammering Man* (1992) by Jonathan Borofsky. Doll figure on back cover represents the Royal Canadian Mounted Police (the "Mounties") circa 1930–40. Courtesy of the Vancouver Museum.

Sasquatch Books
615 Second Avenue
Seattle, WA 98104
(206)467-4300
books@SasquatchBooks.com
www.SasquatchBooks.com

# Credits

of the University of Oregon Museum of Art.

page 189: These beaded leather Métis mittens (length 30 cm) reflect the dual heritage of the Métis people, descended from Native American women, mostly Cree or Ojibwa, and French or English fur traders. Collected by S. M. Washburn, 1897-1905; gift of Jessie B. Sterne. Photo by Jack Liu; courtesy of the University of Oregon Museum of Natural History. Below: Photo by Steve Bonini; courtesy of the University of Oregon Museum of Natural History.

page 191: Courtesy of the Dolly Wares Doll Museum.

page 212: Photo by Ron Richmond; courtesy of the Jensen Arctic Museum.

page 215: Photo by Mary Catherine Lamb.

page 217: Courtesy of the Oregon Coast History Center.

page 226: Courtesy of the Tamastslikt Cultural Institute Museum.

page 228: Photo by Gary Tarleton, Corvallis, Oregon; courtesy of the Benton County Historical Museum.

page 229: Courtesy of the American Advertising Museum.

page 231: Courtesy of Kidd's Toy Museum.

page 232: Courtesy of Lilah Callen Holden Elephant Museum.

page 233, 234: Courtesy of the Oregon History Center.

page 237: Photo by Burt Peterson; courtesy of the Oregon Museum of Science and Industry.

page 239: Above: Le Petit Patisserie (circa 1922), oil on canvas by Chaim Soutine. Right: Helen with Apples (1981), painted plaster and wood sculpture by George Segal (243.6 cm). Both courtesy of the Portland Art Museum.

page 241: Photo by Ross Reynolds.

page 251: Egyptian male coffin mask, late period. Sycamore wood with black underpainting and traces of white plaster and green and red paint (12 3/4 x 7 1/2 inches). Gift of Mark and Janeth Hogue Sponenburgh, 1990; courtesy of the Hallie Ford Museum of Art.

page 253: Courtesy of the Mission Mill Village and Mission Mill Museum.

page 265: Courtesy of the Union County Museum.

page 267: Native American saddle, beaded bag, parfleche, and leather whip. Courtesy of The Museum at Warm Springs.

## British Columbia

Section opener, page 267: Top: Wool button blanket of Kwagiutl origin (Canada). Courtesy of the Museum of Anthropology, University of British Columbia. Middle: Doll figure representing the Royal Canadian Mounted Police (the "Mounties"), circa 1930-40. Courtesy of the Vancouver Museum.

Bottom: Argillite panel of Haida origin (Canada), circa 1890. Gift of Dr. Walter Koerne; courtesy of the Museum of Anthropology, University of British Columbia.

page 270: Courtesy of the B.C. Museum of Mining.

page 274: Untitled work (1994) by ceramic artist Steven Heinemann. Courtesy of the Canadian Craft Museum.

page 275: Courtesy of Granville Island Sport Fishing and Model Ships Museums.

page 277: Top: Coast Salish (Canada/U.S.) wooden mat creaser on loan from the Canadian Museum of Civilization, Hull; courtesy of the Museum of Anthropology, University of British Columbia. Bottom: Red cedar totem poles in Great Hall of Haida and Tsimshian origin (Canada). Courtesy of the Museum of Anthropology, University of British Columbia.

page 279: Indian House Interior with Totems (1912) oil on canvas by Emily Carr (30 x 40 inches). Courtesy of the Vancouver Art Gallery.

page 281: Photo of model courtesy of the Vancouver Maritime Museum.

page 284: Right: Courtesy of the Art Gallery of Greater Victoria. Below: Above the Gravel Pit (1936) oil on canvas by Emily Carr (30 x 40 inches). Courtesy of the Art Gallery of Greater Victoria.

page 287: Courtesy of the Maritime Museum of British Columbia.

page 289: Courtesy of the Royal British Columbia Museum.

page 291: First three baskets are made of cedar with cherry bark imbrication, far right basket made of cedar with cherry bark and reedgrass imbrication. Photo courtesy of the White Rock Museum and Archives.

# CONTENTS

# BRITISH COLUMBIA

## ACKNOWLEDGMENTS

Giant thanks to the collectors and curators who make sure these museums are open to the public and filled with wonderful things; to Adam Woog, a generous soul who first suggested sharing these stories on paper—and then made it happen; and to 'tipsters' and museum-lovers including Mary Catherine Lamb, Donna Bishop, Barbara "Biscuit" Hansel, Bea Nickel, Rachel Price, Bart Ripp, Bob Rini, Cheryl Smalley, and the folks at KBCS, KSER, and KUOW.

Special thanks also to Anne Depue, who made sure the path was clear and ventured out there herself; to keen-eyed and good-humored Meg Heffernan, who saw the project through; to Kate Rogers, who barely flinched when I brought word of a newly discovered cache of taxidermied two-headed calves; to copyeditor Sherri Schultz, who insisted I learn the difference between a highway and a state route; to industrious proofreader Amy Smith Bell; and to the rest of the talented folks at Sasquatch who made sure this book reads right, looks good, and is in your hands.

And, finally, I thank my mom and dad and my brothers, who are proud of me no matter what curious path I take; and most especially, my husband, Ross, who's sick and tired of hearing about that giant hairball and all those two-headed calves. Thank goodness he's not sick and tired of me.

# A Few Notes about This Book

Many museums in this book are quite small and are staffed by volunteers. The author has gone to great lengths to ensure that all of the information listed for each museum is accurate and up-to-date, but there may be inconsistencies as to when a museum is open. Please call ahead to confirm **hours.** Many smaller museums and collections will also open for visitors by special appointment if given prior notice. The author has listed which museums are open "by appointment," but if you plan to be in an area when a specific museum will be closed, don't hesitate to call and ask about its policies—you may get lucky and receive a private narrated tour!

Museum **admission** charges vary widely. As such, the author has indicated whether a museum admits visitors for free, by donation, or by admission fee. Most admission prices fall between $3-10 and usually there are **discounts** for kids or seniors; call ahead for specific prices. Many larger museums have a "free day" once a month (and sometimes an additional "free day" for kids and/or seniors); the author has also included this information when available.

Finally, many museums offer **special events:** classes, readings, musical recitals, film series, lectures, tours, performances, and so on. Often the prices for these events are quite reasonable and occasionally events or special exhibits are free. Take advantage of the wonderful treats offered by your local museum or any collections or exhibits you encounter while traveling through the Pacific Northwest.

## INTRODUCTION

The giant hairball came later.

First it was the taxidermied bucking horse, the freeze-dried cats, the rosary made of giant Styrofoam balls, and the carefully-mounted barbed wire samples. These treasures, each proudly displayed and lovingly cared for, are just a few of the gems that caught my eye when I first moved west in 1980 and started visiting museums throughout the region.

My museum visits turned into adventures once I started reading labels and asking questions. I learned, for example, that the bucking horse was well-known on the rodeo circuit, and that those freeze-dried cats were once well-loved pets. I heard the story of how the Styrofoam rosary came into being as a prop in a school play, and how, back in the days before electric fences, every knot of barbed wire was named and registered.

By examining the old tools, vintage clothing, and assorted memorabilia that citizens save and display in their town museums, I also learned about local history, agriculture, economics, and business; the power of true love and determination; and heard stories of the sort of experiences that can bind together the citizens of a small community. At the Forks Timber Museum in Forks, Washington, for example, there's no questioning the community's reliance on timber and its reverence for loggers. And at the Oregon Coast History Center in Newport, Oregon, it's clear that folks still have bright memories of Lulu Miller (Nye), who posed in a tiara of lightbulbs for a portrait commemorating her role as "Miss Electricity 1891."

These museum adventures turned serious (some might say a bit obsessive) when I began insisting that others hear detailed accounts of my discoveries. First it was over dinner with friends, then it was on the radio in a series heard nationally on public radio. In 1993 I hooked up with Seattle writer Adam Woog to write *Atomic Marbles and Branding Irons,* a book highlighting 130 of our favorite offbeat museums, curiosities, and collections throughout the Northwest. You now hold in your hands my far more inclusive guide to (almost) all the Northwest museums, which I hope you'll take with you on the road as you head out on your own adventures.

The book lists more than 325 Northwest museums. That seems like a lot. It certainly *felt* like a lot when I was out on the road doing site visits. And it was way too many for my husband who drove with me, in an un-air-conditioned car, to 35 museums in eastern Washington over one stiflingly hot weekend. Despite my determination to include every possible collection, there remain dozens of museums that were missed and others that we just didn't have room to include. So I apologize ahead of time if I passed over one of your favorite spots, and beg you to drop me a note to let me know what jewels I've missed.

Please enjoy reading this book and don't forget to bring it along as you explore the Northwest. Oh, and don't pass up the opportunity to visit my favorite museum exhibit: the giant hairball at the Mount Angel Abbey Museum in Mount Angel, Oregon. This 2 1/2-pound behemoth was discovered in the belly of a hog slaughtered at a meatpacking plant back in 1941, and has been under curatorial care at the monastery for quite some time. Why is it there and why do they keep this thing around? It doesn't really matter. I just love that it *is* there, nestled in among the museum's rare religious artifacts, military memorabilia, and assorted "collectobelia" that includes a really big ear of corn and a taxidermied eight-legged calf.

*Harriet Baskas*

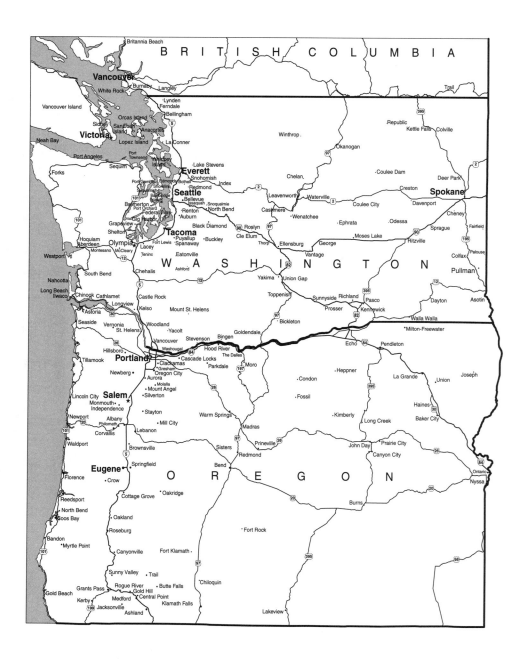

# Washington

■ **Aberdeen Museum of History**
111 E Third Street
Aberdeen, WA 98520
(360)533-1976

Maybe it's because the town was "pretty much wiped out by the 1903 fire," mused one Aberdeen Museum of History volunteer, "that we not only have a miniature model of what Aberdeen looked like before the fire, but also a collection of antique fire trucks and firefighting equipment. We have an old steam pumper used to help fight the 1903 'big one,' an Old Tiger hand pumper built in 1855, and a 1926 Ahrens Fox. They weren't going to get burned again."

Located in a historic National Guard armory, the museum also displays an extensive canoe collection, vintage photographs from in and around Aberdeen, farming equipment, and well-stocked, full-size dioramas of an early-day kitchen, bedroom, schoolhouse, church, and general store. A narrated slide show relates highlights in Aberdeen history, a video shows old steam locomotives in action, and the logging exhibit includes tools and detailed information about the days when more than 28 sawmills operated in the area.

> *Hours: Mid-June to mid-Sept: Wed–Sun 11am–4pm. Rest of year:*
> *Sat–Sun noon–4pm.*
> *Admission free.*
> *Directions: From northbound Highway 101, turn right on Broadway and*
> *right on E Third Street.*

■ **Anacortes Museum**
1305 Eighth Street
Anacortes, WA 98221
(360)293-1915

Amos Bowman had big plans for Anacortes. By 1876 he'd moved to the eastern area of Ship Harbor, established a post office, and named the town for his wife, Anna Curtis. Then he set about trying to get the town selected as the terminus for the transcontinental railroad. This led to a boomtown atmosphere, with sky-high speculation boosting the population, the price of building lots, and hopes for great fortunes. By late 1890, though, it was clear that Anacortes would not be chosen as the terminus. Folks left, fortunes were lost, and the future looked grim. But a year later, Anacortes incorporated as a city and began re-creating itself as a fishing and logging town.

The Anacortes Museum, housed in an old Carnegie library building, features changing exhibits as well as permanent displays of artifacts and archival materials ranging from colorful cannery labels to a full-size recreation of the offices of the Fidalgo Island Cannery Company, one of a dozen or more fish-processing facilities that once operated in the area.

One wall sports a large six-by-five-foot oil-on-canvas painting titled *Anacortes in 1891*, depicting a view of Cape Sante, Fidalgo Bay, and Mount Baker. It's unsigned but was supposedly painted by a down-on-his-luck artist in exchange for room and board at a local hotel. Out front is a drinking-fountain statue dedicated to Carrie White, a hardworking local temperance activist. The statue includes a basin for dogs at the bottom, one for horses in the middle, and another for people on top.

The collection also includes a National Historic Landmark vessel, the *W. T. Preston*. Preserved in a dry berth four blocks from the museum headquarters, the *W. T. Preston* offers visitors a close-up look at a snagboat that was used to remove navigational hazards (such as logs) from Puget Sound rivers and tributaries. When the *W. T. Preston* was retired in 1981, it was the last working sternwheeler on Puget Sound and is now one of only two remaining snagboats in the United States.

In addition to tours of the snagboat, the museum offers educational workshops and sponsors special events such as the Steam and Gas Engine Day in September.

> *Hours: Museum: Thurs–Mon 1pm–5pm.* W. T. Preston: *Memorial Day to Labor Day: Daily 11am–5pm. April–May, Sept: Sat–Sun 11am–5pm.*
> *Admission by donation.*
> *Directions: From I-5, take exit 230 (westbound State Route 20) and turn right on Commercial Avenue. For the museum, turn left on Eighth Street and follow it three blocks to M Avenue. For the* W. T. Preston, *turn right on Ninth Street and drive two blocks to R Avenue.*

## ASHFORD

### ■ Longmire Museum (Mount Rainier National Park)
State Route 706
Ashford, WA 98304
(360)569-2211 ext 3314

If you're visiting Mount Rainier National Park, it's probably the outdoors you're interested in seeing. But take a moment to visit the Longmire Museum, just inside the Nisqually Gate entrance, and you'll be treated to exhibits featuring taxidermied animals, large Native American baskets, and information about the history, geology, and naming of Mount Rainier.

In case you don't get to see them live and up close in the park, the museum displays a variety of animals that were caught and taxidermied as far back as the 1930s, including a cougar, a beaver, a bobcat, an owl, a snowshoe hare, and a porcupine. In the history exhibit you'll learn about the first people who settled the park, the mountain's first climbers, and the story of how George Vancouver named Mount Rainier and many other Northwest peaks in honor of his buddies back home in England.

> *Web site: www.nps.gov/mora/interp.htm*
> *Hours: Daily 9am–5pm.*
> *Admission free with park entry fee.*
> *Directions: The museum is just inside the Nisqually Gate, at the southwest entrance to the park. From I-5, take exit 141 to State Route 161. Drive through Eatonville and head south on State Route 7 to Elbe. When State Route 7 turns into State Route 706, continue straight ahead to the park. The museum is a small structure across from the park administration building.*

## ASOTIN

### ■ Asotin County Historical Museum
Third and Filmore (PO Box 367)
Asotin, WA 99402
(509)243-4659

Headquartered in a former funeral home, the Asotin County Historical Museum displays a wide assortment of community artifacts, including an old printing press, a treadmill-powered washing machine, an old telephone switchboard, vintage photographs, tools, and about a dozen timepieces from a 400-piece clock collection that once belonged to a local resident.

Stepping stones lead visitors to historic structures that have been restored and relocated to the museum grounds. These include a sheep-

Ask about a tour on the sternwheeler *Jean,* docked in Asotin's Snake River

herder's cabin built in the 1930s, a schoolhouse built in 1927, a log cabin built in 1882, a windmill, and a "country toilet" from a nearby ranch. The *Salmon River* barge is a reproduction of the ones used on the Salmon River years ago to bring supplies to miners and homesteaders. Few original barges of this type exist because once they arrived at their destination and offloaded their shipments, the barges were torn apart so the lumber could be used for other purposes.

Don't miss the 1901 Pole Barn, officially the "Ziegler, Lightfoot, Gordon, Thiessen" barn. It houses several buggies, including a classic surrey with a fringe on top, as well as Bob Weatherly's collection of close to 200 branding irons from Asotin, Garfield, and Nez Perce Counties.

*Hours: Tues–Sat 1pm–5pm.*
*Admission by donation.*
*Directions: From Clarkston, follow southbound State Route 129 for five*
*miles to Asotin. The museum is two blocks from the courthouse*
*on Filmore.*

## AUBURN

### ■ White River Valley Museum
918 H Street SE
Auburn, WA 98002
(253)939-4523

Auburn, known these days as the home of the Supermall and the Emerald Downs racetrack, was a hop farming center in the late 1800s and later served as the western freight terminus of the Northern Pacific Railroad.

Located in the city's Les Gove Park, the White River Valley Museum, which was renovated in 1998, features interpretive exhibits depicting the Auburn area as it might have looked from the 1860s through the 1920s. Along the way, visitors learn about farming and logging, visit a 1915 Japanese American farmhouse, and stroll through re-creations of shops in downtown Auburn circa 1920.

Almost all the exhibits feature some interactive and hands-on activity. For example, in the *Auburn Depot* you can warm up near the potbellied stove and get your picture taken with the conductor. In the *Japanese-American Farmhouse* you can learn to fold origami, listen in on a conversation about the food being prepared for a Buddhist holiday dinner, and leaf through a family scrapbook. And in *Downtown's* shops you can try on hats, look over the entries to a photo contest, and hear customers in James Cugini's public market discuss all the changes happening in town.

In addition to these exhibits, the museum houses South King County's largest collection of artifacts and archival material regarding the Japanese American (Nikkei) experience and the history of Japanese Americans in the White River valley.

*Hours: Wed–Fri 9:30am–4:30pm, Sat–Sun noon–4:30pm.*
*Admission charged.*
*Directions: From I-5, take State Route 18 exit east to Auburn, then take*
*    the Auburn Way exit. Turn left on Auburn Way and follow the brown*
*    MUSEUM/LIBRARY signs into Les Gove Park.*

## BAINBRIDGE ISLAND

### ■ Bainbridge Island Historical Museum
7650 NE High School Road
Bainbridge Island, WA 98110
(206)842-2773

It's a rare day that offers up a chance to inspect a creosote chamber. But you'll find one of these huge shiny cylinders sitting out in front of the restored 1908 one-room schoolhouse that's now the Bainbridge Island Historical Museum.

The timber-savvy folks inside will tell you how the chamber was used to treat large timbers, and how the site where the ferry now docks was once home to one of the world's largest sawmills. You'll also find turn-of-the-century photos, maps, and other artifacts that revisit the town's glory days, when vast cargoes of timber were loaded onto big ships and when hotels and stores dotted the bustling waterfront.

Other exhibits relate the sad story of the internment of the island's Japanese residents during World War II, and how Bainbridge became the first community to send American-born Japanese people to such camps.

*Hours: May to Sept: Wed–Sun 1pm–4pm. Oct to April: Call for hours.*
*Admission by donation.*
*Directions: From the Bainbridge Island ferry dock, follow Highway 305,*
*    turn left at NE High School Road (at the Safeway), continue past*
*    the four-way intersection to the STRAWBERRY HILL PARK sign, and*
*    turn right.*

## BELLEVUE

### ■ Bellevue Art Museum
Bellevue Square, Third Floor
NE Eighth Street and Bellevue Way NE
Bellevue, WA 98004
(425)454-3322

The Bellevue Art Museum (BAM) is a nontraditional museum. Not only is it on the third floor of a mall, but it owns no art and has no plans to acquire any, despite the fact that it will be moving into its very own, considerably larger $20 million facility just east of the mall at the end of the year 2000. Instead of acquiring art, BAM focuses on offering an ambitious schedule of five changing exhibitions each year as well as a wide variety of special events, held both inside and outside the museum.

Exhibitions might be single-artist retrospectives, group shows of work created around a theme, or touring exhibits from museums around the country. Each summer BAM hosts the Pacific Northwest Annual, which highlights the work of artists from throughout the region, as well as the Pacific Northwest Arts Fair. The fair, which is more than 50 years old, features art demonstrations, visual art exhibitions, the work of more than 300 artists, and a children's fair that lets young artists make their own creations.

Special programs include an evening series of readings and lectures by area artists and poets, performances, artists-in-action, art history classes, videos, and a variety of hands-on workshops for children and adults throughout the year. The museum also offers docent-led tours of selected exhibitions in eight different languages (not all at the same time): English, French, German, Italian, Japanese, Russian, Spanish, and American Sign Language.

BAM's new facility will be located at the corner of NE Bellevue Way and NE Sixth Street, directly across the street from its current location in Bellevue Square. Architect Steven Holl, who also designed the Chapel at St. Ignacius at Seattle University and the Museum of Contemporary Art in Helsinki, Finland, is designing the new 36,000-square-foot building. Scheduled to open at the beginning of the year 2001, the bigger BAM still won't own any artwork, but it will have three exhibition galleries, four permanent classrooms, an artist-in-residence studio, and a two-story-high Explore Gallery devoted to the aesthetics of art, the elements of visual art, and visual literacy.

> Web site: www.bellevueart.org
> Hours: Tues and Fri 10am–8pm, Mon, Wed–Thurs, Sat 10am–6pm, Sun 11am–5pm.
> Admission charged. Free Tues.
> Directions: The museum is in downtown Bellevue, four miles east of Seattle and across Lake Washington. From I-405, take the NE Eighth Street (westbound) exit and continue to Bellevue Square, the shopping mall at the corner of NE Eighth Street and Bellevue Way NE.

### ■ Rosalie Whyel Museum of Doll Art
1116 108th Avenue NE
Bellevue, WA 98004
(206)455-1116

"Really cool old dolls" or "fine, priceless antiques"—call them what you may: From rare bisque baby dolls and fine dollhouse miniatures to the latest Barbie or G.I. Joe, there's something for everyone at the Rosalie Whyel Museum of Doll Art.

Two bisque dolls, circa 1890, made by Jules Steiner

Whyel, the daughter of a wealthy coal family in Alaska, started collecting dolls at 21. Her collection grew to include doll accessories and furniture, toys, games, miniatures, and dollhouses. In 1992 she opened the 13,000-square-foot museum to share her collection with others, in a building that resembles a grand Victorian-style dollhouse.

Whyel's collection comprises more than 3,000 items, and at least half of them are on display at any one time. Related dolls are often grouped in whimsical vignettes: For example, 20 baby dolls fill one case, while a dozen or so early homemade and manufactured dolls are used to explain how doll-making technology evolved in response to the materials available, from rubber, metal, and porcelain to plastic.

Whyel's collection is strong in Victorian-era French and German bisque dolls, but it also includes tiny Egyptian tomb dolls, mechanical dolls from the 1700s, and a papier-mâché English doll from 1690 that's the oldest and perhaps rarest doll in the museum. Other unusual dolls on display include those with multiple faces. Some variously walk, talk, eat, sleep, laugh, cry, and, of course, wet their diapers. One rare doll, the anatomically incorrect Bebe Gourmand model made in 1881, was designed to "eat" a biscuit inserted into her mouth. The biscuit fell down a tube in the doll's body and came out a hole in one of her feet.

There are other surprises throughout the museum in the pullout drawers and closets that help to stretch the available display area and to somewhat satisfy the urge to touch something. Patient visitors to the magical Toy Attic will be rewarded when the train set, rocking horse, and rocking chair come to life.

In addition to the permanent displays, one gallery highlights three or four special, changing exhibits each year. Special programs include seminars and workshops on doll making, doll restoration, and related activities that complement gallery exhibits.

*Web site: www.dollart.com/dollart*
*Hours: Mon–Sat 10am–5pm, Sun 1pm–5pm.*
*Admission charged.*
*Directions: The museum is near downtown Bellevue. From I-405, take the*
*　　NE Eighth Street (westbound) exit and look for signs to the museum.*

## BELLINGHAM

### ■ Bellingham Antique Radio Museum
1315 Railroad Avenue
Bellingham, WA 98225
(360)671-4663

Located in a narrow storefront not too far from a feed store, the Bellingham Antique Radio Museum is stuffed floor to ceiling with more than 1,000 vintage radios and a smattering of old televisions, movie projectors, and audio odds and ends. Jonathan Winter put this collection together, and he helps set the scene by playing vintage radio programs and dressing in vintage outfits.

Ask to see the old crystal sets made from oatmeal boxes, the 1918 DeForest crystal radio built for the U.S. Army Signal Corps, and the rare submarine radio from 1917. Then poke around and try to spot Edison phonographs, vintage microphones, and the 1928 Visionola, a contraption that combined a movie projector with a screen and a sound system that played only records.

*Web site: www.antique-radio.org*
*Hours: Wed–Sat 11am–4pm.*
*Admission free.*
*Directions: From I-5, take the Lakeway Drive exit and turn west on*
*　　Lakeway Drive. Continue for about four blocks to a four-way stop*
*　　where the street turns into E Holly Street. Go west on Holly to Rail-*
*　　road Avenue and turn right. The museum is on the west side of the*
*　　street in the middle of the block.*

### ■ Mindport Exhibits
111 Grand Avenue
Bellingham, WA 98225
(360)647-5614

If your kids liked the hands-on exhibits at the Whatcom Children's Museum (see next listing), head just one block east to Mindport Exhibits, a discovery museum that also features artwork, photography, a Washington native plant display, and a rare static-electricity generator from the 1880s—on loan from the Bellingham Antique Radio Museum (see previous listing).

Exhibits such as *Backwards Speech*, *Eye Mirror*, and *Magnetic Molasses* all teach something about history, construction, logic, math, or science, but it's a painless way to learn—and lots of fun. Museum staff claim they get inspiration for the entertaining exhibits from "odd things and ordinary, serious and silly; elaborate, simple, technical, and artistic." It's true: Everything from computers and magnets to Ping-Pong balls and gnarled driftwood has been drafted into service here. Look for Burl Jives—a wood burl wired for a surprising array of sounds.

*Web site: www.mindport.org/~mindport*
*Hours: Wed–Sun 10am–5pm.*
*Admission free or by donation.*
*Directions: From I-5, take exit 253 and follow the signs to the Whatcom*
*    Museum of History and Art; Mindport Exhibits is one block east.*

■ **Whatcom Museum of History and Art**
**Whatcom Children's Museum**
121 Prospect Street
Bellingham, WA 98225
(360)676-6981

Headquartered in a late Victorian–style building that once served as a city hall, the Whatcom Museum of History and Art now spreads its offerings among four separate buildings.

Head for the main building (Old City Hall, 121 Prospect Street) to see changing history and contemporary art exhibits and, on the third floor, woodworking tools, toys, vintage clothing, and the inner workings of the large clock visible on the building's facade.

Then visit the museum's Syre Education Center (201 Prospect Street), where the Edson-Booth taxidermied bird collection is displayed. This collection, put together by museum founder John Edson, taxidermist Edward Booth, and former Lynden mayor Edward Edson (no relation to John Edson), is composed of more than 500 specimens of taxidermied birds: 28 species of local wild ducks alone, plus owls, loons, woodpeckers, hawks, eagles, and more. The Syre Education Center also displays Victorian-era period rooms and carvings, masks, tools, basketry, and other items from the museum's Northwest Coast First Nations Ethnography Collection.

The Arco Exhibition Gallery (206 Prospect Street) houses major changing art and history exhibitions and often features works chosen from the museum's own collection of contemporary Northwest artists, which includes nearly 1,000 examples of painting, sculpture, photography, and crafts.

Kids will no doubt want to begin their visit at the fourth building, the Whatcom Children's Museum (227 Prospect Street), where the hands-on and interactive exhibits serve as an introduction to the larger themes represented elsewhere in the museum complex.

Special programs include a lunchtime series of lectures, readings, and demonstrations and, at the Whatcom Children's Museum, a variety of "wonder workshops" and daylong fairs.

*Web site: www.cob.org/museum.htm*
*Hours: Museum of History and Art: Tues–Sun noon–5pm. Children's Museum: Sun and Tues–Wed: noon–5pm; Thurs–Sat 10am–5pm.*
*Admission by donation (Museum of History and Art); admission charged (Children's Museum).*
*Directions: From I-5, take exit 253, follow Lakeway Drive west to E Holly Street, and turn right on Prospect Street.*

---

### While You're in Bellingham:

Western Washington University's Western Gallery features changing exhibitions throughout the year, but the permanent outdoor sculpture collection features work by major national, international, and regional artists, including Richard Serra, Isamu Noguchi, Robert Maki, James Fitzgerald, and others. Ask for a map at the University Visitors Center or at the Western Gallery. Both places should also have a brochure offering a self-guided tour of the city's collection of outdoor art and a walking-tour guide to the historic Fairhaven neighborhood.

*Western Gallery, Western Washington University, Fine Arts Complex, Bellingham, WA 98225; (360)650-3963.*
*Gallery Hours: When the university is in session: Mon–Fri 10am–4pm, Sat noon–4pm. Sculptures accessible daylight hours all year round. Admission free.*
*Directions: From I-5, take exit 252 to McDonald Parkway. Turn north, toward the campus, onto S College Drive.*

---

## BICKLETON

■ **Whoop-N-Holler Museum**
1 Whitmore Road
Bickleton, WA 99322
(509)896-2344

Curators from small museums in central and eastern Washington have been known to take field trips themselves to the Whoop-N-Holler Museum in Bickleton, a treasure trove of antiques, curios, whatnots, and exotic memorabilia on Lawrence and Ada Ruth Whitmore's ranch.

"You have to see it to believe it!" exclaims one pioneer-museum curator. "We thought we had a lot of stuff, but this takes the cake!" says another. This is strong praise from the museum community, where local pride and family roots often take a front seat to historical etiquette.

Speaking of a front seat, one of the attractions of the Whoop-N-Holler Museum is Lawrence Whitmore's collection of antique and classic cars. He's filled a large barn with Model T Fords, antique pickup trucks, horse-drawn wagons, and other vintage modes of transportation, including the 1927 Studebaker he drove when he was courting Ada Ruth.

The attraction here isn't just cars. The 1900 Fairview schoolhouse and several other buildings around the property are filled with pioneer memorabilia, historical photographs, and thousands of artifacts that entwine the Whitmores' family tree with the history of eastern Klickitat County. Ask how the Whitmores got that pipe organ, the tin bathtub, the hand-carved doll furniture, or that collection of dubious home remedies, and you'll be treated to an entertaining afternoon of stories that bring local history to life.

*Hours: April 1 to Sept 30: Daily 10am–4pm. Closed rest of year. Admission charged.*

*Directions: From Bickleton, take East Road south for 12 miles to Whitmore Road. The museum is on the Whitmores' ranch on East Road, and is 11 miles north of Roosevelt.*

## BINGEN

### ■ Gorge Heritage Museum
202 E Humboldt Street
Bingen, WA 98605
(509)493-3228

Located in the former Bingen Congregational Church (dedicated in 1912), the Gorge Heritage Museum features a replica country store filled with objects ranging from medicine bottles and jars to original containers of foodstuffs and household implements. Museum curators are proudest of their bottle collection, donated by a well-known bottle expert, and their historical photo collection, which includes early pictures of fishing at Celilo Falls, portraits of early area residents, photos of old sawmills and early buildings, and street scenes. Display cases feature pioneer clothing, logging and farming tools, medical and surgical equipment, and Native American artifacts and crafts. Kids will enjoy the dollhouse and toy collection.

*Hours: Last weekend in May to Sept: Thurs–Sun 11am–4:30pm. Closed rest of year.*

*Admission charged.*

*Directions: The museum is one block north of State Route 14 at Maple and E Humboldt Streets.*

## BLACK DIAMOND

### ■ Black Diamond Historical Museum
32627 Railroad Avenue
Black Diamond, WA 98010
(360)886-2142

The town of Black Diamond was established back in the early 1880s when the Black Diamond Mining Company of California sent miners north in search of high-quality coal. The extremely rich vein that spread from Franklin to Ravensdale established Black Diamond as the largest producer of coal in King County by 1895. Earlier, in 1884, the Black Diamond company had sent 101 people, including Welsh miners and their families, to settle the town and start mining, but by the turn of the century more than 3,000 people lived here, making Black Diamond the fourth-largest city in the state.

Ann Steiert, the curator of the Black Diamond Historical Museum, has lived in Black Diamond since 1926. She remembers the days before community volunteers restored the old railroad depot for a museum, when it was used as a restaurant, a library, a telephone exchange, an office for the water department, and, finally, a storage shed for the city maintenance department. Now it houses a wide array of clothing, tools, and other artifacts relating to the town's coal-mining history, historical photographs of local places and people, and displays showing how households, schools, and businesses were operated in days gone by.

*Hours: Thurs 9am–4pm, Sat–Sun noon–3pm.*
*Admission by donation.*
*Directions: From State Route 169, turn west onto Baker Street and turn*
   *south onto Railroad Avenue.*

## BOTHELL

### ■ Bothell Historical Museum
9919 NE 180th Street (PO Box 313)
Bothell, WA 98041
(425)486-1889

The Bothell Historical Museum is housed in the restored 1893 home of William Hannan, a local businessman who owned a mercantile store. The building has been moved from its original site, on Main Street, to the lovely park at Bothell Landing.

Each room in the house features turn-of-the-century furnishings and artifacts from the community, such as vintage clothing, toys, and quilts. The 1885 Beckstrom Log Cabin, which once housed a pioneer family of 10 and later served as Bothell's first one-room schoolhouse, sits next door to the Hannan House and is filled with school-related memorabilia.

*Hours: Mar to mid-Dec: Sun 1pm–4pm.*
*Admission by donation.*
*Directions: From I-405, take the Bothell/Beardslee exit and follow Beard-*
   *slee Boulevard, which turns into Main Street, which turns into Bothell*
   *Way. Turn left on NE 180th Street. The museum is on the right, par-*
   *allel to the river.*

### ■ Bremerton Naval Museum
130 Washington Avenue
Bremerton, WA 98337
(360)479-7447

Established in 1954 by Rear Admiral Homer N. Wallin, the Bremerton
Naval Museum explores the history of the U.S. Navy, with a particular
focus on the history of the Puget Sound Naval Shipyard.

Exhibits include a wide variety of aircraft-carrier models ranging in
size from four inches to more than 20 feet in length, knotboards, ship's
bells, naval uniforms from around the world, and an assortment of
weapons, including an unexploded mine and two torpedoes.

In addition to exhibits honoring Pearl Harbor, the USS *Washington,*
and other battleships, the museum has a diorama of the Puget Sound
shipyard as it looked during World War II, items that once belonged to
Admiral George Dewey, a bamboo cannon dating from the 1400s, and a
piece of a mastodon tusk that was unearthed when the shipyard was
built.

Kids will enjoy the hands-on replica of a ship's bridge area, complete
with ship's wheel, signaling devices, and heavy mounted Big Eyes, or
binoculars.

> *Hours: Memorial Day to Labor Day: Mon–Sat 10am–5pm, Sun*
> *1pm–5pm. After Labor Day to before Memorial Day: Tues–Sat*
> *10am–5pm, Sun 1pm–5pm.*
> *Admission by donation.*
> *Directions: From the Bremerton ferry dock, follow Washington Avenue. The*
> *museum is on the right at the end of the block.*

### ■ Kitsap County Historical Museum
280 Fourth Street
Bremerton, WA 98337
(360)479-6226

Originally housed in a single room at the courthouse, the Kitsap County
Historical Museum now has its own building in downtown Bremerton,
large enough to display its collection of textiles, Native American artifacts, archaeological finds, and historical objects. Its themed exhibits
include a timeline of Kitsap County, a series of re-created storefronts and
street scenes, and a hands-on kids' area.

The timeline begins with the end of the last ice age and continues
with the history of the local Native people prior to contact with white
settlers, the growth of local industries such as logging and stump
farming, the story of the regional transportation system known as the Mosquito

Fleet, and the establishment of military installations such as the Puget Sound Naval Shipyard.

Visitors can study a scale model of the Suquamish Indian log house known as Old Man House, peer into a floating loggers' bunkhouse, meander along artifact-filled historical street scenes, count the rings on an old-growth tree slab, and feel what it's like to handle a bucksaw.

The interactive children's exhibit offers a mock navy vessel, a working telephone switchboard, and a playhouse full of old-time games, clothes, and furnishings.

*Web site: www.waynes.net/kchsm/*
*Hours: Memorial Day to Labor Day: Daily 10am–5pm, first Fri of the*
  *month 10am–8pm. Rest of year: Tues–Sun 10am–5pm.*
*Admission by donation.*
*Directions: From the Bremerton ferry dock, take Washington Avenue north*
  *to Fourth Street. The museum is three-quarters of the way down the*
  *block, next to the Roxy Theater.*

## BUCKLEY

### ■ Foothills Historical Museum
175 Cottage Street (PO Box 530)
Buckley, WA 98321
No phone

The folks at the Foothills Historical Museum would love for you to stop by and see their "still lifes": a doctor's office, an old still, two different kitchen arrangements, and a turn-of-the-century playroom. They'd also love to show off the old fire engine and buggy on the front lawn and the display cases inside filled with crystal, tools, and other items donated by community members. Then again, if you want to just sit and visit in the comfortable chairs in the front parlor, that's all right too.

Just be sure you don't miss the museum annex across the street. It includes a log cabin built in 1923 as the Forest Service headquarters, two buildings salvaged from the old Lester logging camp, a blacksmith shop, an old Vulcan steam donkey, and other logging equipment.

*Hours: Thurs noon–4pm, Sun 1pm–4pm.*
*Admission free.*
*Directions: From Sumner, take State Route 410 to the center of Buckley.*
  *Turn right on Main Street, drive one block, and turn left on River*
  *Avenue. The museum is in the brown-and-white building a block*
  *down on the right (entrance is on River Avenue).*

## ■ Chelan County Historical Society Museum and Pioneer Village
600 Cotlets Way (PO Box 22)
Cashmere, WA 98815
(509)782-3230

In April 1941, Mrs. Lois Cooke was ready to begin her springtime ritual of preparing her garden for summer. She'd been working the same garden plot behind her home, just downriver from Wenatchee, for more than 50 years, but this spring morning, before she could take shovel to soil, Cooke noticed a black tip sticking out of the ground. It turned out to be a black stone double cross, a rare Native American artifact estimated to be 1,500 to 2,000 years old. Today the stone cross and a photo of Mrs. Lois Cooke in her garden are prominently displayed in the Chelan County Historical Society Museum's main

Visit the kitchen of the Weythman Cabin

exhibit hall, alongside an impressive collection of central Washington artifacts dating back 9,000 years.

The museum's well-known Willis Carey Collection of American Indian and pioneer artifacts on the upper level includes photos of the Wenatchi tribe and other Northwest Coast Native Americans, as well as stone tools, baskets, and headdresses made of porcupine hair and buffalo horn. These items were no doubt exchanged at times for some of the colorful Hudson's Bay Company trading items that are also on display: shiny brass, glass, and copper buttons, thimbles, blankets, and twists of tobacco. The exhibit hall also includes a far-ranging archaeological collection with early tools, personal objects, and artwork ranging from stone and whalebone clubs to petroglyphs or rock art.

Down on the lower level, in the natural history wing, are petrified wood and semiprecious stones from north-central Washington, as well as mineral specimens from around the world. A wide range of taxidermied birds and forest animals populates dioramas depicting various Northwest landscapes during all four seasons. In the Pioneer History Exhibit Hall are tools, household items, musical instruments, and other personal belongings that illustrate the early pioneer lifestyle.

The museum is huge, but save some time and energy to wander out back to the Pioneer Village, which boasts 20 original pioneer structures, relocated here from sites all over Chelan and Douglas Counties. Each building, including the blacksmith shop, the school, the hotel, the saddle shop, and the general store, are furnished with turn-of-the-century artifacts.

Special events include Founder's Day, celebrated with a parade during the last weekend in June, and Apple Days, featuring an apple pie contest, during the first weekend in October.

*Hours: Mar to Oct: Tues–Sun 9:30am–5pm. Closed rest of year.*
*Admission charged. Free first Sat of the month.*
*Directions: From Highway 2, take the Cotlets Way exit into Cashmere. Turn onto Museum Road, which leads right to the museum parking lot.*

## CASTLE ROCK

■ **Castle Rock Exhibit Hall**
147 Front Avenue NW (PO Box 721)
Castle Rock, WA 98611
(360)274-6603

Before 1980, Castle Rock was a classic Northwest fishing and logging town. Timber, smelt, sawmills, and pulp and paper operations kept folks busy. The town was also one of the places tourists passed through on their way to visit nearby scenic Mount St. Helens. All that changed, of course, with the mountain's eruption on May 18, 1980.

Castle Rock Exhibit Hall manager Roberta Dickerson remembers that when the mountain blew, "ash turned the nearby Toutle River thick as pancake batter, and made the water so hot that fish got cooked while they swam!" Area bridges, homes, and businesses were destroyed, and mud and debris from the Cowlitz River overflowed the banks and covered the town's high school football and track field, the motorcycle track, and the fairgrounds. In the aftermath, giant banks of lights burned around the clock while the Army Corps of Engineers worked to dredge the ash and gunk out of the rivers and set things back in order.

Castle Rock ("Where Mount St. Helens Happened") uses its exhibit hall to tell the story of how the mountain changed the town. The museum also documents "pre-mountain days," from the early Cowlitz Indian era to the logging heyday, when area timber workers brought home more than 80 world championship titles in events such as speed climbing, tree topping, women's log rolling, axe throwing, shingle bucking, and Jack-and-Jill bucking.

You'll definitely want to inspect the "before and after" mountain photos, leaf through the scrapbook of newspapers clippings documenting the eruption, and shake your head in wonder at what's left of a particular giant tree splintered by the force of Mount St. Helens. For an unusual perspective on the event, pick up one of the red telephone handsets on the back wall. You'll hear actual radio transmissions that went back and forth between 911 dispatchers and the police.

*Hours: Memorial Day to Sept: Daily 9am–6pm. Oct to May: Wed–Sat 10am–2pm.*

*Admission free.*

*Directions: From I-5, take exit 49 to State Route 504. The museum is in downtown Castle Rock.*

## CATHLAMET

### ■ Wahkiakum County Historical Museum
65 River Street
Cathlamet, WA 98612
(360)795-3954

Wahkiakum County took its name from a Kathlamet Indian village that once stood on the north bank of the Columbia River, near what is now the town of Cathlamet. When Meriwether Lewis and William Clark's expedition came through here, canoes were needed to travel across the river, but today travelers can take a bridge from Cathlamet to Puget Island and continue across the river to Oregon on the Wahkiakum, the last remaining ferry servicing the lower Columbia River.

Cathlamet is also the home of the Wahkiakum County Historical Museum, a museum built by local volunteers on the site of an old Native American burial ground. The museum is filled with Native American artifacts, community photographs, guns, logging equipment, and exhibits about agricultural activities, fishing, and the pioneer way of life.

The museum displays a variety of very early dolls, toys, and doll buggies as well as vintage clothing, sewing machines, medical implements, and the window from an old post office. There are milk cans and coolers in the agricultural exhibit, and a display of nets in the fishing exhibit that help describe the seine fishing done on the river with the aid of horses.

*Hours: May to Oct: Tues–Sun 11am–4pm. Nov to April: Thurs–Sun 1pm–4pm.*
*Admission by donation.*
*Directions: From State Route 4, turn onto Main Street in Cathlamet. The museum is on the corner of River and Division Streets. From Highway 30 at Westport, take the ferry to Puget Island and head toward Cathlamet.*

> ### While You're in Cathlamet:
> To learn more about the history of Cathlamet and the surrounding area, pick up a flyer at the Wahkiakum County Historical Museum describing historic sites around town. The map will point you toward the Pioneer Cemetery, where Chief Wahkiakum is buried, and to the James Birnie Trading Post site. Birnie, the town's first white settler, came to the area around 1846 with the Hudson's Bay Company and named the community Birnie's Retreat. The spot in town where Ulysses S. Grant pitched his tent when he stopped by to visit Birnie is also on the map.

## CHEHALIS

### ■ Lewis County Historical Museum
599 NW Front Way
Chehalis, WA 98532
(360)748-0831

Lewis County, the oldest county in Washington state, once stretched west to the Pacific from the Cowlitz River and north from the Columbia River to the border of Russian Territory. The county is smaller now, ranking sixth in the state, but its role in regional history is celebrated in a big way at this museum in Chehalis.

Housed in the historic 1912 Chehalis railroad depot (where 40 trains still rumble by daily), the Lewis County Historical Museum features four galleries filled with exhibits and information about Chehalis Indian culture, pioneer settlement of Lewis County, and the area's agriculture and logging industries. Well-stocked, life-size dioramas depict everything from a Chehalis Indian village as it might have looked before the arrival of white settlers to a Victorian parlor, a fire lookout post, and early-day schoolrooms and 1920s-style kitchens. In the comfortable hands-on children's area, kids can dress up in vintage clothes, shop in the Mayfield

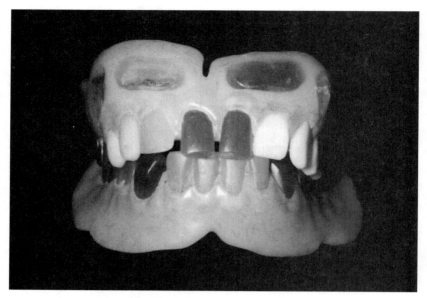

Rockhound Basil Mulford made
and wore these dentures of jade, tiger's eye, and agate

Mercantile, and take home a raised imprint from the seal used by the Chehalis Furniture and Manufacturing Company, which in 1915 was one of the largest plants in the county.

The agricultural exhibits relating to the county's logging and farming history contain some unusual items. Look for the vintage egg incubator capable of coddling 750 eggs at a time, the harpoon hay fork, a set of bejeweled teeth, and the vintage 1906 corn husker designed to be worn on the hand and fastened around the waist. Back among the dioramas depicting everyday life, look for the wooden Indian from the Chehalis Cigar Store and the stage curtain from the John Arnold Grange. Elsewhere in the museum are Northern Pacific Railroad and mining memorabilia, toys, dolls, fashion accessories, and lots of early tools.

Some of those tools might have been used in 1962, when the folks in Centralia built their own version of the Space Needle in an attempt to attract tourists on their way to the Seattle World's Fair. According to a newspaper clipping displayed in the *Celebrating the '60s* exhibit, Centralia's 150-foot Space Needle had its own "astronaut," 18-year-old Loren Wolff, who chatted with tourists on the telephone during his two months' residency in the capsule.

*Hours: Tues–Sat 9am–5pm, Sun 1pm–5pm.*
*Admission charged.*
*Directions: From Olympia, take I-5 to exit 79 and turn left on Chamber Way. Turn right at State Street and left at West Street. Cross two sets of railroad tracks and turn right into the museum parking lot.*

## CHELAN

■ **Lake Chelan Historical Museum**
204 E Woodin Avenue
Chelan, WA 98816
(509)682-5644

Chelan gets plenty of visitors, but few take time to stop by the Lake Chelan Historical Museum, right on the town's main street. Too bad, because this two-story, volunteer-staffed community museum is filled with community treasures—and some surprises.

By far, the highlight is the collection of area apple-crate labels, all neatly arranged in a tall wall-mounted scrapbook. Wenatchee's North Central Washington Museum (see listing) has many more labels in its collection, but I found some new favorites here, including Appletizin, Don't Worry, Young Love, Plen-Tee Color, and Quality Talks.

Along with a large arrowhead and mineral collection, the museum displays a five-foot-wide slab of what is said to have been the area's largest pine tree. The movie projector and the advertisement-filled stage curtain from the town's old Ruby Theater have also found a home here. Downstairs are quilts, a transportation display, dioramas portraying pioneer life, Knut Hjelvik's six-pound raccoon coat, Hudson's Bay Com-

An inventive apple-crate label

pany trading items, a homemade banjo with a woman's head carved on the back, and a handmade cap and flintlock rifles.

Two exhibits remind visitors of the importance of cluttered, attic-like museums like this to a town's collective memory. One, sadly, is the scrapbook filled with newspaper clippings documenting a 1944 school bus accident that killed 15 children. Less tragic, but just as meaningful, is a knickknack-filled display case exhibiting not only valuable glass and porcelain antiques donated by local citizens, but also a wind-up plastic penguin, a yellow rubber lizard, and a small, well-used pincushion. "The connection," a museum volunteer points out, "is that each item is something that was important to someone in our community. Sometimes, though, we forget just who and why."

*Hours: June 1 to Oct 1: Daily 10am–4pm. Closed rest of year.*
*Admission by donation.*
*Directions: The museum is on the corner of E Woodin Avenue and*
*   Emerson Street in downtown Chelan.*

## CHINOOK

### ■ Fort Columbia State Park Interpretive Center
Highway 101
Chinook, WA 98614
(360)777-8221

Three military posts—Forts Canby, Columbia, and Stevens—were built at the mouth of the Columbia River during the Spanish-American War. At Fort Columbia, now a 600-acre Washington State Parks Heritage Site, you can see a dozen original structures from the former army base, including bunkers, searchlight stations, gun batteries, lookouts, a fire station, a theater, and the commanding officer's house, stocked with period antiques.

Historical displays in the Fort Columbia State Park Interpretive Center (in the former Enlisted Men's Barracks) include a mess-hall table set with period silver and china, a kitchen equipped with three coal-fired ranges, an oak refrigerator and a variety of utensils, and a squad room furnished with beds, wall lockers, and tables. Exhibits dedicated to the Chinook Indians include stone tools, baskets, trade items, a replica dugout canoe, and panels describing the tribe's successful fishing strategies.

The building that once served as the commandant's quarters is now the Columbia House, furnished with items that might have been here at the turn of the century. The former quartermaster's storehouse depicts the offices of the *Chinook Observer* as they might have looked during the days when the newspaper was reporting on the activities of the fort.

*Web site: www.parks.wa.gov/ftcolumb.htm*
*Hours: April 1 to Oct 15: Daily 6:30am–dusk. Closed rest of year.*
*Admission by donation.*

*Directions: Fort Columbia State Park is two miles east of Highway 101 in Chinook.*

## CLE ELUM

### ■ Cle Elum Historical Telephone Museum
221 E First Street
Cle Elum, WA 98022
(509)674-5702

Housed in Cle Elum's old Pacific Northwest Bell telephone building, the Cle Elum Historical Telephone Museum takes pride in the fact that Cle Elum was not only the last place in the Pacific Northwest to switch over from operator-assisted phone calls to automatic direct-dial, but the last Northwest town where touch-tone service was implemented.

Cle Elum got its first telephones in 1901. To complete a call back then, residents turned a crank on their telephone at home, which made a small numbered tab drop at the telephone switchboard in town. That signaled an operator to plug in a connecting cord and help complete the call. The process remained pretty much the same until 1966, when direct-dial arrived, and it gave the telephone operators an important role: They were often the first to be notified of illnesses, fires, and other emergencies. When the area was bustling with mining activity, operators needed to understand more than one language, because folks had flocked to the area from more than 25 countries to work in the mines.

> **While You're in Cle Elum:**
> The Cle Elum Historical Society also operates the Carpenter House, a turn-of-the-century banker's mansion with spacious rooms, Tiffany lamps, and a ballroom on the third floor.
>
> *Carpenter House, 302 W Third Street, Cle Elum, WA 98022; (509)674-5702.*
> *Hours: Memorial Day to Labor Day: Sat–Sun noon–4pm. Closed rest of year. Admission by donation. Directions: From I-90, take the Cle Elum exit. The Carpenter House is at the corner of N Third Street and Billings Avenue.*

The museum displays the town's increasingly sophisticated telephone switchboards, telephone wire insulators, early telephone directories, and a progression of telephones and telephone equipment, including a calcula-graph, an early device used to track long-distance phone calls.

In addition to the telephone displays, the museum has a case of miners' tools, old post office fixtures, pioneer family memorabilia, and other artifacts. A display recognizing Cle Elum–born heroes honors astronaut Francis (Dick) Scobee, who perished in the explosion of the Challenger in January 1986.

*Hours: Memorial Day to Labor Day: Tues–Fri 9am–4pm, Sat–Mon noon–4pm. Closed rest of year.*

*Admission by donation.*
*Directions: From I-90, take the Cle Elum exit. The museum is on the*
*corner of E First Street and Wright Avenue in downtown Cle Elum.*

## COLFAX

### ■  Perkins House and Cabin
623 Perkins Avenue
Colfax, WA 99111
(509)397-2555

This Victorian-style home was built in the mid-1880s by Whitman County pioneer and Colfax founder James A. Perkins. The Whitman County Historical Society restored and refurbished the interior of the Perkins House in a turn-of-the-century manner. The society now offers tours and organizes several changing exhibits in the home each year. For a contrast, check out the more spartan Perkins Cabin, behind the house.

Special events include a theme tea in mid-April and an annual ice cream social the last Sunday in June.

*Hours: June 1 to Labor Day: Thurs and Sun 1pm–4pm and by appoint-*
*ment. Closed rest of year.*
*Admission by donation.*
*Directions: From Main Street, turn right on Last Avenue, then right on*
*Perkins Avenue.*

## COLVILLE

### ■  Keller Heritage Center: Stevens County Historical Museum and Pioneer Machinery Museum
700 N Wynne Street (PO Box 25)
Colville, WA 99114
(509)684-5968

Several artifact-filled buildings sit in the seven-and-a-half-acre park that makes up the Keller Heritage Center. Scattered around the park grounds are a farmstead cabin, Colville's first schoolhouse, a sawmill, a blacksmith shop, a trapper's cabin, the Graves Mountain Lookout tower, and the impressive historic 1910 Keller House, complete with original furnishings, beveled glass windows, and red-birch beams. The center also contains two official museums: the Pioneer Machinery Museum and the Stevens County Historical Museum.

The Machinery Museum contains examples of horse-drawn and steam-powered farming equipment, including a 1925 Twin City grain separator and a sandwich hay baler. The museum also displays the cart and wagon in which a Mr. Wilson traveled around the country during the 1930s promoting Jumbo, a buffalo-cattle hybrid (which he called a "catalo") that he hoped would catch on as a good source of meat.

A bison bull and a domestic cow produced this "catalo" named Jumbo

The Stevens County Historical Museum, at the entrance to the park, contains more than 3,000 items depicting the history and development of northeast Washington. Exhibits are arranged chronologically, describing the area's geological history, Native American communities, Fort Colville, and the mining and forest-products industries.

The museum also displays the printing press and other print-shop equipment from the *Colville Examiner,* a fully stocked pharmacy, and equipment from Mount Carmel Hospital. Look for the painting by local artist Mike Somerlott depicting Kettle Falls in the days before construction of the Coulee Dam covered the area with 90 feet of water.

> *Hours: June to Aug: Mon–Sat 10am–4pm, Sun 1pm–4pm. Sept to May:*
> *Daily 1pm–4pm.*
> *Admission by donation.*
> *Directions: The museum is on N Wynne Street, just off Highway 395 in*
> *Colville.*

## COULEE DAM

### ■ Colville Confederated Tribes' Museum
512 Mead Way
Coulee Dam, WA 99116
(509)633-0751

The Colville Confederated Tribes' Museum honors the culture and history of the tribe's 12 bands with photographs, artifacts, murals, and dioramas.

The most prominent display is a life-size 3-D diorama that depicts the traditional salmon fishing grounds at Kettle Falls. The scene features a multipaneled mural of the falls, a man spearfishing from scaffolding, and a mounted 65-pound salmon on loan from the Cheney Cowles Museum in Spokane (see listing).

The museum also features beadwork, dance regalia, arrowheads, basketry, corn husk bags, the work of tribal artists, and an impressive photographic display. Special artifacts include an 1801 Thomas Jefferson Peace Medal, a dress dyed purple—using huckleberries—that is more than 75 years old, and photographs of people participating in ceremonies while wearing some of the elaborately beaded dresses, tunics, and other items on display.

> *Hours: April to Dec: Mon–Sat 10am–6pm. Jan to March: Tues–Sat 10am–6pm.*
> *Admission by donation.*
> *Directions: Traveling west in Coulee Dam on State Route 155, continue on Roosevelt Way instead of following the turn of the highway. Drive two blocks to Mead Way. The museum is in a church building.*

## DAVENPORT

### ■ Lincoln County Historical Museum
Seventh and Park Streets (PO Box 869)
Davenport, WA 99122
(509)725-6711

Davenport, just 35 miles west of Spokane, promotes itself as a "darn nice place to visit." For a sneak preview, stop by the Lincoln County Historical Museum and learn a bit about the area's agricultural and cultural history. A shed out back is full of farm machinery, steam engines, and covered wagons, while inside are charming displays chock-full of local memorabilia. But, human nature being what it is, you'll probably find yourself rooted to the floor by the Harry Tracy display.

Tracy was a notorious outlaw who escaped from prison in 1902 and successfully evaded capture by a posse from the nearby town of Creston. Rather than allow himself to be captured, Tracy killed himself while hiding from the posse. The museum's Tracy artifacts include his plaster death mask, a frying pan he used while on the run, a bullet from his cartridge belt, and lots of gruesome photos.

Most other exhibits are intriguing but far less grisly. There's a meteor discovered in Egypt (the town 20 miles north), a photo gallery of area farms, schools, and downtown buildings, and a re-created section of a well-stocked general store. Other offerings include a lovely button display, mannequins modeling vintage clothing, and assorted local artifacts, including 14 neatly framed used spark plugs.

Don't forget to go out back to see the farm machinery and the two newly acquired vintage fire engines. And don't be shy about asking someone to unlock the other buildings out there for you too: A building

Death was preferable to jail for outlaw Harry Tracy

that was once a brewery now houses Native American artifacts, taxidermied birds, and vintage printing and office equipment. Another building stores baggage carts, trunks, and other railroad items, including the loop the stationmaster once used to give orders to the engineer and conductor on a moving train.

> *Hours: May to Sept: Mon–Sat 9am–5pm, Sun 1pm–4pm. Closed rest of year.*
> *Admission by donation.*
> *Directions: The museum is just off Highway 2, at the intersection of Park and Seventh Streets, right next to the park.*

## DAYTON

■ **Dayton Depot**
222 E Commercial Street (PO Box 1881)
Dayton, WA 99328
(509)382-2026

Although it's small, Dayton has a lot going for it. It's the Columbia County seat, and its recently restored courthouse, built in 1887, has been in operation longer than any other in the state. The law may rule downtown, but out in the fields asparagus rules. Much of the world's asparagus gets canned here, which is why you'll spot the image of the Jolly Green Giant on a hillside just west of town.

The lovely restored two-story Dayton Depot, the oldest railroad station in the state of Washington, is just a block from the courthouse. Built in 1881 by the Oregon Railroad and Navigation Company, it was moved to its present site in 1899 and now serves as a museum. On the main floor are a variety of changing exhibits as well as a permanent display honoring Dayton pioneers, a photographic timeline of the history of Dayton, and a display of locally made furniture. Of course, there's also railroad memorabilia, including caboose lanterns, message hooks, a train crossing bell, and caps worn by station agents and engineers. The depot's second floor, with a wraparound balcony on three sides, is decorated to look much as it might have when it served as the stationmaster's living quarters.

The depot is always part of the Dayton Historic Homes Tour, held on the second Sunday in October, and each year during Thanksgiving weekend a craft show is held in the depot.

*Hours: Tues–Sat 9am–5pm.*
*Admission charged.*
*Directions: From Walla Walla, take State Route 12 east to Dayton and turn left on Second Street. The depot is a half-block down, by the railroad tracks.*

## DEER PARK

### ■ North Spokane Farm Museum—The Red Shed
W 6223 Ridgeway Road
Deer Park, WA 98006
(509)466-2744

Bob Greiff's family started farming 83 years ago. Now Greiff's working farm is also the North Spokane Farm Museum, designed to honor the memory of his dad and to show city folk just what sorts of tools, machinery, and just plain hard work it takes to keep a farm going.

Greiff's collection of farm machinery dates from 1890 through the 1950s and includes corn planters, farm wagons, hay rakes, potato diggers, walking plows, and cultivators. He's also got a shed, known as the Red Shed, with more than 500 farm-related items hanging on the wall, 26 sets of ironstone dishes dating back to 1875, and hundreds of household items displayed in a 1920s kitchen, a 1940s bedroom, and a Queen Victoria room.

*Hours: Open by appointment or if Bob Greiff is around.*
*Admission by donation.*
*Directions: From Spokane, take Highway 395; turn west on Monroe Road and follow it to Ridgeway Road. Look for the signs.*

## DUPONT

### ■ DuPont Historical Museum
207 Barksdale Avenue
DuPont, WA 98327
(253)964-2399

DuPont is an old company town established in 1906 by explosives manufacturer E. I. du Pont de Nemours Company. The dynamite works built here operated for almost 70 years, and during that time pretty much all the men (and some of the women) in town worked making explosives. To find out just what goes into making dynamite and what precautions folks took to keep the whole darn town from blowing up on a regular basis, stop by for a visit at the DuPont Historical Museum.

Housed in a building that once served as a butcher shop and later as the town's city hall, the museum displays photographs of early DuPont and artifacts from the factory, including historical photographs, work clothing and tools, the machine used to mix and press dynamite into sticks, shell casings, and the specially padded boxes used to ship the fragile cargo. The "recipe" for dynamite is here too, but it's probably not something you'll want to whip up at home on a slow Tuesday night.

In addition to the dynamite department, the museum has several exhibits describing Fort Nisqually, the trading-post settlement built in this area in 1833 by the Hudson's Bay Company. Outside, in the small park area next to the museum, are four cars from the narrow-gauge train that once ran through the DuPont plant.

> *Hours: June to Aug: Wed 7pm–9pm, Sun 1pm–4pm. Sept to May: Sun 1pm–4pm.*
> *Admission by donation.*
> *Directions: From southbound I-5, take exit 119. At the top of the off-ramp, turn right on Barksdale Avenue (it may not be marked). Stay in the middle (nonturn) lane; the museum is the second building on the right.*

## EATONVILLE

### ■ Pioneer Farm Museum and Ohop Indian Village
7716 Ohop Valley Road
Eatonville, WA 98328
(360)832-6300

Tours of this 1880s pioneer farm make it clear that pioneer life was tough. Don't believe it? Then accept the Pioneer Farm Museum tour guide's invitation to dress up as a pioneer and try your hand at all sorts of farm chores. Find out what it's like to churn butter, grind coffee, knead dough, shave with a straight-edge razor, milk a cow, gather eggs, work in a woodshop, and, for relaxation, ride in a bumpy wagon.

If you're here on a summer weekend, you'll also have a chance to visit the Ohop Indian Village next door and learn about the daily chores performed by Native Americans in this area before white settlers started moving in. Here you can gain some hunting and fishing skills, see how food items were prepared, and get a lesson in several Native American craft activities.

> *Hours: Father's Day to Labor Day: Farm: Daily 11am–4pm. Village Tours: Sat–Sun 1pm and 2:30pm. Closed rest of year.*
> *Admission charged.*

*Directions: The facility is between State Routes 161 and 7, three miles north of Eatonville, on Ohop Valley Road.*

## EDMONDS

### ■ Edmonds Museum
118 Fifth Avenue N (PO Box 52)
Edmonds, WA 98020
(425)774-0900

In the old days, folks visited Edmonds's Carnegie library not only to read and check out books, but to conduct important business: City hall was on the building's lower floor. Now the building is home to the Edmonds Museum, and, appropriately enough, there's a research library upstairs and at least one exhibit downstairs that pays tribute to the building's role in civic history.

The *Changing Face of Edmonds* exhibit includes a diorama showing what the city's bustling downtown and surrounding areas looked like during the early 1900s (when shingle mills filled the waterfront), a working model of a shingle mill, and a reproduction of a bedroom from the Stephens Hotel circa 1894.

Downstairs, the Marine Room is filled with photographs of early-day Puget Sound sailing vessels, nautical instruments, navigation lights and charts, and, according to one museum docent, "ship models that just won't quit!"

*Hours: Wed–Sun 1pm–4pm.*
*Admission by donation.*
*Directions: From either I-5 or State Route 99, head west on State Route 104 (Edmonds Way) and follow it as it becomes Sunset Avenue. Turn right on Main Street and left on Fifth Avenue N. The museum is half a block north of Fifth Avenue N and Main Street in downtown Edmonds.*

## ELLENSBURG

### ■ Clymer Museum of Art
416 N Pearl Street (PO Box 1002)
Ellensburg, WA 98296
(509)962-6416

As a high school student in Ellensburg, John Ford Clymer was already selling his artwork. Later, Clymer earned a living, and gained a reputation as an accomplished artist, by painting a total of 80 covers for the *Saturday Evening Post,* covers and ads for *National Wildlife* and *Field & Stream,* and illustrations for many other publications. It wasn't until he was 57 that Clymer turned to creating artwork he truly loved: historically correct paintings of the Old West that many art critics rank up there alongside the work of C. M. Russell and Frederic Remington.

With his wife, Doris, Clymer would visit sites he hoped to paint. He'd make detailed sketches, and she'd research the spot's historical aspects. Then Clymer would get to work, creating paintings that evoke everything from the days of the Lewis and Clark expedition, fur trading, and frontiersmanship to the search for gold and the experiences of cattlemen and other early pioneers.

The Clymer Museum of Art displays a large collection of John Clymer's art and memorabilia, including many of his original *Saturday Evening Post* covers. The museum also features a variety of changing exhibitions throughout the year focusing on the art, industry, and culture of the Pacific Northwest. Past exhibitions have showcased contemporary western artists, fruit-crate label art, local collections, and that classic western icon: the cowboy boot.

*Hours: Weekdays 10am–5pm, weekends noon–5pm.*
*Admission charged.*
*Directions: From I-90, take exit 109 or 106. The museum is in historic*
 *downtown Ellensburg on the corner of N Pearl and Fourth Streets.*

## ■ Kittitas County Historical Museum
114 E Third Avenue (PO Box 265)
Ellensburg, WA 98926
(509)925-3778

The Kittitas County Historical Museum is housed in the 1889 Cadwell Building, one of the sturdy downtown structures built after the July 4, 1889, fire that destroyed much of the city. The museum's holdings include early pioneer artifacts as well as a large collection of Kittitas Indian treasures that features beaded and corn-husk bags, baskets, and other beautiful items. The museum is also home to the vast Rollinger Brothers Collection of petrified wood, mineral samples, and polished rocks. Look carefully among the cases for the unusual Ellensburg blue agate and assorted pieces of miniature furniture made from petrified wood.

Display cases near the front entrance celebrate the establishment of the Ellensburg County Fair in 1885

### While You're in Ellensburg:
If you happen to be downtown, don't pass up the chance to stop at Dick and Jane's Spot. It's clear right away that artists live here: The house, the fencing, and the surrounding yards are decorated with wacky and whimsical found art, folk art, and homemade creations.

*Dick and Jane's Spot, 101 N*
 *Pearl, Ellensburg, WA*
 *98296.*
*Hours: Always open (public space), but be respectful of the private residence the art surrounds. Admission free. Directions: The house is right across from the fire station, just a few blocks down N Pearl from the Clymer Museum of Art (see listing).*

and the addition of the Ellensburg Rodeo in 1923. Both events continue today. Other exhibits feature antique dolls, vintage toys, and displays evoking early area businesses, including a blacksmith shop, a doctor's office, and a bank. In the center room, look for the large statue of RCA's mascot, Nipper. This friendly pooch has made Ellensburg his home since 1928.

> *Web site: www.ellensburg_wa.com*
> *Hours: May to Sept: Mon–Sat 10am–4pm. Oct to April: Tues–Sat 11am–3pm.*
> *Admission by donation.*
> *Directions: From I-90, take exit 109 (Canyon Road, which turns into Main Street). Turn right on E Third Avenue and continue for two blocks.*

## EPHRATA

### ■ Grant County Historical Museum and Village
742 Basin Street NW (PO Box 1141)
Ephrata, WA 98823
(509)754-3334

The artifacts at the Grant County Historical Museum and Village range from Native American basketry to a velvet-lined carriage that once belonged to cattle baron Lord Blythe. Behind the museum is an entire pioneer village, with 29 authentic and reconstructed buildings, including everything from a saloon to a schoolhouse.

The Native American exhibit focuses on the Wanapum and Sinkiuse tribes and includes a miniature sweat lodge, beadwork, jewelry, baskets, and a mural depicting these two tribes at Trading Rock, on the historical Lord Blythe House property at Rocky Ford Creek. Furniture, pictures, and other memorabilia from the historic Grant County Courthouse are displayed, along with toys, porcelain dolls, crystal bowls, and school-related items. A formal dining room, parlor, bedroom, and country kitchen are each furnished with items donated by members of the community and populated by mannequins dressed in fine vintage clothing. Down in the basement are military items and a nice collection of carved animals.

Out back, there's more stuff in the 30 buildings that make up the village, including a church, a jail, a bank, a print shop, a livery stable, and a camera shop filled with more than 300 vintage cameras.

In the first part of June and on the last Saturday in September, the village becomes a living museum, with special programs and demonstrations of blacksmithing, cooking, and other pioneer activities.

> *Hours: May to Sept: Mon, Tues, Thurs–Sat 10am–5pm; Sun 1pm–4pm. Closed rest of year.*

*Admission charged.*
*Directions: From eastbound I-90, take exit 151 (State Route 283) to NW*
  *Basin Street in Ephrata (283 turns into Basin Street) and head north.*
  *From westbound I-90, take exit 179 (State Route 17) to Basin Street*
  *NW in Ephrata and head north.*

EVERETT

■ **Snohomish County Museum**
2817 Rockefeller Avenue (PO Box 5556)
Everett, WA 98206
(425)259-2022

The Snohomish County Museum draws on its eclectic collection of photographs, furniture, textiles, logging tools, household items, and community memorabilia to create regularly changing exhibits reflecting the history and culture of the county. Museum staffers promise at least four new exhibits each year.

*Web site: www.snonet.org/discover/snocomuseum/*
*Hours: Wed–Sat 1pm–4pm.*
*Admission by donation.*
*Directions: From I-5, take the Hewitt Avenue exit. Head west about one*
  *mile to Rockefeller Avenue and turn right. The museum is on the first*
  *floor of the Betty Spooner Dance Studio.*

FAIRFIELD

■ **Southeast Spokane County Historical Society Museum**
Main Street
Fairfield, WA 99012
(509)283-2512 (library)

Prison bars on one wall of this museum attest to the fact that the building once served as the town's jail. At other times, the structure housed the city hall and a fire station. Now it's the Southeast Spokane County Historical Society Museum, which displays household goods, military uniforms, hats, buggies, toys, Native American artifacts, and every southeast Spokane County senior class picture since 1910. Other exhibits include a bank teller's window and vault, an old-time dentist office, and a great old fire cart.

*Hours: Summer: Tues and Thurs afternoons, or stop by the library for a key.*
  *Closed rest of year.*
*Admission by donation.*
*Directions: From eastbound I-90, take State Route 27 south to Fairfield.*
  *The museum is on Main Street, next to the library.*

## ■ Pacific Rim Bonsai Collection
Weyerhaeuser Company
33663 Weyerhaeuser Way S
Federal Way, WA 98003
(253)924-5206

To honor its trade relations with the Pacific Rim nations and as a tribute to the Washington State Centennial in 1989, the Weyerhaeuser Company established the Pacific Rim Bonsai Collection not as a garden but as an "outdoor museum of living art." The "museum" features more than 100 quality bonsai artworks from the Pacific Rim nations of Canada, China, Japan, Korea, Taiwan, and the United States, displaying them in a tropical conservatory and on 50 outdoor tables, set in groups of two or three.

Now, these aren't just stunted trees in pots. Freely translated, bonsai (pronounced "BONE-sigh") is the Japanese word for the horticultural practice of planting something—anything—in a shallow container. "But while there are many kinds of potted plants," notes collection curator Dave DeGroot, "bonsai are trees, vines, or shrubs used as an artistic medium. The common thread is that artists use the plants to create a small-scale representation of something in nature." In Japan, bonsai can be tiny enough to be grown in thimble-size pots, but the Weyerhauser collection features mostly medium and large bonsai, up to four feet tall.

In the process of shaping a plant to the desired size and shape, the roots may be clipped and branches may be wired or cut, but the result, says De-Groot, "is that a bonsai can mature and have a personality, like an old but very powerful person. It can also evoke a fine painting, tell a story, send you on an imaginary journey, or convey an emotion such as balance or drama." And because these living works of art continue to grow and

## While You're in Federal Way:

Just down the road from the Pacific Rim Bonsai Collection is the 23-acre Rhododendron Species Botanical Garden, operated by the Rhododendron Species Foundation. This is one of the largest collections of species of rhododendrons and azaleas in the world, with more than 2,100 different varieties of "wild" flowering plants on display. Rhododendrons ranging from one-inch Chinese dwarfs to 100-foot giants of the Himalayas grow alongside premier collections of ferns, maples, heathers, and bamboo. Members can purchase seeds, pollen, and plants propagated from the collection.

*Rhododendron Species Botanical Garden, Weyhaeuser Way S (PO Box 3798), Federal Way, WA 98063; (253)661-9377. Hours: March to May: Fri–Wed 10am–4pm. June to Feb: Sat–Wed 11am–4pm. Admission charged. Directions: Same as the Pacific Rim Bonsai Collection.*

A delicate bonsai from the museum's collection

change, they're never really "finished": The artistic process of tending and shaping the plant or tree continues as long as the plant is alive.

Many of the bonsai plants in this collection have won prizes and been featured in books and magazines. Some are in their third country of residency, and others have had four generations of owners. To learn more about the story behind each plant, pick up a copy of the collection guidebook when you visit, or attend one of the free lectures offered on weekends throughout the spring and early fall.

> *Hours: March to May: Fri–Wed 10am–4pm. June to Feb: Sat–Wed 11am–4pm.*
>
> *Admission free.*
>
> *Directions: From southbound I-5, take exit 143, turn left on S 320th Street, turn right on Weyerhaeuser Way S and follow it to the east entrance, and then follow the signs. From northbound I-5, take exit 142A onto State Route 18, turn left on Weyerhaeuser Way S, proceed to the east entrance, and follow the signs.*

## FERNDALE

### ■ Pioneer Park

c/o Ferndale Heritage Society
Pioneer Park, First Avenue (PO Box 3127)
Ferndale, WA 98248
(360)384-6461

Ferndale's Pioneer Park boasts a wonderful collection of original pioneer log cabins, each lovingly restored by members of the hardworking Ferndale Heritage Society. Many of the cabins had been abandoned and left to rot in the woods, but over the course of several decades a dozen were rescued and moved to Pioneer Park, next to the Nooksack River.

Each cabin is furnished with period artifacts: the 1887 granary building, for example, is filled with the sort of farm tools that would have been used to harvest and mill grain; the 1879 Parker House is filled with general store merchandise; and the 1890 Holeman House is set up as a typical one-room schoolhouse. Sprinkled throughout the other buildings are a collection of old typewriters, a complete print shop, and several "gold pokes," leather pouches that once held gold.

No doubt each artifact in each building has a story to tell, but the story behind the Foster Piano is a gem: In 1890, James Robert Foster Jr. ordered a piano from the East Coast as a wedding gift for his bride, Ella Mae Orchard. The piano traveled "around the Horn" of South America to San Francisco, where it was loaded onto another ship for its trip north to Whatcom County. Over the next 100 years the piano followed various family members and their friends around the Northwest. Finally, at a Foster family reunion in the early 1990s, it was decided that the piano should go back to its "proper place" in the original Foster cabin, which was the first log house to be assembled at Pioneer Park. Today a photograph of Ella Mae Foster, the original recipient of the piano, hangs on the wall above it.

The piano, the picture, the cabins, and thousands of other artifacts help create a villagelike setting that portrays what life was like for the county's pioneer settlers. The site is all the more meaningful because back in 1897, early settlers used this park to convene their second Old Settlers' Picnic, and such picnics have been held here ever since, on the last week in July, as part of a weeklong celebration that includes concerts, parades, and cabin tours.

*Web site: members.aol.com/logcab1997/Ferndale*
*Hours: May 15 to Sept 15: Tues–Sun 11:30am–4:30pm. Closed rest*
*of year.*
*Admission charged.*
*Directions: From I-5, take exit 262, drive one mile west (crossing the*
*Nooksack River), and turn left on First Avenue. The park is at the*
*end of the street.*

## FORKS

### ■ Forks Timber Museum
1421 S Forks Avenue (PO Box 873)
Forks, WA 98331
(360)374-9663

There's no questioning that what's important to the folks in Forks is wood. The two-story Forks Timber Museum was built from wood (what

Welcome sign at the museum

did you think?) by a crew that included a high school carpentry class and inmates from the a nearby correctional center. The sign welcoming visitors out front features loggers and was carved by a noted local chain-saw artist, and next to the museum is a 12-foot-tall loggers' memorial honoring people who worked in the woods on the Olympic Peninsula.

Go inside for more timber history. Exhibits cover everything from area mills and log-hauling trucks to the 1951 fire and a lesson in loggers' lingo. Displays include a loggers' bunkhouse complete with work clothing; a stove used in a logging camp cookhouse; and a wide variety of logging equipment such as single- and two-man power saws and a scale model of a steam donkey.

Upstairs, resting in the beams above the Native American artifact exhibit, is a 30-foot-long, unfinished Makah canoe found abandoned in the woods. Visitors can step outside on this upper level onto the fire-watch tower and learn how important a job it is to watch for "smokes" from the forest mountaintops.

Before you leave, ask for your very own "Dictionary of Logging Terms." Otherwise, how will you remember that a "bindle" is a bedroll and "hen skins" are what loggers call light summer underwear?

*Web site: www.forks-web.com/fg/timbermuseum.htm*
*Hours: Mid-April to Oct: Daily 10am–4pm. Closed rest of year.*
*Admission by donation.*
*Directions: The museum is on Highway 101, one mile south of Forks, just across from the airport.*

### ■ Fort Lewis Military Museum
Off I-5 at exit 120
Fort Lewis, WA 98433
(253)967-7206

During World War I thousands of doughboys trained at what was originally named Camp Lewis, the country's first military installation created
as a result of an outright gift of land from private citizens. Now all private
citizens who want to visit the Fort Lewis Military Museum must show ID
and get a pass authorizing them to be on base. But if you're interested in
the army and the role it played in the exploration, settlement, and defense
of the Pacific Northwest, the museum's exhibits are worth the trouble.

The museum is housed in the historic Red Shield Inn, a white ski
chalet–inspired structure built by the Salvation Army during World War I
as a lodge and social center for Camp Lewis soldiers. Now the building is
divided into the Soldiers of the Northwest, America's Corps, Fort Lewis,
and Ninth Infantry Division galleries.

The Camp Lewis piano is here, along with a wide variety of military
uniforms, decorations, swords, pistols, rifles, toy soldiers, classic posters
advertising war bonds, and other military memorabilia. Don't be surprised to find a dugout canoe in the main gallery. It's a reminder that the
story of the American soldier in the Northwest began in 1804, when
Meriwether Lewis and William Clark, both ranking members of the U.S.
Army, led the Corps of Discovery's infantrymen to the mouth of the
Columbia River. Corps members learned how to make these canoes
from the Native Americans they met in the Northwest.

There's a large vehicle park outside the museum, displaying tanks,
cannons, missiles, and other military hardware, including tanks captured
from Iraqi forces occupying Kuwait during Operation Desert Storm by
the 864th Engineer Battalion, also known as the Pacemakers.

*Hours: Wed–Sun noon–4pm.*
*Admission free.*
*Directions: From I-5, take exit 120 to the main gate of Fort Lewis. After*
*showing a driver's license and vehicle registration, you'll be issued a*
*base pass and directed to the museum.*

### ■ Fox Island Historical Society Museum
1017 Ninth Avenue
Fox Island, WA 98333
(253)549-2239

The Fox Island Historical Society Museum displays dioramas of early
Northwest life, Native American artifacts from the Pacific Northwest,

pioneer artifacts, and objects relating to Fox Island history. The museum is especially proud of its collection of restored farm equipment and machinery, its exhibit about the life of former Washington governor Dixy Lee Ray, and their 400-piece pulley block collection. Other items on display include early radios, record players, cameras, seashells, and two cases full of military items dating from the Civil War to the present.

The museum sponsors a speakers' program, holds a spring bazaar and quilt show each April, and welcomes Santa each December.

*Hours: Mon and Sat 1pm–4pm, Wed 11am–3pm.*
*Admission charged.*
*Directions: From Tacoma, take State Route 16 toward Bremerton, across the Narrows Bridge. Take the first overpass and head west, following the signs for Fox Island. Turn left on Wollochet Drive (beside Peninsula Gardens); the main road becomes 40th. Turn left on 70th, drive to the end, and turn right at the bottom of the hill; this takes you to the Fox Island Bridge. Continue for a mile, turn right on Ninth Avenue, and follow it to Camas Drive. After crossing that intersection, you'll see a fire station; the museum is right behind it.*

## GIG HARBOR

### ■ Gig Harbor Peninsula Historical Museum
4218 Harborview Drive (PO Box 744)
Gig Harbor, WA 98335
(253)858-6722

In 1951 and again in 1953, Gig Harbor resident Clarence E. Shaw held a round-rock contest, offering cash prizes for the five rocks or stones judged to be the most perfectly rounded. Qualifying stones had to come from Washington state and be naturally round—no scratching or shaping allowed.

Want to know who won? Stop by the Gig Harbor Peninsula Historical Museum, where the winning rocks from 1953 are on display. Think you have a competition-worthy rock in your collection? The museum recently revived the round-rock contest, and winning rocks are displayed each June, during the area's Maritime Gig Festival.

Of course, there's more to see at this museum than just those round rocks. Explore the changing exhibition gallery and the permanent *Gig Harbor Peninsula* exhibition, which offers a great overview of local history, with sections on the fishing industry, logging, wooden-boat building, the Narrows Bridge, steamboat and ferryboat operations, and agricultural efforts including poultry, dairy, and berry farming. Many of the artifacts on display belonged to area fishermen, farmers, and businesspeople. There are steamboat and fishing-boat journals, fishing equipment, boatbuilding tools, a two-ton safe, bedroom and living room furniture, children's games, and a huckleberry cleaner.

Gig Harbor's "Roosterettes" pose for a photo

An outdoor display features a large trough and pot once used to tar cotton fishing nets in order to make them last longer in the salt water. Other fishing gear, such as nets, floats, blocks, brailers, and plungers, is arranged as it might be found inside a fisherman's net shed.

Inside the museum, community life is portrayed through photographs, rooms furnished with vintage curios, memorabilia from garden clubs and other civic groups, and entertaining ephemera that includes the rules for that round-rock contest, a curious invitation to an early ball game that pitted the area's "fat ladies against the lean ladies," and items relating to Shaw's popular rooster-racing contests. According to museum records, Shaw not only sponsored the round-rock contests and the area's popular rooster racing, "he also had a miniature village called Roosterville and invited young women to wear majorette-style uniforms and become Roosterettes."

*Web site: www.peninsula-art.com/ghphsm/ghphsm.html*
*Hours: Tues–Sat 10am–4pm.*
*Admission by donation.*

*Directions: From State Route 16, take the City Center exit and drive straight on Stinson Avenue. Turn left on Harborview Drive and cross N Harborview at a three-way stop; the museum driveway is on the left.*

## GOLDENDALE

### ■ Maryhill Museum of Art
35 Maryhill Museum Drive
Goldendale, WA 98620
(509)773-3733

In 1907, Northwest entrepreneur Sam Hill purchased 7,000 acres of land along the Columbia River for a Quaker agricultural colony that was never built. Hill also commissioned a massive three-story poured-concrete "country getaway" in the area, but he lost interest in that too.

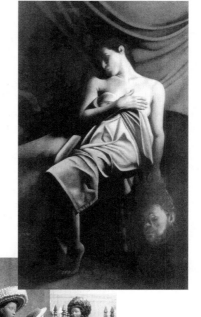

Hill's friend Loie Fuller, the flamboyant pioneer of modern dance known in Paris as "La Fée Lumineuse" (the Fairy of Light), convinced Hill to turn the house—called Maryhill after Hill's daughter, Mary—into a museum; and their friend Queen Marie of Roumania agreed to dedicate

Right: *Judith* (1996) by Gloria De Arcangelis
Below: Some of the miniature fashions from Théâtre de la Mode

it. But in 1926, after Queen Marie made a much-publicized 37-day train trip across the United States on the Royal Roumanian, the first queen ever to visit the United States arrived at Maryhill only to discover that after 10 years of "work," the museum was little more than a concrete shell!

The museum didn't open until after 1940—and by then, Sam Hill, Loie Fuller, and Queen Marie were all dead. It was another of Hill's friends, sugar heiress Alma Spreckels, who got the job done. Thank goodness! Today the Maryhill Museum of Art, a castle-like chateau overlooking the Columbia River Gorge, is a showcase for an eclectic array of collections ranging from royal Roumanian artifacts to fine art and sculpture.

The museum's holdings feature a collection of Queen Marie's regalia that includes ballgowns, furniture, jewels, and other objects. A large Native American artifact collection features rare baskets, beadwork, and rock carvings. The museum also owns many Classical Realist paintings, including *Indian Buffalo Hunt* by Charles Russell, and more than 52 large sculptures by Auguste Rodin. Ornate and imaginative chess sets from around the world are displayed to show how designers have used the game to reflect the rivalries of their time.

Maryhill is also the home of the Théâtre de la Mode, a rare set of miniature French fashion mannequins created by the top Paris costume houses after World War II in an effort to reclaim their status as the arbiters of fashion. The finely attired mannequins toured Europe and the United States wearing only the best jewelry, clothing, and accessories, all made to scale. The traveling fashion show, which had its own small sets and specially composed incidental music, was eventually abandoned in San Francisco. In 1952, Alma Spreckels arranged for Maryhill to provide shelter for it.

In addition to ongoing exhibits, the Maryhill Museum also presents classes, workshops, and other programs to coincide with special exhibitions and uses some of its 26 acres of exquisitely landscaped grounds, where peacocks roam, to host summertime concerts and an annual Outdoor Sculpture Invitational.

### While You're in Goldendale:

Three miles east of the Maryhill Museum is a full-size replica of England's Neolithic Stonehenge. Sam Hill ordered this monument built as a World War I memorial for the fallen soldiers from Klickitat County, Washington. Like the museum, construction of the memorial took a long time. Although the altar stone was dedicated on July 4, 1918, the memorial wasn't completed until 1929. Still, Hill's Stonehenge was the first World War I memorial constructed in the United States. If you'd like to pay your respects to Sam Hill, you'll find his crypt directly south of Stonehenge, overlooking the Columbia River.

*Web site: www.maryhillmuseum.org*
*Hours: March 15 to Nov 15: Daily 9am–5pm. Closed rest of year.*

*Admission charged.*
*Directions: From eastbound I-84, take exit 104 and follow the signs to the*
*museum.*

■ **Presby Museum**
127 W Broadway (PO Box 86)
Goldendale, WA 98620
(509)773-4303

In the early 1900s, Winthrop Bartlett (W. B.) Presby served stints as mayor of Goldendale, district U.S. land commissioner, and state senator. His ornate 20-room mansion is now the Presby Museum, filled with furniture, clothing, utensils, personal effects, and unusual collections gathered by the Klickitat County Historical Society to illustrate what life might have been like for well-to-do folks living in the area during the late 1800s and early 1900s.

There's Mr. Presby's home office, Mrs. Presby's parlor and pump organ, a dining room table set and ready for guests, clothes laid out in the bedroom, and toys set out and ready for playtime in the children's room. The photographs on the walls show Goldendale, the Columbia River Gorge, and early settlers of the area.

All this is charming and lovely, but according to museum "hostess" Terry Durgan, what draws the most attention from visitors seems to be the coffee grinder display on the second floor. The collection of more than 124 grinders from all over the world is neatly labeled and attached to display cases. One grinder, probably made for use in a shop, is more than five feet tall. Another made the trip in a covered wagon heading west and remains attached to the piece of wood it traveled here on.

Don't forget to make your way up to the attic. Decorated like an authentic homestead cabin, it contains branding irons, Washington state's brand registry books, and hundreds of pieces of branded leather that ranchers used to register their brands.

*Hours: April to Oct: Daily 9am–5pm. Closed rest of year.*
*Admission charged.*
*Directions: From Highway 97, turn west on State Route 142. Follow State*
*Route 142 to Goldendale. The museum is on the corner of W*
*Broadway and Grant Avenue.*

GRAPEVIEW

■ **Museum of Puget Sound**
170 E Stretch Island Road S
Grapeview, WA 98546
(253)858-7971

When Bill Somers was in college, studying for a maritime-related degree, he spent his summers working on freight and passenger boats in the

Puget Sound. During World War II he served on air/sea rescue boats. Now he's captain of the Museum of Puget Sound, a maritime heritage gallery in an old winery building on Stretch Island, near Tacoma.

Set up like a ship, with fun things like a pilot wheel, an engine room, foghorns, and lots of other hands-on artifacts, this is a place both kids and more serious maritime fans will thoroughly enjoy. The pilot wheel, for example, is from the ferry *Defiance,* which originally ran between Gig Harbor and Tacoma; the steam whistle (cover your ears!) is from the *Tyrus,* which became the *Virginia IV.* Keep your ears covered if you see Somers heading for one of the museum's six ship foghorns.

Other items on display include original ship nameboards, deck gratings, searchlights, portholes, more than 100 ship models (including some in bottles), and a 10-foot-long model of Colman Dock in downtown Seattle. The collection of shadow boxes, says Somers, is the most popular item with young and old alike. Located in the museum hallway, the three shadow boxes are artist-made dioramas depicting a variety of Puget Sound ferries en route. Each scene was first painted on a board, and an ice pick was then used to punch hundreds of "pinholes." This helps create a magical nighttime scene when the hallway lights are dimmed and a white light is shown from behind.

> *Hours: June to Oct: Sat–Sun 10am–4pm. Closed rest of year.*
> *Admission by donation.*
> *Directions: From Tacoma, cross the Narrows Bridge to Gig Harbor. Turn*
> *left toward the town of Purdy on State Route 302, drive to the town of*
> *Allyn, and turn left on Grapeview Loop Road. At the Grapeview*
> *store, turn left and cross the bridge to Stretch Island. At the foot of the*
> *hill, turn right. The museum is at the next right, on E Stretch Island*
> *Road S.*

## HOQUIAM

■ **Polson Museum**
1611 Riverside Avenue (PO Box 432)
Hoquiam, WA 98550
(360)533-5862

In the 1880s the Polson family began logging operations in the woods near Hoquiam. By the 1920s the Polson Brothers Logging Company, along with its subsidiary lumber and shingle mills, had become the world's largest timber production company and a powerful, influential force on the economic, social, and cultural scene in the Grays Harbor community. Now the Polson family's grand mansion in Hoquiam is the Polson Museum. The exhibits here reminisce about Grays Harbor during "better days" and do a fine job of documenting the area's colorful history.

Seventeen of the 26 rooms house exhibits that include everything from local Quinault and Makah Indian artifacts to the 11-foot Howard 60-beat clock, made in 1870, that once adorned downtown Hoquiam's jewelry store. Visitors can tickle the ivories of the 1875 Steinway square grand piano, crank the handle on an old Victrola record player, and thumb through sheet music that belonged to Hoquiam's opera star, Minnie Carey Stine.

And then, of course, there's the logging equipment and machinery. An assortment of saws, axes, and other tools are displayed in the Polson family's master bedroom, along with a large working model of a turn-of-the-century railroad logging operation. There's also a vintage railroad velocipede (a four-wheeled railroad cycle) and a giant two-man chain saw in the sitting room.

Upstairs, in what were once the Polson daughters' bedrooms, are a huge dollhouse, a 1920s telephone switchboard, and exhibits honoring historic area sports teams. Local celebrities, including champion log roller Diane Ellison, Captain Matt Peasley, and aforementioned opera star Minnie Carey Stine, all merit special displays.

After peeking into all the hallways and exhibit rooms in the mansion, stroll the grounds: There's a replica blacksmith shop next to the museum, large pieces of logging machinery, picnic tables, and a lovely rose garden.

*Hours: Mid-June to Sept: Wed–Sun 11am–4pm. Oct to mid-June:*
*Sat–Sun noon–4pm.*
*Admission charged.*
*Directions: The museum is on northbound Highway 101 in Hoquiam, at*
*Riverside Avenue.*

### ILWACO

### ■ Ilwaco Heritage Museum
115 SE Lake Street (PO Box 153)
Ilwaco, WA 98624
(360)642-3446

If you're driving north up the Long Beach Peninsula, be sure to stop and get a tour of the Ilwaco Heritage Museum from one of its community volunteers. You'll learn how important fishing, logging, and cranberry growing was to the area and how early salmon traps worked so well that they were eventually outlawed. You'll also find out how the funny-looking shoes on display made it possible to harvest cranberries. In the "Land of the Canoe People" Gallery, your guide will point out the rare section of an 800-year-old canoe that was found in an archaeological dig and describe how local Chinook Indians might have used that canoe to conduct business with other Northwest Coast tribes at the mouth of the Columbia River. Then you'll be gently prodded to look closely at the

Lifeboat on display

carved duck decoys in the Exploration Gallery, the working model of the Columbia River estuary in the Water Adventure Gallery, and the scale-model railroad out back.

The Exploration Gallery tells the story of non-native exploration of the Northwest Coast. The Water Adventure Gallery explains wetlands, tides, and Columbia River history. A model of the boat that adventurer Gerard d'Aboville rowed across the Pacific to Ilwaco is here too, along with documentation of his treacherous journey and, not coincidentally, an exhibit on lifesaving. Out back, in the restored Ilwaco railroad depot, is a 50-foot-long scale model of the Long Beach Peninsula, complete with an operating miniature railroad and buildings made of cereal boxes and old lottery tickets. The railroad depicted is the "Irregular, Rambling & Never-get-there Railroad." It's modeled on the Ilwaco Railroad & Navigation Company, also known as the Clamshell Railroad, which served the towns along Washington's Long Beach Peninsula from 1889 until 1930. The line had a reputation for being somewhat irregular because in order to meet the river steamers at either end of its line, it adjusted its schedule to the tides. There's another train exhibit with hand-made cars on the mezzanine level.

And then there's the Seaside Village, which represents an old-time Long Beach Peninsula town in miniature, complete with furniture and artifacts belonging to area residents. Shops come and go, so you might see a turn-of-the-century kitchen, a barbershop, a school, a church, or a dressmaker's shop. If the Ilwaco post office's furniture is on display, look carefully at the office desk. It's made out of packing crates from the salmon cannery; one old-timer claimed he knew the cannery night-watchman who'd made it, as a gift for the postmistress, who didn't have a desk "or a husband."

The Ilwaco museum sponsors several events each year, but it's most proud of the Cranberrian Fair, held each year during the second weekend in October. The festival began as a local agrarian fair back in the 1920s and now features regional cultural exhibits, cranberry-related food and gifts, and bog tours of area cranberry operations via bus.

> *Hours: Summer: Mon–Sat 9am–5pm, Sun noon–4pm. Rest of year:*
> *Mon–Sat 10am–4pm.*
> *Admission charged.*
> *Directions: The museum is one block south and a half block east of the*
> *stoplight on Highway 101 in Ilwaco, at the corner of First Avenue and*
> *SE Lake Street.*

## ■ Lewis and Clark Interpretive Center
Fort Canby State Park
Fort Canby Road
Ilwaco, WA 98624
(360)642-3029

A visitors center in Fort Canby State Park commemorates the Lewis and Clark expedition and the day in 1805 when the intrepid crew got their first view of the Pacific Ocean from this very spot. A five-minute hike uphill from the parking lot takes determined visitors to an incredible bluff overlooking the Columbia River's rush into the Pacific Ocean and a trail leading to the Cape Disappointment Lighthouse, the state's first.

At the Lewis and Clark Interpretive Center, you can follow the 8,000-mile journey Meriwether Lewis and William Clark took across the Badlands, the Rockies, and the wild American West to this very cliff. It's a bit dark inside and the exhibit runs along a ramp, but the story is well told with journal selections, artifacts, and replicas of items that describe the team's medical treatment, meals, entertainment, and the valuable assistance provided by the Chinook and other Native American tribes along the way. Be sure to look for the large dugout canoe that commands renewed respect for the term "portaging."

Other exhibits describe the history of Fort Canby, the construction of the area's historic lighthouses, and the story of the many shipwrecks that occurred at the mouth of the Columbia.

> *Web site: www.parks.wa.gov/ftcanby.htm*
> *Hours: Daily 10am–5pm.*
> *Admission by donation.*
> *Directions: Fort Canby State Park is three miles southwest of Ilwaco off*
> *Highway 100.*

Photo of the town's main intersection by Lee Pickett, circa 1910

INDEX

■ **Index Pickett Museum**
510 Avenue A (PO Box 299)
Index, WA 98256
(360)793-1534

From 1910 until the 1940s, Great Northern Railway photographer Lee Pickett took thousands of photographs. Many, of course, documented the progress and impact of the Great Northern Railway, but Pickett also captured impressive scenery as well as aspects of everyday life.

The Index Pickett Museum is housed in Pickett's former home, and his photos form the core of the collection. Whenever the curator plans a new exhibition, she begins with images from the Pickett archives and builds from there. Look for exhibits illustrating small-town life, Native American history, early-day tourism, mountain climbing, river adventuring, and the industries—such as granite quarrying, logging, and mining—that kept this early railroad boomtown alive.

*Hours: Memorial Day to Sept: Sat–Sun noon–3pm. Closed rest of year.*
*Admission by donation.*
*Directions: From Highway 2, take the Index/Galena exit and drive one*
   *mile to Index.*

■ **Gilman Town Hall Museum**
Issaquah Historic Depot
165 SE Andrews Street (PO Box 695)
Issaquah, WA 98027
(425)392-3500

The building that houses the Gilman Town Hall Museum served as the original town hall from the early 1890s, when Issaquah was still called Gilman, until 1928. Later the building did duty as a meeting hall, a library, and a storage space for firefighting equipment.

These days the building is filled with costumed mannequins, dolls, toys, and other treasures donated by local pioneer families, as well as artifacts relating to early local industries. Vintage household items on display include a wood-burning cookstove, a vintage refrigerator, and selected items from a "rotating" collection of washing machines.

Go out the back door and you'll come upon the town's old two-cell jail, constructed in 1914 and used until 1928. Made of concrete, the jail has eight-inch walls and a forged iron lockbar weighing at least 80 pounds. If you continue farther down the road, you'll come to the Issaquah Historic Depot, featuring vintage photographs, railroad memorabilia, an HO-gauge model railroad, and a vintage caboose. Railroad, logging, and mining exhibits are displayed in the depot's museum annex, a restored World War II troop kitchen car.

Look for a vintage steam donkey and yet another logging display one block south of the depot, along the Community Center Green.

Each July, the Issaquah Historic Depot is the gathering spot for the Issaquah Pioneer Reunion.

*Web site: www.issaquah.org/comorg/past/mpast.htm*
*Hours: Sat 11am–3pm.*
*Admission free.*
*Directions: From I-90, take exit 17 (Issaquah/Front Street). Follow Front Street south to downtown Issaquah (about a mile) and turn left at the depot. The depot is at the first left, near the library. To get to the museum, turn right on First, drive half a block, and turn left on SE Andrews Street.*

■ **Cowlitz County Historical Museum**
405 Allen Street
Kelso, WA 98626
(360)577-3119

An 1884 log cabin built and lived in by a Toutle River valley settler, a wide variety of Native American artifacts, a Model T truck, and a re-created general store, loggers' bunkhouse, and steamboat dock, and railroad depot are just some of the artifacts this Cowlitz County Historical Museum uses to introduce visitors to the people and history of the county. A hands-on section about the fur trade includes beaver pelts, trade goods, and iron tools. The logging exhibit features saws, axes, and an intriguing eight-by-six-foot photomural of a crew of hungry loggers standing around a log eating lunch.

Cowlitz County history is also presented thematically. Changing exhibits have focused on recreation, wartime activities, smelt fishing, and lace. The permanent *Cowlitz Corridor: Footpath to Freeway* exhibit centers on the confluence of the Columbia, Coweeman, and Cowlitz Rivers and explores how the area's transportation choices have changed over time—from the canoes of the Cowlitz Indians to the Model T truck of the 1920s. The exhibit includes photographs of the construction of I-5 during the early 1960s; according to one museum staffperson, folks in Kalama dubbed the road "our Berlin Wall" because the highway divided Kalama in two.

It's not just history buffs who'll enjoy this museum: Carvers, hunters, and folk art enthusiasts flock here to see the extensive exhibit of working waterfowl decoys and to use the well-stocked library of waterfowl- and decoy-related books, magazines, and art objects that are part of the collection.

*Hours: Tues–Sat 9am–5pm, Sun 1pm–5pm.*
*Admission by donation.*
*Directions: From I-5, take exit 39 and follow Allen Street a quarter-mile*
*west to the museum.*

## KENNEWICK

### ■ East Benton County Historical Museum
205 Keewaydin Drive
Kennewick, WA 99336
(509)582-7704

Even before you enter the East Benton County Historical Museum, you'll encounter some historical treasures: Scattered around the grounds are Native American petroglyphs recovered from the Columbia River in 1939, pioneer farm implements, and the bell from the old Finley School south of town. Inside are photographs, Native American arrowheads and stone tools, exhibits dealing with rail, water, and auto travel, the Jay Perry Columbia River Gem Point Collection, and agricultural displays devoted to wheat, fruit, and other crops. Period rooms portray an early schoolroom, various businesses and professions, and daily life in the early days of the county. The building features an unusual petrified wood floor created by a local ironworker.

*Hours: Tues–Sun noon–4pm.*

*Admission charged.*
*Directions: Take eastbound State Route 240 into Kennewick, where it turns*
  *into Columbia Drive. Turn right on Fruitland Street, left on First*
  *Avenue, and right on Dayton. Keewaydin Drive will be on the left,*
  *and the museum is on Keewaydin Drive, between the library and the*
  *senior center, across from Keewaydin Park.*

## KETTLE FALLS

■ **Kettle Falls Interpretive Center**
c/o Kettle Falls Historical Center
Juniper–Greenwood Road
Kettle Falls, WA 99141
(509)738-6964

For thousands of years, Native Americans gathered at Kettle Falls to fish
for salmon. In 1825 the Hudson's Bay Company set up a trading post—
Fort Colville—at this popular Columbia River site, and it soon became
the company's chief Northwest trading center.

Exhibits at the Kettle Falls Interpretive Center describe the daily life
of the Native American tribes whose lives were centered around the falls,
and present historical photographs as well as bottles, traps, and tools used
by early European trappers.

St. Paul's Mission, one of the few remaining examples of the
Hudson's Bay Red River construction style, is a short drive from the
center. A trail here leads past a cemetery and a huge stone used by Native
fishermen to sharpen their fishing tools. At the end of the trail is an overlook of the now-submerged falls.

*Hours: May 15 to Sept 15: Wed–Sun 11am–5pm. Closed rest of year.*
*Admission by donation.*
*Directions: From Highway 395/State Route 20, drive north past Kettle*
  *Falls. The center is one-eighth of a mile from Kettle Falls, on*
  *Juniper–Greenwood Road.*

## KEYPORT

■ **Naval Undersea Museum**
1 Garnet Way (PO Box 408)
Keyport, WA 98345
(360)396-4148

Located next to the Keyport naval base, which supplies the Pacific fleet
with torpedoes, the Naval Undersea Museum tells the history of
undersea warfare and sea exploration. Outside stands a conning tower
from a nuclear attack submarine called the USS *Sturgeon* as well as the *Tri-
este II,* a deep-sea research vessel that has descended 35,000 feet to the
bottom of the Pacific Ocean. Inside are more pieces and parts of sub-

mersibles, from diving suits to human-powered submarines and the control room of a nuclear-powered sub.

And then there are the torpedoes: glossy, long, and lethal. The history of their development and deployment is quite fascinating; even if you're not a war buff, you can't help but be intrigued to learn that it was the Germans in World War II who figured out how to power a torpedo so it didn't leave a telltale bubble trail. History buffs will enjoy the exhibits relating undersea mythology and maritime legends, and the sea exploration timeline that reminds us that it was Benjamin Franklin who invented the first (wooden) flippers for swimmers back in the 18th century.

A room of hands-on experiments demonstrates the science of navigating the deep, and piped-in spooky sounds, pings and echoes, help create an atmosphere of life below the surface. Many of the volunteers have had experience on subs and are happy to share their stories.

> *Hours: June to Sept: Daily 10am–4pm. Oct to May: Wed–Mon*
> *10am–4pm.*
> *Admission by donation.*
> *Directions: From State Route 3, travel east three miles on State Route 308*
> *and follow the signs.*

## LACEY

### ■ Lacey Museum
829 1/2 Lacey Street SE
Lacey, WA 98503
(360)438-0209

Located in a 1926 home that was later used as a city hall and headquarters for the volunteer fire department, the Lacey Museum traces local history back from present-day residents to the pioneer settlers who crossed the Oregon Trail.

An old rowboat and vintage photographs celebrate the days, between the 1920s and the 1950s, when Lacey was a popular lake resort area. Another exhibit features original equipment from radio station KGY. Founded in the 1920s by Father Sebastian Ruth from St. Martin's College, KGY was one of the first radio stations in Washington state.

The grounds around the museum have been designated as a special place of remembrance where trees and bushes are planted in memory of pioneer Lacey families.

> *Hours: Thurs–Sat 10am–4pm.*
> *Admission by donation.*
> *Directions: From Olympia, take northbound I-5 to exit 108 (College*
> *Street). Turn right on College and follow it to Pacific Avenue.*
> *Turn left on Pacific and follow it one block past Clearbrook Drive SE*
> *to Lacey Street SE. The museum is on the left, behind the Lacey*
> *Women's Club.*

## LA CONNER

■ **Museum of Northwest Art**
121 S First Street (PO Box 969)
La Conner, WA 98257
(360)466-4446

Located in the heart of downtown La Conner, the Museum of Northwest Art (MoNA) features works by, you guessed it, Northwest artists. Originally, when it was founded back in 1981, the museum planned to showcase only major Northwest artists, but over the years it has expanded its mission to include exhibitions by a wide range of Pacific Northwest artists and emerging regional talent. In 1995, the museum moved from its location (for 14 years) in the historical Gaches Mansion to a bright, contemporary space downtown; a well-stocked museum store is on the first floor.

MoNA's upper gallery showcases items from the permanent collection, which includes work by Morris Graves, Mark Tobey, Kenneth Callahan, and Guy Anderson, a group credited with creating the Northwest School, a style of painting that reflects Asian influences, philosophy, and spirituality. The main floor features up to eight new exhibitions of paintings, drawings, sculpture, photography, and studio glass each year.

Special programs include classical concerts, chorale performances, artist-led tours and discussions, and glass-blowing demonstrations.

*Hours: Tues–Sun 10am–5pm.*
*Admission charged.*
*Directions: From I-5, take exit 230*
*at Burlington. Head west on*
*State Route 20 to La*
*Conner/Whitney Road. Turn*
*south and follow that road as it*
*curves into La Conner. Drive to*
*S First Street, turn left, and go*
*half a block.*

---

**While You're in La Conner:**
The La Conner Quilt Museum, which opened in 1997, fills two floors of the restored Gaches Mansion with changing exhibits of new and antique quilts. Themed exhibitions have included Celtic quilts, a display of quilts made by local quilters for orphans in Bolivia, and treasured quilts on loan from local quilters and area residents. Each spring, when the tulips are in bloom, the museum features quilts with a floral theme.

*La Conner Quilt Museum,*
*703 S Second Street*
*(PO Box 1270),*
*La Conner, WA 98257;*
*(360)466-4288.*
*Hours: April to Sept: Wed–Sat*
*11am–5pm, Sun noon–5pm.*
*Oct to March: Wed–Sat*
*11am–4pm, Sun noon–4pm.*
*Admission charged. Directions:*
*From I-5, take exit State Route*
*20 west and turn south on*
*La Conner/Whitney Road and*
*follow it into La Conner. Head*
*west on Morris Street.*
*The museum is in the Gaches*
*Mansion.*

## ■ Skagit County Historical Museum
501 S Fourth Street
La Conner, WA 98257
(360)466-3365

La Conner's Skagit County Historical Museum presents a variety of changing exhibits along with its continuing Skagit Legacy show. Housed in both the north and south wings, Legacy takes visitors on a tour of the birth of the county, beginning with Native American artifacts. Then it's on to the area's early logging history; a look at early agricultural efforts; and a peek inside a settler's home, an early parlor, a kitchen, a general store, and a bedroom. Once you've viewed the past, step onto the observation deck for a great view of the Skagit Valley today.

Special programs include evening Skagit Topics lectures the third Thursday of each school month; as well as events surrounding Treaty Day in January, which honors the treaty signed on January 22, 1855, between the U.S. government and the tribes of Western Washington; the Tulip Festival in April; and Old Fashioned School Days in May.

*Hours: Tues–Sun 11am–5pm.*
*Admission charged.*
*Directions: From I-5, take State Route 20 west to La Conner/Whitney Road and drive south to La Conner. In downtown La Conner, follow Second Street to Benton Street. From Benton Street, drive uphill to S Fourth Street, turn left, and drive to the top of the hill. The museum is on the right.*

## LAKE STEVENS

## ■ Lake Stevens Historical Museum
1802 Main Street
Lake Stevens, WA 98258
(425)334-3944

The Lake Stevens Historical Museum features hundreds of historical photographs, a film projector from one of the town's old movie theaters, and a series of glass-fronted "vignettes" depicting a lumberjack's shack filled with tools, an early schoolroom, local shingle mills, and the swimming, ice skating, water skiing, and fishing that brought folks here for year-round recreation.

According to museum organizers, the most popular exhibit recreates a scene from Mitchell's Pharmacy, complete with soda fountain, milk shake machine, ice cream parlor tables, medicine bottles, and prescription books. "That was the hub of the town in the old days," recalls museum officer Anne Whitsell. "Folks went to Mitchell's for ice cream, to pay their bills, and for social gatherings after high school games. It was the place to be!"

*Hours: Fri–Sat 1pm–4pm.*
*Admission by donation.*
*Directions: From northbound I-5, take the Highway 2 exit (toward Stevens*
*Pass) and cross the trestle. Turn left on State Route 204 and, at the*
*second stop light, turn left on Highway 9 and right on Lundeen*
*Parkway. Follow that through the four-way stop and continue up the*
*hill (20th Street) to Lake Stevens. At the Viking Drive-In, turn right*
*on Main Street. The museum is on your right, behind the library.*

## LONG BEACH

### ■ Marsh's Free Museum
State Route 103
Long Beach, WA 98631
(360)642-2188

No trip to the Long Beach Peninsula is complete (or, if you have kids, allowed) without a stop at Marsh's Free Museum, an intriguing shop filled with unusual and bizarre items such as shrunken heads, historical artifacts, and—oh yeah—souvenir T-shirts, saltwater taffy, and other vacation baubles.

Marsh's is most famous, however, for being the home of Jake the Alligator Man. Jake, the museum's mascot, is supposedly half man and half alligator, and to see him you have to make your way to the back corner of the shop. Along the way there's plenty to distract you, including a coin-operated music box urging you to hear the warbling of the mechanical "imported French canary"; the Throne of Love, which promises to test your passion; and displays that feature early mousetraps, turn-of-the-century valentines, and oodles of stuff that elicits an "Oh my, what's that!?" response.

Toward the front of the shop, above the souvenir racks, are shelves displaying a two-headed pig and a menagerie of taxidermied and freeze-dried animals. The kitty that for years lounged lazily by the store's front register is now part of the display; and store owners claim that, not long after the first cat was "put on the shelf," a startlingly similar-looking cat walked in the front door and plopped himself down by the register. One way or another, we suspect he'll be sticking around.

*Hours: Summer: Daily 9am–10pm. Rest of year: Daily 9am–6pm.*
*Admission free.*
*Directions: From northbound Highway 101, head west on State Route 103,*
*which becomes the main drag in downtown Long Beach. Once down-*
*town, look for the faded wood building with a low porch strewn with*
*giant carved wooden cowboys, old pig-scalding kettles, and assorted*
*farm equipment.*

■  **Pacific Coast Cranberry Foundation Museum**
Pioneer Road
Ilwaco, WA 98264
(360)642-4938

Don't assume that Cape Cod has the corner on the cranberry market. Northwest farmers have been growing cranberries since the late 1800s and now at least 7 percent of the North American cranberry crop is grown in Bandon and Seaside, Oregon, and in Long Beach and Grayland, Washington.

The Pacific Coast Cranberry Foundation Museum, next to a 10-acre demonstration cranberry farm, offers a historic view of cranberry production on the West Coast. Vintage photographs explain the steps involved in growing and cultivating cranberries, from bog preparation and planting to harvesting and marketing. The historical equipment on display includes cranberry beaters, tools, and vintage cranberry boxes. There's a variety of picking equipment, from old-fashioned hand-picking tools to more modern sorters, separators, and mechanical pickers, including the Furford cranberry picker, invented in 1956 by Grayland cranberry farmer Julius Furford. The museum also displays examples of "cranberry money," the tokens and tickets that farmers once used to pay the cranberry pickers and that were honored only "in town."

Once you've learned how the cranberry industry evolved, pick up a brochure and take a walking tour of the adjacent cranberry bog, which offers a firsthand look at different varieties of cranberries, irrigation systems, and cranberry cultivation.

> *Hours: Museum: May 1 to Dec 15: Fri–Sun 10am–3pm. Closed rest of year. Walking tour: Year-round dawn to dusk.*
> *Admission by donation.*
> *Directions: The museum is on Washington's Long Beach Peninsula. Take northbound State Route 103 through Long Beach and turn right on Pioneer Road.*

■  **World Kite Museum and Hall of Fame**
Third Street NW (PO Box 964)
Long Beach, WA 98631
(360)642-4020

Each August, hundreds of kite fliers and thousands of spectators show up at Long Beach hoping for just enough wind to make the Kite Festival another sky-filled success. The more people who show up the better, because each year festival organizers try to break the Western Hemisphere record for the most kites in the sky at one time. They usually do.

Long Beach is not only a great place to go fly kites, it's also the home of the World Kite Museum and Hall of Fame, a small building filled with kites of all sizes, shapes, colors, and purposes. The collection includes kite books, colorful photographs of kites in flight, and more than 600 kites representing over two dozen countries and practically every state. Some kites are no bigger than a matchbox, while others seem way too big to achieve liftoff, and several elaborate handmade kites from China and Japan seem too beautiful and fragile to throw into the sky.

Not only does the museum display colorful modern-day kites, but it also tells the story of kites in history, from Benjamin Franklin's electricity experiment with a kite and a key in 1752 to the kites emblazoned with pictures of enemy airplanes that were used to train World War II gunners. During this time box kites, known as Gibson Girl kites, were also standard equipment on lifeboats—not to provide entertainment at sea, but to raise an aerial so rescue signals could be transmitted.

The museum's Hall of Fame honors famous kite flyers and kite inventors, including Arthur Batut, a French photographer who in the late 1880s became known as the father of aerophotography. One day, the story goes, he noticed a butterfly floating by with perfectly still wings. From this, he somehow got the notion to attach a camera to a kite so he could take photos from the air. But once the kite and camera were aloft, how did Batut snap his shots? According to museum notes, before the contraption lifted off, he simply lit a wick; when the wick burned down, voilà!—the SkyCam was born.

> *Hours: June to Aug: Daily 11am–5pm. Sept to Oct: Fri–Mon 11am–5pm. Nov–May: Sat and Sun 11am–5pm.*
> *Admission charged.*
> *Directions: Take northbound State Route 103 to Long Beach. After the traffic light, take the second left, on Third Street NW. The museum is on your right.*

## LOPEZ ISLAND

### ■ Lopez Historical Museum
Lopez Village
Corner of Weeks and Washburn Roads (PO Box 163)
Lopez, WA 98261
(360)468-2049

Look for the reef-net boat, the tractor, and the beckoning picnic tables outside the Lopez Historical Museum. Go inside to see historical photographs, household items, kitchen utensils, tools, and other artifacts chronicling local farming activities and the daily lives of area pioneer families. Other exhibits feature maritime and fishing paraphernalia such as a fish trap and models of steamboats, and Native American artifacts including two dugout canoes.

> *Hours: July to Aug: Wed–Sun noon–4pm. May, June, Sept: Fri–Sun noon–4pm. Closed rest of year.*
> *Admission by donation.*

*Directions: From the Lopez Island ferry dock, the museum is four miles south, on the corner of Weeks and Washburn Roads in Lopez Village.*

## LYNDEN

### ■ Lynden Pioneer Museum
217 Front Street
Lynden, WA 98264
(360)354-3675

While all the shops, restaurants, and storefronts in downtown Lynden are done up in cheery Dutch-themed decor, the real attraction here is the Lynden Pioneer Museum, one of the largest and most appealing museums of its kind in the Northwest.

Local pioneer Fred K. Polinder got the ball rolling when he donated more than 40 antique buggies, wagons, and carts to the museum in 1976. His collection, now on display in one section of the basement, includes a milk wagon, a 1929 Reo fire truck, a mail cart, a laundry wagon, and a horse-drawn gasoline wagon. The Puget Sound Antique Tractor and Machinery Association weighs in with a display of old tractors and farm machinery in another section of the basement, not far from a nice selection of vintage cars, radiator caps, spark plugs, rare bicycles, and vintage firefighting equipment.

If cars and tractors don't thrill you, spend your time on the main floor, which celebrates Lynden's dairy, timber, and agricultural history. Look for the locally designed Magic Automatic Egg Cleaner in the dairy exhibit, and learn some logger lingo in the logging exhibit. Sit for a moment on one of the shiny red counter stools in the "Cozy Cafe," pondering the low prices, and then window-shop your way through the 26 storefronts in the charming two-story re-creation of early downtown Lynden. Businesses include the well-stocked Lynden Department Store, city hall, a dentist and doctor's office, a hotel, and a church. Be sure to look in the barbershop, which claims to have the first bathtub to arrive in the Northwest. Each shop's second floor is accessible from the museum's upper level, which also offers a nice collection of Girl Scout memorabilia, old radios, an intriguing assortment of objects from the sea, and a drawing of the stump that served for many years as an area post office.

Don't leave without exploring the "vault." Located just to the left of the entrance, this room contains Civil War artifacts, dolls, guns, a great collection of Native American treasures, and an exhibit of magic lanterns and vintage cameras.

*Hours: Mon–Sat 10am–4pm.*
*Admission charged.*
*Directions: Lynden is 13 miles north of Bellingham, and the museum is on Front Street downtown. From State Route 539, follow the signs to downtown Lynden.*

## McCLEARY

■ **McCleary Museum**
314 Second Street
McCleary, WA 98557
(360)495-3450

Housed in the Carnell House, the McCleary Museum tells the story of McCleary in the days when it was a logging town owned by timber baron Henry McCleary. Exhibits include historical logging photographs dating back to the town's first sawmill in 1898, farming and logging equipment, World War I memorabilia, household items such as washtubs and fruit jars, and a copper moonshine still in complete working order. "Of course we don't make white lightning around here anymore," says museum curator Charles Fattig, "but during the 1920s moonshine was our second industry, after door manufacturing."

Judging from the photographs on the walls, McCleary's third industry might well have been bear hunting. Keeping the trees safe from bears is such a tradition in town that each year, during the second week of July, McCleary hosts a Bear Festival, complete with a parade and a big bear stew cooked up in the park. Alas, no moonshine is served.

> *Hours: June to Aug: Sat–Sun noon–4pm. Closed rest of year.*
> *Admission free.*
> *Directions: From Olympia, take westbound Highway 101. Past Aberdeen, the road becomes State Route 8 (Highway 101 turns north toward Port Angeles). Continue on State Route 8 to the McCleary exit, turn right, and at the T turn left toward town. Turn right at E Pine Street, drive one block, and turn left on Second Street.*

## MOLSON

■ **Okanogan Highlands Museum (Molson School Museum)**
**Old Molson Museum**
Main Street
Molson, WA 98844
(509)422-4272

Molson, a former boomtoom 15 miles east of Oroville, has two museums: the Okanogan Highlands Museum and the Old Molson Museum.

Housed in a three-story brick schoolhouse built in 1914, the Okanogan Highlands Museum (also called the Molson School Museum) features a restored schoolroom, antique hand tools, a pioneer post office, historical photographs, and lots of household items. Look for the horseshoe display and the collection of antique skis, skates, and sleighs.

The Old Molson Museum is a reassembled pioneer town just a mile away. Buildings are filled with farming, mining, and other artifacts and include an original bank, an assay office, and a homesteader's cabin.

*Hours: Okanogan Highlands Museum: Memorial Day to Labor Day:*
*Daily 10am–5pm. Closed rest of year. Old Molson Museum: April to*
*Dec: Daily till dusk. Closed rest of year.*
*Admission free.*
*Directions: From Oroville, head east ten miles on Oroville–Toroda Creek*
*Road, then drive five miles north on Molson Road.*

## MONTESANO

### ■ Chehalis Valley Historical Museum
730 W Pioneer Avenue
Montesano, WA 98563
(360)249-5800

Located in a 1906 Norwegian Lutheran church building, the Chehalis Valley Historical Museum tells the story of the early days of the Chehalis River valley, from Oakville to Montesano. Displays include artifacts and photos from the forest-products industry, pioneer tools and household items, toys, books, and details salvaged from a local high school. Exhibits include items relating to the Clemons Logging Company, founded by Charles H. Clemons and eventually sold to the Weyerhaeuser Company. Weyerhaeuser's first tree farm, in Grays Harbor County, was named the Clemons Tree Farm in his honor.

The museum also has a large collection of scrapbooks, including one documenting what some remember as a "Woodstock-style" rock festival held in the area. According to newspaper clippings, the Satsop River Fair and Tin Cup Races were scheduled over three days on Labor Day weekend in 1971. Despite three days of constant rain, 60,000 people attended the festival on Saturday alone, despite the objections of the Grays Harbor Board of Commissioners, who attempted to block the concert. The festival was so widely attended that when it concluded, the string of cars leaving the site reportedly stretched 40 to 50 miles to Tacoma. No mention is made in the scrapbooks of the bands that performed.

*Hours: Sat–Sun noon–4pm.*
*Admission free.*
*Directions: From Highway 12, take the Montesano City Center exit and*
*turn north on Main Street. At the stoplight (W Pioneer Avenue), turn*
*west and continue to the church, on the south side of the street.*

## MOSES LAKE

### ■ Adam East Museum and Art Center
122 W Third Avenue
Moses Lake, WA 98837
(509)766-9395

In 1955, Adam East donated more than 8,000 Native American and historical artifacts to the city of Moses Lake. Few people were given the opportunity to see this collection—or the fossils, geological specimens, and photographs in the city's collection—until the Adam East Museum and Art Center was created in the early 1990s.

Now the museum has two permanent exhibits, a changing historical exhibition gallery and an art gallery that presents eight or ten shows a year featuring the work of regional artists and touring shows borrowed from other institutions. The permanent exhibits are updated regularly and feature items from the museum's collection. *Our Changing Oasis* is a timeline and cultural history of Moses Lake full of historical photographs and artifacts from geologic times through the present. *Native Cultures of North America* displays many of the finer artifacts from the collection along with information on resource protection and profiles of contemporary Native Americans.

On Family Saturdays (the first Saturday of each month), the museum presents a free workshop, demonstration, or special exhibit. The museum also sponsors art classes, poetry readings, musical performances, films, and a winter lecture series. Art shows include the annual Columbia Basin juried art exhibit each summer, a holiday show in November, and the ever-popular Baked, Mashed, and Fried potato-art show each winter.

*Hours: Tues–Sat 11am–5pm.*
*Admission free.*
*Directions: From eastbound I-90, take exit 176 onto Broadway and follow it to Ash Street (about two miles). Turn right and drive one block to W Third Avenue; the museum is on the corner of W Third and Ash.*
*From westbound I-90, take exit 179 onto Pioneer Way and follow it to W Third Avenue. Turn left on W Third and continue for five blocks to Ash Street.*

### ■ Schiffner Military Museum
4840 Westshore Drive
Moses Lake, WA 98837
(509)765-6374

George and Margaret Schiffner are big collectors of military and law enforcement memorabilia. They've collected so much stuff that they've turned their Moses Lake ranch into a museum that displays more than

100 military uniforms, a wooden flagpole from Larson Air Force Base, military hats, helmets, guns, gas masks, and more.

The Schiffner Military Museum's collection is far-ranging and includes thousands of police badges and law enforcement patches, a World War II Japanese medical kit, a U.S. Army folding field operating table, buttons from a Civil War uniform, a canteen from the Spanish-American War, a Gibson Girl emergency radio complete with a box-kite antenna, the holster used by Moses Lake's first town marshal, and horse-shoes from horses that once pulled caskets at Arlington Cemetery. There are even videotaped World War II training films featuring then-actor Ronald Reagan. In one film he plays a chaplain; in another, he warns soldiers to be careful not to discard any papers containing information that might benefit an enemy.

All this stuff, from matchbooks included in World War II C rations to mannequins dressed in uniforms from a wide variety of military eras, is scattered throughout the Schiffners' home and a building next door.

*Hours: By appointment only.*
*Admission by donation.*
*Directions: From westbound I-90, take exit 175 (State Park) onto West-*
*shore Drive. Follow it north for four miles; when the country road*
*takes a right turn, look for the driveway between two brick pillars.*
*From eastbound I-90, take exit 174 and cross the overpass. Continue*
*one mile to the intersection of Hansen Road and Westshore Drive, and*
*turn left on Westshore.*

## MOUNT ST. HELENS

### ■ Mount St. Helens National Volcanic Monument Visitor Centers
Amboy, WA 98601
Mount St. Helens Visitor Center: (360)274-2100
Hoffstadt Bluffs Visitor Center: (360)274-7750
Forest Learning Center: (360)414-3439
Coldwater Ridge Visitor Center: (360)274-2131
Johnston Ridge Observatory: (360)274-2140

Five visitors centers along the Spirit Lake Memorial Highway (State Route 504) help visitors learn about the May 18, 1980, eruption of Mount St. Helens and its effects on the landscape.

The Mount St. Helens Visitor Center, operated by the U.S. Forest Service, is five miles east of I-5 on Silver Lake. A video, slide program, timeline, and other exhibits give you an introduction to volcanoes, the events leading up to the 1980 eruption, and the cultural history of the area. Kids will especially enjoy the walk-through volcano and the "make-a-quake" seismograph display.

The Hoffstadt Bluffs Visitor Center (at Milepost 27) is mostly a service center, but at the Forest Learning Center (at Milepost 33), you'll learn about the Weyerhaeuser Company's response to the eruption, about how it salvaged timber from its land in the blast zone, and about the exhaustive replanting efforts under way. Look for the life-size *Forest That Was* exhibit and line up for a chance to "fly" a helicopter over the St. Helens Tree Farm.

The Coldwater Ridge Visitor Center (at Milepost 43) is a multi-million-dollar facility that offers an amazing view of the volcano and exhibits detailing the biological side of the eruption. Interactive exhibits here show which plants and animals survived the eruption, how they did it, and what new species have colonized the area in the post-eruption era.

At the end of the highway (at Milepost 52) is the Johnston Ridge Observatory, with great views of the mountain's crater, lava dome, and other geological features. This center interprets the geological story of the volcano and shows how scientists monitor an active volcano. Special features include a relief model of the volcano that uses 65,000 fiber-optic lights to explain the eruption sequence and a dramatic large-screen theater presentation titled *Message from the Mountain.*

> Web site: *www.fs.fed.us/gpnf/mshnvm/*
> Hours: *Call for hours at individual centers, or check at a Forest Service information station.*
> Admission *free at the Hoffstadt Bluffs Visitor Center and the Forest Learning Center. Admission charged at the centers operated by the Forest Service. (One fee covers all three.)*
> Directions: *From I-5, take exit 47 and head east on State Route 504.*

## NAHCOTTA

### ■ Willapa Bay Interpretive Center
Oyster Station House
273rd Street, on the jetty
Port of Peninsula
Nahcotta, WA 98640
(360)665-4547

This full-size replica oyster shack built on pilings in Willapa Bay is actually an oyster museum, created to tell the story of the bay's 150-year-old oyster industry and the Native Americans and early settlers who harvested oysters. Inside the Willapa Bay Interpretive Center, visitors can view an informational videotape and historical photos, including a shot of the unusual local train that "ran by the tide." Artifacts displayed range from the small one-man boats (called bateaus) used for harvesting oysters to oyster knives, oyster baskets, a tide clock, and other oyster-industry equipment. Outside, on the museum deck, are panels with information about local birds, grasses, and wildlife, and a detailed description of the bay.

> *Hours: Memorial Day to Cranberrian Fair (early October): Fri–Sun*
> *10am–3pm. Closed rest of year.*
> *Admission free.*
> *Directions: The center is on the jetty just east of State Route 103 in Nah-*
> *cotta, at 273rd Street (the Port of Peninsula), just east of the Ark*
> *Restaurant.*

## NEAH BAY

### ■ Makah Museum
Makah Cultural and Research Center
1880 Bayview Avenue/State Route 112 (PO Box 160)
Neah Bay, WA 98357
(360)645-2711

In 1998 the Makah Indians announced that, after a seven-decade hiatus and despite protests from animal-rights groups, the tribe would resume its ancient tradition of whale hunting. The decision has drawn worldwide media attention to remote Neah Bay and to the history of the Makah people.

On Neah Bay, at the end of State Route 112, you'll find the Makah reservation and the Makah Cultural and Research Center, also known as the Makah Museum. Visitors making the long trek will be rewarded with a rare sight. The permanent exhibits include artifacts from Ozette, a Makah village partly covered by a mudslide for more than 300 years. In

Makah canoes used for whaling and sealing

1970, when tidal erosion began to reveal the village, it was discovered that the mud had acted like the ash at Pompeii and had perfectly preserved thousands of items used in fishing, hunting, and everyday life. By the time archaeologists closed the Ozette dig in 1981, more than 60,000 artifacts had been excavated, helping to re-create the Makahs' history as whalers, sealers, fishermen, hunters, craftspeople, and warriors.

Unusual artifacts now on display include a cedar carving of a killer whale's dorsal fin embedded with more than 700 otter teeth, early metal tools, cedar bark cradles, basketry, and early fishing gear and nets. Visitors are allowed to handle many of the artifacts, including tools used in whaling and sealing. The museum also displays four cedar dugout canoes as well as dioramas depicting marine environments complete with the sound of birds, waves, and sea lions.

The museum's 60-foot longhouse replica is based on the dimensions of Ozette longhouses. It was allowed to weather outdoors and was then dismantled and reconstructed inside the museum. Step inside to hear conversations and singing in the Makah language and see fish drying on the racks overhead.

Special programs include lectures and demonstrations, but you must make reservations well in advance.

> *Hours: Memorial Day to Sept 15: Daily 10am–5pm. Sept 16 to before Memorial Day: Wed–Sun 10am–5pm.*
> *Admission charged.*
> *Directions: The museum is just inside the gateway to the Makah reservation, on State Route 112 at Neah Bay.*

## NORTH BEND

### ■ Snoqualmie Valley Historical Museum
320 North Bend Boulevard (PO Box 179)
North Bend, WA 98045
(206)888-3200

While some folks still visit this area in search of locations depicted in the troubling *Twin Peaks* television show and movie, these days most visitors are headed for Snoqualmie Falls or the outlet mall in North Bend. Those who take a moment to visit the Snoqualmie Valley Historical Museum, though, will learn a great deal about life in this valley.

Displays describe the history of both the Snoqualmie Indians and the European and American pioneers who came to log and farm in the area. Artifacts include basketry, a dugout canoe, and Fuzzy, a taxidermied bear cub. The museum also has a fully stocked 1912 country kitchen, complete with a baby doll in a high chair waiting for breakfast. Out back, in the farm shed, is a well-labeled collection of farm equipment and old machinery ranging from an industrial egg-grader to a lovely green metal-and-glass Rainbow gas pump.

*Hours: April to Oct: Thurs–Sun 1pm–5pm. Closed rest of year.*
*Admission by donation.*
*Directions: From I-90, take exit 31; the museum is a half mile north, just*
  *down the road from the outlet mall.*

## ODESSA

### ■ Odessa Historical Museum
Elm Street (PO Box 536)
Odessa, WA 99159
(509)982-2539

Back in the 1890s, the Great Northern Railway lured farmers to the Odessa area by offering immigrants free train fare west along with the opportunity to apply for homesteads. Eighty percent of the people who responded were German wheat farmers from Russia, many of whom had friends and relatives who'd already settled into productive wheat farming in the nearby communities of Colfax and Ritzville.

To learn what the mostly German community of Odessa was like at the turn of the century, stop by the Odessa Historical Museum. Exhibits include farm equipment, household items, photographs, and some of the cherished possessions brought west by early immigrants, including a shawl and a Bible.

The museum also displays tools, a printing press, military items from World Wars I and II, cameras, and several re-created rooms, including a kitchen, a parlor, and a general store. Outside in the yard are farm equipment, a working windmill, and three lines of horseshoes for use by anyone who stops by.

*Hours: Memorial Day to Sept: Sun 1pm–4pm. Dec (when the museum is*
  *decorated for an old-fashioned Christmas): Sun 1pm–4pm. Closed rest*
  *of year.*
*Admission by donation.*
*Directions: From I-90, exit onto State Route 28 at the town of George. At*
  *the edge of Odessa are a golf course and a* MUSEUM *sign. Turn right*
  *at the first street past the golf course, turn left on W Fourth Street, and*
  *continue for one block; the museum is on the corner of Elm and W*
  *Fourth Streets.*

## OKANOGAN

### ■ Okanogan Museum
1410 Second Avenue (PO Box 1129)
Okanogan, WA 98840
(509)422-4272

Operated by the Okanogan Historical Society—a busy group of volunteers that also runs the two museums in Molson (see listings in Molson) and the Shafer Museum in Winthrop (see listing)—the Okanogan Museum features dioramas, models, historical photographs, and a wide variety of artifacts that tell the Okanogan County story from earliest to modern times.

Outside, there's a replica of an Old West town. Indoor exhibits focus on the area's geology, pioneer life, mining history, and the activities of the U.S. Forest Service. A section on Native American history features artifacts from the area's early tribes and includes a picture of Chief Joseph of the Nez Perce tribe. Elsewhere in the museum are old schoolhouse furniture, a barbershop complete with an old bathtub, and models of Fort Okanogan and the sternwheeler *Okanogan*.

The Old West town beside the museum features farm equipment and miniature versions of a bank, a saloon, a dressmaker's shop, a hotel, and other businesses. The town also has a log cabin built in 1879 that is believed to be Okanogan's oldest structure, and a replica of the 1910 Okanogan Fire Hall, complete with vintage fire trucks and antique fire-fighting equipment.

> *Hours: Memorial Day to Sept: Daily 10am–4pm. Closed rest of year. Admission charged.*
> *Directions: The museum is on State Route 20, between Okanogan and Omak.*

## OLYMPIA

### ■ Washington State Capital Museum
211 W 21st Avenue
Olympia, WA 98501
(360)753-2580

The Washington State Capital Museum is housed in the Lord Mansion, an impressive red-tile-roofed home with 32 rooms and five fireplaces, built in the early 1920s for the family of banker C. J. Lord, who served a term as Olympia's mayor in 1902–03.

The elaborate wood-paneled bedrooms, living room, library, and dining room now house an eclectic collection that includes objects celebrating the Native Americans of southern Puget Sound, documentation relating to the establishment of the state capital, a 30-day clock that once hung in the state's legislative chambers, and the original state seal.

Sadly, the museum's stuffed platypus is gone, and making arrangements to view the state's chunk of moon rock seems way too complicated. However, the permanent *Traditions and Transitions* exhibit area at the top of the formal staircase features an impressive Native American "welcome figure," much like the ones traditionally placed in front of longhouses to greet guests. This figure welcomes visitors to explore the replica cedar plankhouse, baskets, jewelry, tools, trade goods, and a well-stocked, kids-level hands-on section.

Outside the museum is the Delbert McBride Ethnobotanical Garden, named in honor of the museum's curator emeritus. The garden was created to provide an understanding of the ways in which Indians of Western Washington use plants as food, medicine, and sometimes tools. Flyers available in the garden detail the uses of each plant. For example, wild strawberry makes a refreshing tea, while western trillium is thought of as a love charm.

> *Hours: Tues–Fri 10am–4pm, Sat–Sun noon–4pm.*
> *Admission charged.*
> *Directions: From I-5, take the State Capitol exit and proceed straight*
>    *ahead to the Capitol campus. Turn left on Capital Way and right on*
>    *W 21st Avenue.*

## ORCAS ISLAND (EASTSOUND)

### ■ Orcas Island Historical Museum
5 N Beach Road (PO Box 134)
Eastsound, WA 98245
(360)376-4849

The six homestead cabins that make up this museum were each carefully disassembled at their original locations around the island and creatively reassembled, log by log, into one interconnected structure. Now each cabin is a room offering a window into the culture of the island's early Native American residents and into the daily lives of the settlers who began arriving here in the 1880s.

For example, the 1890 Nels Olson cabin, which now displays woodworking and farming tools, belonged to a Swedish sailor who jumped ship here. The Alexander Jackson cabin houses an *Early Stores and Post Offices* exhibit and features a special cat entrance by the front door; a homestead map shows the original location of each cabin. Other cabins feature early photographs of the island taken by noted local photographer James Geoghegan, early furniture, and collections of artifacts and handcrafted items from Northwest Coast tribes, including the totem pole out front.

> **While You're on Orcas:**
> Orcas Island is also home to the School House Museum. Built in 1888, the structure served as the Crow Valley School until 1918 and became a community club in 1919. Now the museum display artifacts and photographs from early Orcas schools.
>
> *School House Museum,*
>    *Crow Valley Road,*
>    *Eastsound, WA 98245;*
>    *(360)376-4260.*
> *Hours: Memorial Day to Labor Day: Thurs–Sun noon–4pm. Closed rest of year. Admission by donation. Directions: The museum is on Crow Valley Road, between Eastsound and Westsound.*

*Web site: www.orcasisland.org/historicalmuseum/index.htm*
*Hours: May to Sept: Fri 1pm–8pm, Tues–Thurs and Sat–Sun 1pm–4pm.*
  *Closed rest of year.*
*Admission charged.*
*Directions: The museum is on N Beach Road, in the center of Eastsound.*

## PALOUSE

### ■ Roy Chatters Newspaper and Printing Museum
100 E Main Street
Palouse, WA 99161
(509)878-1688

The Roy Chatters Newspaper and Printing Museum is a pioneer newspaper print shop that has an 1890 flatbed letterpress, typesetting machines, an 1888 job press, a large paper cutter, and a variety of other equipment used for linotype and letterpress printing in the American West. The museum also has a large archive of Whitman County and regional newspapers.

*Hours: June 1 to Labor Day: Thurs and Sun 1pm–4pm. Closed rest*
  *of year.*
*Admission by donation.*
*Directions: From Highway 195, take eastbound State Route 272 to*
  *Palouse. The museum is on E Main Street, next to a gift shop.*

## PASCO

### ■ Franklin County Historical Museum
305 N Fourth Street
Pasco, WA 99301
(509)547-3714

Housed in a refurbished 1911 Carnegie library building, the Franklin County Historical Museum features artifacts from the Spokane, Wanapum, Yakima, Umatilla, Nez Perce, and Palouse Indians, historical photographs dating back to 1900, and an exhibit on Lewis and Clark's visit to the area in October 1805. The exhibits reflecting the early days of the community include a little schoolroom, a parlor occupied by mannequins dressed in period clothing, Northern Pacific Railroad memorabilia, and a display on the early steamboats that traveled the local rivers. Embroidered clothing and enameled dishes from the area's early Chinese residents are also on display, along with a buggy from 1910; items describing irrigation, wheat farming, and the area's cattle and sheep ranching industries; antique toys and dolls; and farming and carpentry tools.

The museum hosts lectures on a wide variety of historical topics throughout the year.

*Hours: Tues–Fri 1pm–5pm, Sat 10am–5pm.*
*Admission by donation.*
*Directions: From I-182, take the City Center/Fourth Street exit. The
    museum is five blocks down on  N Fourth Street.*

## PORT ANGELES

### ■ Clallam County Museum
Federal Building
138 W First Street
Port Angeles, WA 98362
(360)417-2364

While it waits for its new home to be completed, the Clallam County
Museum is camped out in temporary quarters in the lobby of the Federal
Building in downtown Port Angeles.

Displays will change from time to time, but the large black Toledo
scale will no doubt stay put. Originally a fixture in the Greyhound depot
on the town's waterfront, the scale still offers "honest exact weight—up
to 300 pounds." Other exhibits explore the county's timber and fishing
industries and provide information about shipwrecks that occurred along
the area's coastline. The museum's archives contain historical photographs
of area towns no longer in existence, artifacts from the Clallam and
Makah Indians, and documentation on the Puget Sound Cooperative
Colony, an 1880s experiment in socialist living. The colony established a
shipyard and lumber mill and, for a while, printed its own money and its
own newspaper and ran its own schools.

Sometime in the year 2001, the museum will have a new home in
the old Lincoln School building on Eighth Street.

*Hours: Mon–Fri: 8:30am–4pm.*
*Admission free.*
*Directions: Follow Highway 101 into downtown Port Angeles. The Federal
    Building is on the corner of N Oak and W First Streets.*

### ■ Port Angeles Fine Arts Center
1203 E Lauridsen Boulevard
Port Angeles, WA 98362
(360)457-3532

The Port Angeles Fine Arts Center is the north Olympic Peninsula's
regional art museum, presenting installations and exhibitions of painting,
sculpture, photography, drawing, functional arts, and mixed media. Each
show runs from four to eight weeks and features both well-known and
emerging artists from the Pacific Northwest and beyond.

The center is on the estate of the late Esther Barrows Webster, a local
artist, publisher, and philanthropist who wanted to be sure Port Angeles
had a stimulating cultural climate. Webster's former home, which contains

the galleries, is a circular contemporary wood and glass structure that offers breathtaking views of the city, the harbor, and the Strait of Juan de Fuca—and, on a very clear day, affords glimpses of Canada. The home is surrounded by five acres of woods that are crisscrossed by trails dotted with permanent and temporary outdoor sculptures.

In addition to its changing exhibitions, the center hosts lectures, musical performances, readings, and other special programs throughout the year.

*Web site: www.olympus.net/community/pafac*
*Hours: Thurs–Sun 11am–5pm.*
*Admission by donation.*
*Directions: From Highway 101 in Port Angeles, take Race Street south to*
  *E Lauridsen Boulevard. Turn east on Lauridsen and drive a short dis-*
  *tance. The center is on the left as you head toward Peninsula College.*

## PORT GAMBLE

### ■ Of Sea and Shore Museum
1 Rainier Avenue (PO Box 219)
Port Gamble, WA 98364
(360)297-2426

Port Gamble native Tom Rice started collecting shells as a kid on beach-combing trips with his grandmother. Later he made seashells the focus of his biology projects for school. Now Rice has a collection of more than 20,000 mollusks (shells) and several thousand specimens of other marine life. Unfortunately, there's room to exhibit only half of them at the Of Sea and Shore Museum he runs in Port Gamble. Fortunately, half of this mammoth collection is quite a lot to see.

On display are giant Australian false trumpet snails, which, at three feet across, are the largest species of shells in the world. You'll also see whale barnacles, whale lice, sand dollars, sea urchins, shark jaws, and just about every shape, size, and color of shell you can imagine. The museum has two lovely painted murals depicting a Puget Sound beach and a trop-ical coral reef, but an exhibit of shells sporting natural dots, circles, spirals, and perfectly formed triangles reminds us that Mother Nature is no slouch at designing either.

Search out the pink, orange, purple, and striped scallop shells, the snails, the beetles, and the starfish, but be careful around the creepy-looking creature by the window at the end of the second-floor balcony. It looks sort of like a shrunken flying monkey from *The Wizard of Oz,* but in Mexico they call these dried skate carcasses "sea devils."

*Web site: www.ofseaandshore.com*
*Hours: Daily 9am–5pm.*
*Admission by donation.*

> *Directions: The museum is on the second and third floors of the General Store Building on Port Gamble's main street. The Port Gamble Historic Museum (see next listing) is on the first floor of the building, on the downhill side.*

## ■ Port Gamble Historic Museum
1 Rainier Avenue, in the rear (PO Box 85)
Port Gamble, WA 98364
(360)297-8074

In 1853, Captain William Talbot and business partners A. J. Pope and Cyrus Walker were in search of a Northwest site that could provide a rich source of timber, a good location for a mill, and a deepwater port. Shipping lumber from Maine around the Horn to San Francisco just didn't seem cost-effective. Port Gamble fit the bill, and the team built a New England–style company town here, complete with homes, a grand hotel, a church, a community hall, a general store, and a Masonic Temple. By 1875 the Puget Mill Company was the largest holder of timberlands in the Washington Territory, and, before it closed in 1995, the mill built at Port Gamble was the oldest continuously operating sawmill in North America.

To learn more about this intriguing chapter in forest-products history, take a walking tour around town, and be sure to stop by the Port Gamble Historic Museum. Port Gamble is still a company town of sorts, but now a Pope & Talbot subsidiary manages it and it's an official national historic site. Museum exhibits include reproductions of both the cargo hold and Captain Talbot's cabin on the *Oriental,* Pope's San Francisco office, and the ornately furnished lobby of the Puget Hotel. Other scenes include an early 1900s saw-filing room, complete with a saw anvil, saw grinders, and other tools, and the master bedroom from Walker's Port Gamble home, Admiralty Hall.

The museum also features an example of the cedar-board homes built by the local Clallam Indian tribe, maps and charts of the port, and the original land-grant deeds signed by Abraham Lincoln and Andrew Johnson granting more than 15,000 acres of timberland to Talbot and Pope. Historic photos include a shot of the last crew that worked at the mill before it closed for good in 1995.

> *Web site: www.ptgamble.com/*
> *Hours: Daily 10:30am–5pm. Call ahead in winter.*
> *Admission charged.*
> *Directions: Port Gamble is one mile east of the Hood Canal Bridge, on State Route 104. The museum is in the General Store Building on Port Gamble's main street; look for it on the downhill side, facing the bay. On the second and third floors of the building is the Of Sea and Shore Museum (see previous listing).*

## PORT ORCHARD

■ **Sidney Art Gallery and Museum**
**Log Cabin Museum**
202/416 Sidney Avenue
Port Orchard, WA 98366
(360)876-3693

When this community was first settled, back in the mid-1850s, it was named Sidney in honor of the fellow who laid out the town. In 1903, after sawmills and shipyards helped establish Sidney as an economic center, the name was "modernized" and Port Orchard became the Kitsap County seat.

You can learn more about the history of Port Orchard at the Sidney Art Gallery and Museum, a historical museum above an art gallery in the town's 1908 Masonic Hall; and at the Log Cabin Museum, just up the hill.

At the museum above the art gallery, life-size displays re-create the town's post office, doctor's office, dry goods store, hardware store, and schoolhouse. Other exhibits display historical photographs, tools, and vintage clothing and celebrate local businesses such as logging and terra-cotta pottery.

At the Log Cabin Museum, a short walk straight up Sidney Avenue, a mannequin family named the Orchards helps tell the story of life in Port Orchard at various points in history. Museum volunteers keep things interesting by creating changing seasonal "sets" for the Orchards and writing a detailed description about what activities each family member might be involved in. You can pick up a flyer with this season's story at the door, or have one of the volunteers "introduce" you to everyone.

> *Hours: Sidney Art Gallery and Museum: Summer: Tues–Sat 11am–4pm, Sun 1pm–5pm. Rest of year: Tues–Sat 11am–4pm, Sun 1pm–4pm. Log Cabin Museum: Sat 11am–4pm.*
> *Admission by donation.*
> *Directions: Take State Route 166 or the ferry from Bremerton to Port Orchard. Sidney Avenue goes straight uphill from Bay Street in Port Orchard.*

## PORT TOWNSEND

■ **Jefferson County Historical Museum**
210 Madison Street
Port Townsend, WA 98368
(360)385-1003

Sharing space in Port Townsend's 1892 city hall building with present-day municipal offices, the Jefferson County Historical Museum features exhibits that occupy the town's original police department, courtroom, jail, and fire hall.

The courtroom, with the original judge's bench, is now filled with exhibits on Jefferson County history, the Chinese community in Port Townsend, customhouse practices, Native American basketry and tools, and Inuit artifacts.

The old fire hall features changing exhibits, shipwreck artifacts, a wonderful photograph collection, and an old safe you can try to crack. At the top of the building, in the old firemen's quarters, are a research library, a local family's collection of seashells, coral and stuffed birds, and just a small part of Mrs. McIlroy's button collection.

The old police headquarters and the city jail seem to be a favorite spot for kids. Most youngsters will sit in a cell just long enough to hear the story of the prisoner who tried to escape by squeezing his body through the slot in the cell door intended for passing prisoners trays of food. The fellow, the story goes, got his head stuck and was found dead in the morning.

### While You're in Port Townsend:

An intriguing display of artifacts relating to Port Townsend's early Chinese community is tucked away on the lower level of an antique mall near the Jefferson County Historical Museum. The items—uncovered during excavation of an empty lot—date back to the late 1800s and include medicine bottles, marbles, rice bowls, coins, gambling buttons, opium pipes, and, mysteriously, a .32-caliber bullet in an ink bottle.

*Port Townsend Antique Mall, 802 Washington Street (lower level), Port Townsend, WA 98368; (360)385-2590. Hours: May to Oct: Daily 10am–5pm. Nov to April: Mon–Tues, Thurs–Fri 10am–5pm, Sat 10am–5:30pm. Admission free. Directions: The antique mall is just a few blocks west of the Jefferson County Historical Museum.*

*Web site: www.olympus.net/arts/jcmuseum*
*Hours: Mon–Sat 11am–4pm, Sun 1pm–4pm.*
*Admission charged.*
*Directions: From Highway 101, follow State Route 20 to Water Street, which passes through downtown Port Townsend. Turn left on Madison Street; the city hall and museum is on the corner of Water and Madison.*

### ■ Puget Sound Coast Artillery Museum
Fort Worden State Park
200 Battery Way
Port Townsend, WA 98368
(360)385-0373

Deactivated as a military post in 1953, Fort Worden is now a 446-acre park overlooking the Strait of Juan de Fuca and Admiralty Inlet. The grounds include officers' houses in a Victorian style, barracks, artillery bunkers, a youth hostel, and a conference center. Visitors can tour the commanding officer's house, which has been restored and furnished with period Victorian pieces, as well as the Puget Sound Coast Artillery Museum, which commemorates the army's 14th Coast Artillery Regiment and the Washington National Guard's 248th Regiment.

For an overview of Fort Worden's role in military history, spend a few moments watching the introductory video, which includes archival footage of activities at the fort and clips of the huge "disappearing guns," kept at the ready from 1910 until 1943. Working models of those guns are displayed.

Other exhibits include a military uniform collection that dates back to the turn of the century, guns, historical photographs, and detailed notes about the resurrection of a steam locomotive that had been buried at the fort for more than 60 years. The locomotive, used between 1890 and 1910 in the construction of both Fort Flagler and Fort Worden, was supposed to be destroyed once the project was completed. But in 1911, according to museum notes, Colonel Garland Whistler turned down a scrap-metal buyer's offer of $30 and instead ordered his men to bury the huge engine in the sand. Some years later, a storage shed was built over the site, and soon folks forgot the locomotive was even there. In 1973, however, when the storage shed was demolished, someone noticed a piece of rusty metal sticking out of the ground; the locomotive was dug back up and is now part of the museum's collection.

*Hours: Memorial Day to Labor Day: Daily 11am–5pm. After Labor Day to mid-Nov: Sat–Sun and holidays noon–4pm. Closed rest of year. Admission by donation.*

*Directions: From Highway 101, follow State Route 20 to Water Street in downtown Port Townsend. Once downtown, follow Cherry Street to Fort Worden State Park.*

## PROSSER

### ■ Benton County Historical Museum
Prosser City Park
Seventh Street (PO Box 1407)
Prosser, WA 99350
(509)786-3842

Prosser, on the Yakima River at the base of the Horse Heaven and Rattlesnake Hills, once served as an oasis for hundreds, perhaps thousands, of wild horses that would come down from the hills to drink at the riverbanks. The horses are gone, but their visits are remembered in an 18-foot curved mural in the Benton County Historical Museum. The mural literally leaps off the wall, with a foreground that includes real sagebrush, bunchgrass, and taxidermied birds and other animals.

The rest of the exhibits in this 5,000-square-foot museum are just as creative. For example, the parlor contains a 40-foot line of mannequins modeling gowns, hats, and high fashion from 1843 through the 1920s as well as an 1867 Chickering square piano, which remains here only as long as the museum allows visitors to tickle the ivories.

In the Farm Room, a re-creation of a homestead shack has been built with boards taken from a real shack built at the turn of the century. The museum found a unique way of dating the original shack: The boards are papered with newspapers dated January 13, 1900. The Farm Room also contains a buggy used by the town's doctor in the late 1880s and an electric miniature carved carousel that museum volunteers will plug in to make the horses move up and down. Volunteers are also happy to play the music boxes or switch on the rare Edison light bulb.

Other exhibits include a well-stocked general store, Native American tools, crafts, and clothing, items that have been to the moon and back, and a narrated slide show detailing early Prosser history.

*Hours: Tues–Sat 10am–4pm, Sun 1pm–5pm.*
*Admission charged.*
*Directions: From Yakima, take eastbound I-82 to exit 80 (Gap Road). Follow Wine Country Road into Prosser and follow Sixth across the bridge. Turn left on Seventh Street and continue through town. The museum is in Prosser City Park at Seventh Street and Paterson Avenue.*

## PULLMAN

## ■ Washington State University Museums and Collections
Pullman, WA 99164
(509)335-6272

More than a dozen museums and special collections, featuring everything from taxidermied antelopes to fine art and antique costumes, are scattered around the Washington State University campus. Take a day—or two—and park the car, unfold the campus museum brochure, and explore. A few favorite museums are further described below.

*Web site: www.wsu.edu*
*Hours: School year: Mon–Fri 8am–5pm. Summer and school vacations: Call for hours.*
*Admission free for all museums.*
*Directions: From Highway 195, head east on State Route 270 to Pullman. The campus is hard to miss once you're in Pullman; follow the signs. You can get a campus map and information about parking from the WSU visitors center in downtown Pullman or at the Public Safety Building in the center of campus.*

### ■ Charles R. Conner Natural History Museum
Washington State University
126 Science Hall
(509)335-3515

The Charles R. Conner Natural History Museum first opened in 1894. Back then it featured highlights from two freight-car loads of specimens the state of Washington had exhibited at the 1893 Chicago World's Fair. Now the museum is touted as the best and largest public collection of birds and mammals in the Pacific Northwest. Among the mounted specimens on display are 570 birds, 225 bird eggs, and more than 145 mammals, including a moose, a huge bison, a freeze-dried cow leg, and a dinosaur skeleton.

*Web site: www.sci.wsu.edu/cm/*
*Hours: Daily 8am–5pm.*

### ■ Culver Memorial
Washington State University
Webster Physical Sciences
Building
(509)335-3009

Containing more than 2,000 pieces, the Lyle and Lela Jacklin Petrified Wood Collection, housed in the Culver Memorial, is the largest display of its kind in the western United States. The Jacklins collected much of the wood themselves on trips around the West, but rumor has it that Lyle also had a forest "connection": a hermit living in the forest who gathered fossilized wood that Lyle polished.

In addition to all the petrified wood, this mini-museum features cut and polished agates, geodes, and dinosaur bones as well as the Culver collection of more than 100 classic rock and mineral specimens. Don't

## While You're at the University:
But wait, there's more—millions more! WSU's collections (all of which are free) include the Mycological Herbarium, featuring more than 70,000 fungi specimens (339 Johnson Hall, (509)335-9541; Mon–Fri 8am–5pm); the Maurice James Entomological Collection, housing more than one million insects (Food Science Building, Room 157, (509)335-5504; hours by appointment only); the Marion Ownby Herbarium, home to more than 340,000 dried plant specimens (G9 Heald Hall, (509)335-3250; Mon–Fri 8:30am–5pm); the Robert P. Worthman Veterinary Anatomy Teaching Museum, with hundreds of dried and skeletal "preparations" of large and small domestic animals (270 Wegner Hall, (509)335-5701; Mon–Fri 8am–5pm); and the Smith Soil Monolith Collection (114 Johnson Hall, (509)335-1859; Mon–Fri 8am–5pm), with more than 150 preserved soil samples—some more than eight feet long! Each collection usually fills a display case or two with prize items, but call ahead and you'll be treated to an educational tour of the collection. WSU's collections also include historic textiles and costumes, rare books, and audio recordings.

pass up the opportunity to step behind a curtain to see a wide variety of fluorescent stones that light up in neon colors under ultraviolet lights.

*Hours: Mon–Fri 8am–5pm.*
*Admission free.*

### ▓ Museum of Anthropology
Washington State University
110 College Hall
(509)335-3441

The Museum of Anthropology features interpretive exhibits that document the record of human evolution and the "lifeways" of people in past and present societies. And though the staff is a bit hesitant to make a fuss about it, the museum also has a display case devoted to the much-loved but ever-elusive Sasquatch. Included are Sasquatch foot- and handprint castings, a map marking sightings throughout Washington and Idaho, and an enlarged photo of a Sasquatch "caught" on film.

*Hours: Mon–Thurs 9am–4pm, Fri 9am–3pm.*

### ▓ Museum of Art
Washington State University
(509)335-1910

The WSU Museum of Art, the largest fine-arts facility in the inland Northwest, presents six to eight changing exhibitions throughout the year featuring work by faculty and graduate students and by nationally and internationally known artists. Exhibits range from the art of antiquity to contemporary art, and from design and photography to sculpture and painting.

In addition, a special exhibition each summer offers highlights from the permanent collection of more than 2,000 American 19th- and 20th-century paintings, drawings, and prints. The collection emphasizes Northwest art, contemporary and Old Master prints, and American paintings. Artists range from Francisco Goya to Andy Warhol. The museum also offers a wide variety of speakers, films, and other special events throughout the year.

*Hours: Tues 10am–10pm, Mon and Wed–Fri 10am–4pm, Sat–Sun*
*1pm–5pm.*

## ■ Three Forks Pioneer Museum
Albion Road
Pullman, WA 99163
(509)332-3889

It takes perseverance and planning to get to the Three Forks Pioneer Museum, a few miles outside of downtown Pullman, but it's without a doubt one of the more magical spots in the Northwest.

When Stella Rossebo first moved to this 420-acre farm more than 60 years ago, there was only a tiny log cabin, built in 1885, on the land. The cabin is still there, but now it's behind the farmhouse and packed full with old pianos, dishes, antique butter churns, and a lamp that once belonged to Stella's grandmother.

Nothing too unusual there. But venture just beyond the cabin and you'll find yourself walking through a pioneer western town—and not a miniature town but a full-size one, built plank by plank by Stella and her son Roger over the past 45 years. There's Marilyn Monroe on the operating table in the doctor's office. The millinery store is stocked with everything from feathers and fabric to a top hat that once belonged to Stella's dad. The town has a barbershop, a general store, a post office, a dentist's office, and a saloon with tin ceilings. Everything you'd expect to see in a "real" old town is re-created here, including the butcher shop, the creamery, and the jail.

Kids will love this place, and very young ones will especially enjoy the peekaboo park with its leprechaun-filled rock garden, miniature dollhouses, plastic chickens, tiny pet cemetery, and two small cottages filled floor to ceiling with toys, dolls, and teddy bears.

*Hours: May to Sept: By appointment only. Closed rest of year.*
*Admission charge.*
*Directions: Call for directions.*

### PUYALLUP

## ■ Meeker Mansion
312 Spring Street
Puyallup, WA 98371
(253)848-1770

Ezra Meeker was a pioneer, author, onetime Hop King of the World, and the first mayor of Puyallup. In 1906 he also became the self-appointed champion of the Oregon Trail when, at age 76, he hitched up two oxen to a wagon and set out from his front yard for Washington, D.C. His goal was to remark the Oregon Trail, which he worried was being obliterated by modern-day civilization. Meeker lived to be 98, long enough to complete several more trips along the trail, including a trip by automobile in 1915 and one by airplane in 1924. Today you can visit Meeker's oxen,

Dave and Dandy, at the Washington State History Museum in Tacoma (see listing).

You can also visit the Meeker Mansion, a 17-room Victorian that Meeker had built in 1890, at his wife Eliza's request, after the couple returned from a hop-selling trip to England. The mansion includes a variety of fine and exotic woods, European fireplaces, a grand staircase, and handpainted ceilings. Permanent exhibits on display highlight Ezra Meeker's 1906 journey over the Oregon Trail, while temporary exhibits contain items from the collections of the Ezra Meeker Historical Society. The grounds include a heritage rose garden and rare trees planted when the Meekers lived in the home.

Special events include a dollhouse and miniature show in April, a Mother's Day tea in May, and Christmas at Meeker Mansion in early December.

*Web site: www.meekermansion.org*
*Hours: Mid-March to mid-Dec: Wed–Sun 1pm–4pm. Closed rest of year.*
*Admission charged.*
*Directions: Take the Pioneer Avenue exit from State Route 512. The man-*
*sion is east of the Third Street bypass, on Spring Street.*

## REDMOND

### ■ Marymoor Museum
6046 W Lake Sammamish Parkway NE (PO Box 162)
Redmond, WA 98073
(425)885-3684

Located in the north wing of the 1904 Clise Mansion in Marymoor Park, the Marymoor Museum highlights the heritage of Bellevue, Kirkland, Redmond, and the east King County region.

In addition to traveling exhibits, the museum displays historic photos, clothing, furniture, and room settings that show the wilderness and rutted roads that gave way to the suburbs and highways we see today. Along the way there were farms, including James W. Clise's Willowmoor Farm, the original name for the estate that once stood on this land, which boasted prize-winning Ayrshire dairy cattle and Morgan horses. A special kids' nook has pioneer dress-up clothing, a marble raceway, and other hands-on activities.

*Hours: Memorial Day to Labor Day: Tues–Thurs 11am–4pm, Sat–Sun*
*1pm–5pm. After Labor Day to before Memorial Day: Tues–Thurs*
*11am–4pm, Sun 1pm–4pm.*
*Admission by donation.*

*Directions: From I-5 or I-405, drive east on State Route 520 to the Mary-moor Park/W Lake Sammamish Parkway NE exit. Stay in the right lane and turn right on W Lake Sammamish Parkway NE. Turn left into Marymoor Park and take the first right into the parking lot. The museum is at the south end of the lot.*

## RENTON

### ■ Renton Historical Museum
235 Mill Avenue S
Renton, WA 98055
(425)255-2330

Housed in a restored art deco fire station built under the Works Progress Administration, the Renton Historical Museum tells the story of the Renton area and its people through artifacts, vintage machinery, home furnishings, period clothing, and an extensive photographic archive.

Cultural artifacts from the Duwamish Indian tribe, which once spent part of each year living on the banks of the (now nonexistent) Black River, are on display, along with a model of a Duwamish village. Also featured are a turn-of-the-century coal car, logging equipment, photos from Longacres racetrack, a 1927 Howard Cooper fire engine, and other items from the time "before Boeing," when the area had so many sawmills, coal mines, and factories that the Chamber of Commerce described it as the Town of Payrolls.

*Hours: Wed–Thurs 9am–4pm, first Wed of the month 9am–4pm and 5pm–8pm.*
*Admission free or by donation.*
*Directions: From I-5, take State Route 900 east to SW Sunset Boulevard (State Route 900). Continue on to S Third Street (State Route 900E) and bear left on Houser Way S, then turn left on Mill Avenue S.*

## RICHLAND

### ■ Columbia River Exhibition of History, Science, and Technology
95 Lee Boulevard (PO Box 1890)
Richland, WA 99352
(509)943-9000

Some folks might remember the Hanford Science Center, which detailed the role Hanford played in the nuclear energy story—from the historic Manhattan Project, which developed the world's first atomic bomb in the 1940s, to the modern-day efforts to clean up the Hanford site.

Those nuclear energy–related exhibits now reside at a new facility with a more welcoming name: the Columbia River Exhibition of History, Science, and Technology (CREHST). The museum offers interactive and hands-on displays designed to tell the story of the Columbia Basin and the surrounding region, from primitive irrigation systems to the development and use of holograms and isotopes.

Non-nuclear exhibits explore the area's early Native American villages and pioneer settlements, the many plants and animals that live within the Columbia Basin, the story of hydroelectric power, and the wide variety of agricultural products grown locally. You'll learn that this region has the largest undisturbed shrub steppe ecosystem left in the United States and that more than 200 varieties of fruits, vegetables, grains, and berries are now grown on land that was once nothing more than a barren desert. Those crops include enough potatoes to produce more than eight billion servings of french fries. (In fact, potatoes are so popular that the agricultural area at CREHST made a potato named the Mighty Spud its mascot.)

The exhibits relating to nuclear energy and the Hanford site are intriguing no matter what political position you take on nuclear power. Here you can find out exactly why Hanford was chosen for that top-secret project back in 1943, what the word "radioactive" really means, and what radiation really can do.

> Web site: www.owt.com/crehst/
> Hours: Mon–Sat 10am–5pm, Sun noon–5pm.
> Admission charged.
> Directions: From westbound I-182, take the George Washington Way exit into Richland. Follow it to Lee Boulevard and turn right; the museum is just east of Howard Amon Park.

## ROSLYN

### ■ Roslyn Museum
Pennsylvania Avenue and Third Street
Roslyn, WA 98941
(509)649-2776

In the early 1900s, job opportunities in the prolific coalfields around Roslyn drew workers from more than 25 ethnic groups. The town bustled with more than 4,000 residents in the 1920s, but it grew sleepy by the 1960s, when the last coal mine was shut down. Things picked up again in the mid-1990s, when Roslyn starred as a stand-in for the fictional Alaskan town of Cicely in the television program *Northern Exposure,* but when the show was canceled a few years later, the town's low-key atmosphere returned.

These days, though, visitors can relive Roslyn's mining glory days at the Roslyn Museum, which displays samples of coal from area mines, an assortment of mining equipment, blueprints from the mine where an explosion killed 45 men in 1892, and beer taps from some of the 23 saloons the mining boomtown once supported. In addition to all the mining memorabilia, this jam-packed museum has pioneer artifacts, old alarm clocks, cameras, pens advertising local businesses, family albums, vintage musical instruments, a homemade bear trap, and the town's first electric refrigerator, which arrived in 1923.

Bing Crosby fans take note: The museum also has a framed letter from Crosby confirming that his family lived in Roslyn for a few years, that his dad worked at the company store, and that his brother, Everett, was born right here in Roslyn.

Outside, next to the museum, are coal cars and the 1932 Kerstetter log cabin, which was moved to this spot from the nearby town of Liberty by a group of Boy Scouts.

*Hours: Daily (or thereabouts): 1pm–5pm.*
*Admission by donation.*
*Directions: From eastbound I-90, take exit 80. The museum is in the center of town, right next to the Roslyn Cafe (the one whose colorful outside wall mural appeared in the opening credits of* Northern Exposure*).*

## SAN JUAN ISLAND (FRIDAY HARBOR)

■ **Pig War Museum**
620 Guard Street
Friday Harbor, WA 98250
(360)378-6495

When the boundary between the United States and Canada was originally established, American and British settlers were murky on just who got the San Juan Islands. Disputes over rightful ownership came to a head in 1859, when an American farmer shot a British pig he discovered rooting in his garden. This pig incident triggered the assignment of American and British troops to the island, the establishment of separate camps, and a standoff that took 13 years to resolve.

Emelia Bave's Pig War Museum features mannequins in intriguing dioramas depicting life on San Juan Island before, during, and after the Pig War. Be sure to get your picture taken with Bave's 700-pound black boar.

*Hours: Memorial Day to Labor Day: Mon–Sat noon–6pm. Closed rest of year.*
*Admission charged.*
*Directions: From the Friday Harbor ferry dock, follow Spring Street to Blair Avenue and turn right. Continue on Blair to Guard Street. The museum is on the corner of Guard Street and Tucker Avenue, across from the Friday Harbor High School tennis courts.*

■ **San Juan Historical Museum**
405 Price Street (PO Box 441)
Friday Harbor, WA 98250
(360)378-3949

Billing itself as the "the most northwestern museum in the continental United States," the San Juan Historical Museum presents a slice of Friday Harbor life from the turn of the century. The museum is on a homestead that's more than 100 years old, amid a complex consisting of an original farmhouse, the first county jail, a turn-of-the-century log cabin, a barn, a milk house, and a carriage house. Furnishings include a 1900s pump organ, a hutch filled with crystal and antique china, and the first sewing machine used in the San Juans.

In addition to temporary exhibits, the museum has an extensive oral history and historical photograph collection and sponsors a variety of activities throughout the year, including a spring lecture series, living history presentations, programs for children, and the Pig War Picnic (also known as the Bite of San Juan).

*Web site: www.sjmuseum.org/*
*Hours: May to Sept: Thurs–Sun 1pm–4pm. Oct to April: Tues and Thurs 10am–2pm.*
*Admission charged.*
*Directions: From the Friday Harbor ferry dock, follow Spring Street southwest through town. Turn right on Price Street and continue for one block.*

■ **Whale Museum**
62 First Street N (PO Box 945)
Friday Harbor, WA 98250
(360)378-4710

Even before all the hullabaloo about the movie *Free Willy* and the campaign to help Keiko return to the ocean, the folks at the Whale Museum were working hard to promote an appreciation for whales and for the earth's marine environment.

Located in a 100-year-old building overlooking the waterfront, the Whale Museum is the place to go for answers to whale-related questions, such as "Just how smart are whales?" and "Are whales fish?" You can get the answers ("Probably as smart as humans" and "No, whales are warm-blooded, air-breathing mammals that bear and nurse live young") from the helpful museum guides. Or unravel the stories yourself as you wander among whale skeletons, comparative displays, whale art, whale lore, and more. You'll see whales in glass, stone, wood, and bone, as well as exhibits that offer insights into the growth, reproduction, migration, acoustic communication, and intelligence of these giant mammals.

Whale skull and Orca model

Hanging from the ceiling is the museum's largest skeleton, a 24-foot-long, eight-month-old gray whale. When grown, these whales can be up to 50 feet long. There's also a life-size model of L8, a 20-foot male orca whose corpse was found washed ashore on Vancouver Island in 1977, as well as L8's entire skeleton—both of which help put the size of whales into perspective.

The museum is extremely kid-friendly. There's a kids' room at the north end that features whale puzzles, windows overlooking the water, and books about the ocean. Kids (and adults) will also enjoy picking up the telephone receiver in the phone booth to hear sounds of bowhead whales, bearded seals, beluga whales, and walruses. The sounds were recorded beneath the Arctic ice and are somehow both eerie and soothing.

On the first floor are the Whalesong Art Gallery and the upstairs Gallery of Whales, which contain exhibits expanded to include information on the Soundwatch boater education program and an unusual visit by orcas to Dyes Inlet in 1998.

Special programs include marine naturalist training, an orca adoption program, a whale hotline, workshops, scientific symposiums and classes for all ages, and public presentations at Lime Kiln State Park, the world's first whale-watching park.

> *Web site: www.whale/museum.org*
> *Hours: Memorial Day to Labor Day: Daily 9am–6pm. After Labor Day to before Memorial Day: Daily 10am–6pm.*
> *Admission charged. San Juan Islanders free Thurs.*
> *Directions: From the Friday Harbor ferry dock, follow Spring Street to First Street, turn right, and follow First uphill for two blocks. Look for the whale mural.*

## SEATTLE

### ■ Burke Museum of Natural History and Culture
University of Washington
NE 45th Street and 17th Avenue NE (PO Box 353010)
Seattle, WA 98195
(206)543-5590

Founded in 1885 by a group of Seattle teens calling themselves the Young Naturalists Society, the Burke Museum of Natural History and Culture is the oldest museum in Washington, housing the largest collection of Northwest Coast Native art and artifacts west of the Mississippi and our state's only real dinosaur skeletons. With room to display less than one-half of 1 percent of its three million artifacts and specimens, how-

This Allosaurus skeleton is 140 million years old,
dating to the late Jurassic period

ever, the Burke had long suffered a reputation as being somewhat dark and stodgy. Now, thanks to a $5 million renovation project completed in 1997, the Burke is an "adventure destination" with interactive displays that appeal to all—kids, teenagers, and adults—who want to learn more about Washington's natural history and culture.

Visitors to the new, improved Burke will find two permanent exhibitions: *The Life and Times of Washington State,* a 550-million-year natural history of the region, and *Pacific Voices,* a showcase of 18 Pacific Rim cultures that help make the Puget Sound region so wonderfully diverse.

*Life and Times* begins when Washington was completely under water and moves forward through the age of dinosaurs, rising volcanoes, and the last ice age. Artifacts that help tell the story include the skeleton of a 140-million-year-old flesh-eating allosaurus, a clutch of 16 real dinosaur eggs in a dinosaur nest, and the world's oldest baleen whale fossil. Kids will especially enjoy standing inside a rumbling 20-foot-tall volcano, crawling inside the replica of a 15-million-year-old two-horned rhinoceros (the original was found smothered upside down under lava near Coulee City), and feeling the blast of ice-cold air that signals the entrance to the ice age exhibit. Along the way there are pullout drawers filled with fossils and skeletons, those now-ubiquitous touch-screen computers, a discovery lab, and a nine-foot-long glass wall filled with thousands of bugs.

The *Pacific Voices* exhibition downstairs was created with the help of more than 100 Chinese, Korean, Japanese, Vietnamese, Laotian, Cambodian, Filipino, Polynesian, Hawaiian, and Native American artists, elders, and community leaders. They chose artifacts, displays, and tape recordings that highlight the stories, ceremonies, languages, and teachings of Pacific and Northwest Coast cultures. Featured items include a Raven headdress for a Tlingit chief; a full-size Quileute canoe and other items from the Burke's extensive Pacific Northwest artifact collection; a boy's initiation mask from Papua, New Guinea; tattooing instruments from Samoa; a table set for a Chinese New Year dinner ceremony; and an elaborately inlaid Vietnamese home altar. Displays feature tape recordings of the cultures' languages, and visitors can listen to community members telling a traditional story or describing an aspect of their culture.

The spiffy newer exhibits are certainly entertaining, but there were some items that museum curators just couldn't bear to put away. Look for longtime favorites in the 40-foot-long *Treasures of the Burke* display case in the lobby.

In addition to its permanent exhibitions, the Burke features a variety of temporary exhibits, family events, workshops, and a lecture series.

*Web site: www.washington.edu/burkemuseum*
*Hours: Thurs 10am–8pm, Fri–Wed 10am–5pm.*
*Admission charged. UW staff and students free. If you plan to visit both the Burke Museum and the Henry Art Gallery across campus (see*

*listing) on the same day, ask for the Burke/Henry Dollar Deal, which*
*lets you visit both for the price of one—plus $1.*
*Directions: The museum is on the northwest corner of the University of*
*Washington campus. From I-5, take the NE 45th Street exit and*
*drive east to 17th Avenue NE.*

■ **Children's Museum**
Seattle Center
Center House (305 Harrison Street)
Seattle, WA 98109
(206)441-1768

Two hours on the parking meter will hardly be enough time if you're taking kids age one or older to the Children's Museum at the Seattle Center, so take the bus or arrange to get picked up later, because this place is full of way too many fun things to do in such a short time.

Some examples: In the forest exhibit, kids can crawl through a nurse log, lift up rocks and find wonderfully icky bugs and slugs, or stop by a tent and transform themselves into black bears with the help of pint-size bear costumes. Cog City provides balls, gears, and a chance to experience what it's like to be a crane operator at the Port of Seattle. Computers offer Mindscape games and activities, and in the history tunnel kids visit Greek and Mayan rooms, where they can make brass rubbings and begin to learn a new language.

Whether it's a visit to a contemporary Philippine village or a ride on the Kobe subway, every exhibit has a hands-on component and plenty of background information to help make an afternoon of play an enjoyable educational experience as well.

In addition to the regular exhibits, the museum also hosts traveling shows and sponsors workshops and special programs in the Imagination Station and the Activity Annex.

*Web site: www.thechildrensmuseum.org*
*Hours: June 15 to Labor Day: Sun–Fri 10am–6pm, Sat 10am–7pm. After*
*Labor Day to June 14: Mon–Fri 10am–5pm, Sat–Sun 10am–6pm.*
*Admission charged.*
*Directions: From I-5, take the Mercer Street exit and follow the signs to the*
*Seattle Center. The museum is on the lower level of the Center House.*

■ **Coast Guard Museum Northwest**
Pier 36
1519 Alaskan Way S
Seattle, WA 98134
(206)217-6993

Here's a chance to go inside the Coast Guard facility down on Seattle's Pier 36. The small white building just inside the gate is the Coast Guard

Museum Northwest, home to an eclectic nautical collection ranging from uniforms, swords, and scale models of Coast Guard cutters to a piece of wood from the USS *Constitution,* also known as *Old Ironsides.*

On display is the Coast Guard flag carried on the first shuttle flight, a lighthouse service clock from 1860, photographs from the museum's archives dating back to the 1800s, and lenses from lighthouses and buoys. There are some rare items here too, most notably the bell from Admiral Peary's steam tug *Roosevelt* and a piece of the rudder from the HMS *Bounty* with a note from Rear Admiral R. E. Byrd confirming its authenticity. Ask a museum guide to tell you the story of how it got here.

*Hours: Mon, Wed, Fri 9am–3pm, Sat–Sun 1pm–5pm.*
*Admission free.*
*Directions: The museum is just inside the gate at Pier 36, on the waterfront just south of downtown.*

---

### While You're in Seattle:

Across the way from the Coast Guard Museum Northwest, on the fourth floor of the Coast Guard's main building, is the Coast Guard's Puget Sound Vessel Traffic Center, a maritime version of an air-traffic control center. Pier 36 is also the homeport for two 400-foot Polar Class Icebreakers and two 378-foot High Endurance Cutters. When they're not in service, they're open to the public on weekend afternoons. To find out which ships are in, call the Coast Guard Museum Northwest.

*Puget Sound Vessel Traffic Center and ships, Pier 36, 1519 Alaskan Way S, Seattle, WA 98134; (206)217-6050.*
*Hours: Traffic Center: Daily 8am–4pm. Ships: Sat–Sun 1pm–4:30pm (when not in service). Admission free. Directions: The traffic center and ships are at Pier 36, on the waterfront just south of downtown.*

---

■ **Experience Music Project**
Seattle Center
325 Fifth Avenue N
Seattle, WA 98109
(425)990-0575

Although it's not scheduled to open at the Seattle Center until mid-2000, here's what's in store at the Experience Music Project (EMP), the $100-million interactive music museum founded by investor Paul G. Allen, designed by noted architect Frank O. Gehry, and stocked with more rock memorabilia than you can shake a drumstick at.

To put it simply, the place is gonna rock! For starters, EMP has assembled the largest collection of Jimi Hendrix artifacts in the world, from the guitars he played at Woodstock and the Monterey Pop Festival

Jimi Hendrix's famous double-breasted green
velvet jacket, circa early 1967

to handwritten lyrics for his songs. The Hendrix Gallery will showcase the collection and detail the career of Seattle's most noted rock musician. The Guitar Gallery will showcase rare, unique, and just plain odd guitars; allow visitors to sample various guitar styles and models; and recount the history of the electric guitar. The Northwest Passage Gallery will delve into the history of music in the Pacific Northwest, covering everything and everyone from Seattle's 1920s jazz scene to Ray Charles, Heart, Kurt Cobain, and Pearl Jam. A *Milestones* exhibit will look behind the scenes of the music industry, from the competing claims for "first" rock 'n' roll record to fans and fan culture.

This museum will celebrate rock music, so don't expect it to be quiet and mellow. A performance space is part of the facility, and exhibits will provide plenty of opportunities to hear music, compare music, and, in the Sound Lab, create your own music.

The magical mystery tour doesn't have to end with the exhibits in the museum. EMP promises a multimedia, interactive, "ridelike" experience that will explore the "path" taken by many of the world's greatest artists.

*Web site: www.experience.org*
*Hours: To be determined.*
*Admission charged.*
*Directions: From I-5, take the Mercer Street exit and follow the signs to the*
*Seattle Center. The museum is along Fifth Avenue N, next to the*
*Space Needle.*

## ■ Frisbee Museum
Seattle, WA
(206)364-9808

You might assume that someone who spent their entire career working around airplanes would have some ideas about what it takes to keep something floating in air. But at a picnic one fine Sunday afternoon, retired Boeing engineer Ralph Williamson discovered that he couldn't keep a Frisbee afloat. "I didn't sleep too much after that picnic back in 1969," he recalls. "I stayed awake trying to figure out what it was that made that darn Frisbee fly." The neighborhood kids took pity on him and shared some tossing tips. Soon he was zealously pursuing flying platters.

Now Williamson has the world's second-largest Frisbee collection and is the curator of his own Frisbee Museum. At last count, there were more than 5,000 Frisbees in the far-ranging collection, which stretches from early metal Frisbee Baking Company pie tins tossed around by college students back East in the late 1800s, to the colorful modern-day plastic models that might glow in the dark or whistle as they fly by. Highlights of the collection include Frisbees that are as small as bottle caps and others as large as garbage can lids. Some sport rock band logos, while others advertise shops or events.

And while they're all carefully labeled and cataloged, not all these Frisbees are just for show. When Ralph Williamson isn't showing visitors through his museum, he's usually out playing Frisbee: Williamson is a six-time World Disc-Golf Champion (a game whose object is to throw small Frisbees into a metal basket) and attends dozens of tournaments a year. He welcomes visitors to the Frisbee Museum by appointment.

*Hours: By appointment only.*
*Admission free.*
*Directions: Provided when you make an appointment to see the museum.*

## ■ Frye Art Museum
704 Terry Avenue
Seattle, WA 98144
(206)622-9250

As you enter the Frye Art Museum through its dramatic two-and-a-half-story rotunda, remember that this lovely spot is made possible by meat—lots of meat and lots of poultry.

Interior of the Frye home, before the museum was renovated

Husband and wife Charles and Emma Frye were well-known Seattle art patrons who made their fortune in the meat-processing business. While they were alive, they were big supporters of Seattle-area religious, musical, cultural, and educational organizations. In their wills, they established a museum to display the artwork they'd been earnestly collecting ever since their first purchase of a European painting at the Chicago World's Fair in 1893.

Over a 40-year period, Charles and Emma Frye traveled frequently to Europe and the East Coast, amassing an impressive selection of 19th- and 20th-century American, German, and French representational paintings, including one of the nation's most important collections of Munich School paintings. Their original collection has been expanded, and the 1,200-piece permanent collection now features works by Mary Cassatt, Thomas Eakins, Winslow Homer, John Singer Sargent, and Andrew Wyeth.

The original museum building was expanded too, and thankfully, the architects for the addition honored Charles Frye's will, which mandated the use of natural light in the museum. Even on a gray day, the high-ceilinged galleries offer a comfortable environment in which to view selections from the permanent collection and from national and international touring exhibitions.

A cafe, a reflection pond, a lovely garden courtyard, and a small auditorium that features weekend concerts, lectures, and poetry readings complement the Frye's art collection. The two-story education wing hosts a wide variety of art classes, workshops, and demonstrations, with an emphasis on drawing, painting, and the ceramic arts.

*Web site: www.fryeart.org*
*Hours: Thurs 10am–9pm, Tue–Wed and Fri–Sat 10am–5pm, Sun noon–5pm.*

*Admission free.*

*Directions: The museum is just east of downtown Seattle, on the corner of Cherry Street and Terry Avenue. There's free parking in a lot on Terry Avenue across from the museum. From southbound I-5, take the James Street exit, turn left on Cherry, go uphill to Terry, and turn left. From northbound I-5, take the James Street exit, turn right on James, go uphill to Terry, and turn left.*

## ■ General Petroleum Museum
1526 Bellevue Avenue E
Seattle, WA 98101
(206)323-4789

You can take a bus, but to really get in the mood to visit this museum, go ahead and drive. If you can get the keys to a real old gas-guzzler, all the better—just this once.

The General Petroleum Museum, a colorful neon- and ephemera-filled warehouse, celebrates the days when gasoline fueled the nation. Appropriately enough, the late Jeff Pederson established this museum here because in 1907 the world's first gas station opened for business down on Seattle's waterfront.

The collection of petroliana features an impressive number of gasoline pumps, ranging from the earliest, unadorned "blind pumps," which dispensed a generic brand of gasoline, to the fancier clock-face and all-glass showcase pump, a model that unfortunately had to be discontinued because folks kept driving into it.

The rest of the room is filled with colorful gas station advertising signs, antique oil cans, keys, signs and fixtures from service station restrooms, packages of petroleum by-products marketed for use in the home, and examples of just about every gas-station giveaway item ever created, from toys, trucks, and holiday candles to complete cups, saucers, and plates. There's even a full-scale replica of an art deco–era service station that was supposed to make drivers feel as if they had just pulled up to a Roman temple.

Don't miss the red neon Pegasus in the window, which once advertised a Mobil gas station, and the mechanical riding-toy version of that flying horse, named Peggy.

You'll need to call ahead for an appointment to see the collection because, more often than not, the museum space is rented out for catered events and parties. All meals are served on—you guessed it—gas-station giveaway china.

*Hours: By appointment only.*

*Admission by donation.*

*Directions: From downtown Seattle, follow eastbound Pike Street to Bellevue Avenue E, turn left, and follow it to E Pine Street. The museum is in the brick building on the corner; look for the red flying horse in the second-floor window.*

Giant boot and friend

■ **Giant Shoe Museum**
Pike Place Market
Second Level Down Under
1501 Pike Place #424
Seattle, WA 98101
(206)623-2870

As a young boy, Dan Eskenazi was understandably intrigued by the giant boots (size 37AA!) on display in his grandfather's downtown shoe-repair shop window. The world's tallest man, 8'11" Robert Wadlow, had given those boots to his grandfather when Wadlow came through town on a promotional tour in the 1930s. But when Eskenazi's grandfather died in the 1960s, the giant shoes disappeared from the store window—and haven't been seen since.

Eskenazi now collects big shoes and is the curator of the Giant Shoe Museum in Pike Place Market. Dedicated to the preservation of outsized and oversized footwear, the museum features Eskenazi's collection of more than 20 giant shoes arranged in a series of sideshow-inspired, coin-operated, curtained display windows.

Highlights include a four-foot-long giant lace-up boot originally displayed at the 1893 Chicago World's Fair, the World's Largest Loafer, and an enormous clown's shoe. The World's Largest Military Boot is here too, along with a three-foot-long wooden shoe adorned with a gold-leaf painting. Then there's the Colossus: a 150-pound, five-foot-long handmade black leather wingtip from the 1920s that Eskenazi believes may be the world's largest shoe.

"All these giant shoes," explains Eskenazi, "were display items once used in a shoe store window, displayed as a promotional gimmick, or mounted on the roof of a delivery truck. They were well made, just like a regular-size shoe, only much, much bigger!"

*Hours: Daily 10am–6pm (or whenever Pike Place Market is open).*
*Admission free, but some window displays open only if you put in a quarter.*
*Directions: Pike Place Market is at First Avenue and Pike Street in downtown Seattle. The museum is on the second level of the Down Under area (the levels below the Main Arcade of Pike Place Market), in the windows of Old Seattle Paperworks.*

## ■ Henry Art Gallery
University of Washington
15th Avenue NE and NE 41st Street (PO Box 353070)
Seattle, WA 98195
(206)543-2280

While it's not the state's biggest public art museum, the Henry Art Gallery holds the title of the state's first public art museum. Established at the University of Washington in 1927 by Seattle builder and philanthropist Horace C. Henry, the original 10,000-square-foot building, with exhibition space laid out in a series of skylit interconnecting galleries, was designed by architect Carl F. Gould as the first wing of a much-larger museum complex that was never built.

The Henry is best known for its progressive exhibition program, which focuses on modern and contemporary art and its historical precedents. By the early 1990s, however, the ambitious programming offered by the Henry, as it's affectionately known, had seriously outgrown its facilities. So noted architect Charles Gwathmey teamed with a local Seattle architectural firm to create a striking three-story modernist addition (the Faye G. Allen Center for the Visual Arts) to the original brick and cast-stone building. The Henry now boasts significantly increased exhibition space, an outdoor sculpture court, an auditorium, a gallery dedicated to video and digital art, and classroom and studio spaces.

The museum also houses a fine permanent collection of close to 20,000 objects: paintings, photography, works on paper, ceramics, and textiles. The collection includes important American and European paintings of the 19th and 20th century by Winslow Homer, Stuart Davis, and others; the Monsen Photography Collection; and prints by masters including Rembrandt and Daumier. There are also wonderful ethnic costumes, Western dress, and textiles that include ceremonial clothing, hats, shoes, and underwear. Look for selected works from the permanent collection among works in special exhibitions.

*The Builders No. 1* (1970) by Jacob Lawrence

The museum offers gallery concerts, seminars, lectures, films, workshops, and a wide variety of programs for children and families.

*Web site: www.henryart.org*
*Hours: Wed–Thurs 11am–8pm, Tues and Fri–Sun 11am–5pm.*
*Admission charged. Free Thurs 5pm–8pm. High school and college students with ID always free. If you plan to visit both the Henry Art Gallery and the Burke Museum of Natural History and Culture across campus (see listing) on the same day, ask for the Burke/Henry Dollar Deal, which lets you visit both for the price of one—plus $1.*
*Directions: The museum is on the western edge of the University of Washington campus. From I-5, take the NE 45th Street exit, drive east to 15th Avenue NE, and turn south on 15th. The Henry is on the left between NE 41st Street and NE Campus Parkway.*

## ■ Hydroplane and Raceboat Museum
1605 S 93rd Street, Building E-D
Seattle, WA 98108
(206)764-9452

Since 1950, Seattle has had a love affair with hydroplane racing. Seattle native Jimi Hendrix was a big hydroplane fan, and even the most casual local sports fan knows that *Miss Budweiser* and *Miss Bardahl* are racing boats, not beauty pageant winners. So it's no surprise that Seattle is home to the nation's only museum dedicated to powerboat racing.

The Hydroplane and Raceboat Museum has a collection of restored vintage hydroplanes spanning seven decades, including boats that have won 17 Gold Cups between them. Hulls displayed change each season but often include the Atlas Van Lines *Blue Blaster, Slo-Mo-Shun IV,* and the *Hawaii Kai III* replica.

Exhibits pay tribute to legendary hydroplane drivers, such as Bill Muncey, Ron Musson, Mira Slovak, and Wild Bill Cantrell, and honor some of today's top drivers such as Chip Hanauer. The collection also includes vintage racing films, books, magazines, race programs, pit passes, trophies, and other hydroplane memorabilia, some of which date back to the turn of the century.

If these loudest and fastest of boats aren't your thing, don't worry: The museum doesn't limit itself to hydroplanes. They're interested in all categories of powerboat racing, from radio-controlled models to drag boats.

> *Hours: June to Aug: Tues 10am–5pm, Thurs 10am–10pm, Sat 10am–4:30pm. Sept to May: Thurs 10am–10pm, Sat 10am–4:30pm. Admission free.*
>
> *Directions: From southbound I-5, take exit 162 (Corson Avenue). Follow Corson to E Marginal Way, turn left, and continue over the 16th Avenue S Bridge. Drive about six blocks and, just before the road crosses over Highway 599, turn left on 14th Avenue S, and take a quick second left on S 93rd Street. Go one block to Marx's Landing restaurant and turn right into the parking lot.*
>
> *From northbound I-5, take exit 156 to State Route 599. Take the 14th Avenue S exit; turn left on 14th Avenue S and make an immediate right on S 93rd Street. Turn right into the parking lot for Marx's Landing Restaurant. The museum is a few doors down from the restaurant.*

■ **Kingdome Sports Museum**
Kingdome
201 S King Street
Seattle, WA 98104
(206)296-3124

Slated to be dismantled along with the Kingdome in 2000, the Kingdome Sports Museum features hundreds of sports-related items the late *Seattle Post-Intelligencer* sports writer and editor Royal Brougham once displayed in his office. Brougham's collection was big, but the museum's collection has grown even larger with contributions from sports fans and sports stars.

If you can visit before it's closed down for good, you'll see Muhammad Ali's boxing shorts, Steve Largent's football jersey, and baseballs autographed by Babe Ruth, Jackie Robinson, Joe DiMaggio, Ty Cobb, and Hank Aaron. Displays include Brougham's collection of press passes (including passes from the 1936 Berlin Olympics), a baseball mitt from the 1880s, Pele's soccer jersey, Evel Knievel's helmet, Jim Whittaker's climbing equipment, a polo mallet used by Will Rodgers, and much, much more.

When the new baseball stadium opens next door—sometime in the summer of 2002—it may have an on-site baseball museum featuring some of the baseball-related artifacts from the Kingdome Sport Museum.

> *Hours: Open before all games; also a stop on the Kingdome tour.*
> *Admission free for those attending a Mariners or Seahawks game at the Kingdome; but there's a charge for Kingdome tours.*
> *Directions: The museum is on the arena level of the Kingdome in downtown Seattle, on the southwest side near Gate B.*

### ■ Klondike Gold Rush National Historical Park
117 S Main Street
Seattle, WA 98104
(206)553-7220

On August 16, 1896, George Washington Carmack, Skookum Jim, and Tagish Charlie struck gold near Dawson City in Canada's Yukon Territory. However, it wasn't until 11 months later, when the SS *Portland* arrived in Seattle with a hefty two-ton cargo of gold, that word got out and the Klondike gold rush began in earnest.

According to park rangers at the Klondike Gold Rush National Historical Park, few of the 100,000 fortune seekers who headed north ever got there, and just 50 lucky dogs returned rich. It was savvy businessmen in Seattle, the jumping-off point for stampeders heading for the goldfields, who cashed in with a vengeance. Less than two weeks after word got out about Carmack and company's gold strike, Seattle merchants had sold more than $325,000 worth of goods to the thousands of gold seekers who began pouring into the city to outfit themselves for their journey north. A year later, merchants had sold more than $25 million worth. Sales were spurred by a requirement imposed by the Canadian Mounted Police: Due to a shortage of supplies in the Yukon, especially during the winter, miners were required to show that they had a year's worth of provisions before they could enter Canada.

A display featuring the ton of food, clothing, equipment, and other supplies stampeders set out with is one of the more striking exhibits at this urban, indoor park in Seattle's historic Pioneer Square district, which was the center of gold rush activity. Other displays feature actual gold nuggets, mining artifacts, and intriguing historical photographs and murals showing would-be prospectors hiking the rugged Chilkoot Trail and some of the grizzly, lucky few who actually filled their pans with gold.

Throughout the year, a small auditorium exhibits films and slide shows about the gold rush period. During the summer months, gold-panning demonstrations are held throughout the day. If you're around on the first Sunday of any month, stop by for a showing of the classic Charlie Chaplin film *The Gold Rush*.

*Web site: www.nps.gov/klgo/*
*Hours: Daily 9am–5pm.*
*Admission free.*
*Directions: The park is in downtown Seattle's Pioneer Square district.*

## ■ Log House Museum
3006 61st Avenue SW
Seattle, WA 98116
(206)938-5293

On November 13, 1851, about two dozen settlers, known today as the
Denny party, rowed toward Alki Point from a schooner named the *Exact*.
Exactly 146 years later, the Southwest Seattle Historical Society opened
the Log House Museum in a renovated turn-of-the-century log structure that once served as the carriage house of the Bernard family's Fir
Lodge beach estate. The museum commemorates the Denny party's
landing, celebrates the heritage of the Duwamish Indians, and tells how a
west Seattle amusement park became such a popular destination in the
early 1900s that it was dubbed the Coney Island of the West.

Exhibits include Native American artifacts, a whiskey bottle and
other items documenting the building's renovation, historical photographs, newspaper clippings, and a video of the documentary *Alki: Birth-
place of Seattle,* created by Dr. B. J. Bullert. The main exhibit, which has
explored topics such as the interaction between the native Duwamish
people and the early white pioneers, is scheduled to change each
November on the anniversary of the day that settlers landed on Alki Point.

*Hours: Summer: Tues noon–7pm, Fri–Sat 10am–4pm, Sun noon–3pm.*
*Rest of year: Thurs noon–6pm, Fri 10am–3pm, Sat–Sun noon–3pm.*
*Admission by donation.*
*Directions: The museum is one block from Alki Beach. From I-5 or*
*Highway 99, cross the West Seattle Bridge and exit onto Admiral Way*
*SW. Turn right on 61st Avenue SW and follow it to SW Stevens*
*Street, where you'll see the museum on the corner.*

## ■ Memory Lane Museum
Seattle Goodwill
1400 S Lane Street
Seattle, WA 98144
(206)329-1000

Most of the good stuff people donate to Seattle Goodwill gets put out
on the shelves for sale at reasonable prices. Some of the more unusual
donations, however, are saved and displayed in the Memory Lane
Museum, smack-dab in the middle of the store.

The *Miss Bardahl* hydroplane is here, along with a taxidermied
Alaskan brown bear, old sheet music, photographs, vintage clothing, and
an exhibit of military items that includes uniforms and letters home.

Memory Lane also has a great collection of Seattle World's Fair memorabilia, fishing gear, and a "garage" filled with license plates, hubcaps, tools, and hood ornaments.

> *Hours: Mon–Fri 10am–8pm, Sat 9am–8pm, Sun 10am–5pm.*
> *Admission free.*
> *Directions: From I-5, take the Dearborn Street exit and head east on*
>    *Dearborn for a few blocks. Seattle Goodwill is on the left, on the*
>    *corner of Rainier Avenue S (don't bother looking for S Lane Street—*
>    *it's tiny).*

## ■ Museum of Flight
9404 E Marginal Way S
Seattle, WA 98108
(206)764-5720

Before Seattle-area coffee and computer software went global, the city was perhaps best known as the home of the Boeing Company and its airplane manufacturing business. After touring the giant Museum of Flight complex, even folks who fear flying will understand the allure of air and space travel.

To get the most out of your visit, tag along with one of the fact-filled, docent-led tours offered throughout the day. Or decide for yourself whether to start in the Red Barn, Boeing's original manufacturing plant; in the Great Gallery, which chronicles the story of flight from mythology through the latest accomplishments in air and space technology; or outside, where the original—if somewhat dowdy—*Air Force One* (a Boeing VC-137B) and other aircraft are parked.

It's hard to resist a visit to Air Force One, which was delivered to President Eisenhower in 1959 and used by Presidents Kennedy, Johnson, and Nixon for assorted official trips. By today's high-tech standards, the communications station up front isn't all that impressive. But keep an eye out for the official doggie door and the First Family's lavatory, which was redesigned for Jackie Kennedy.

The glitzy aviation gems are housed in the giant steel and glass exhibit hall called the Great Gallery. More than 50 full-size aircraft are on display here—with more than 20 suspended from the ceiling, so don't forget to look up! Everyone has their favorites, but some highlights include a replica of the B & W, Boeing's first airplane; the world's only Lockheed M/D-21 Blackbird and drone; and a rare World War II FG-1D Corsair that was rescued from Lake Washington.

Then there's Moulton B. Taylor's bright red Aerocar III. With detachable wings and a rear propeller that are easily towed when using the Aerocar on the highway, it's a commuter's dream come true. Another "getaway" item is the Apollo Command Module "Serial Number 007," which astronauts used for splashdown practice. After its training stint, this module spent a decade abandoned and abused in a Houston Department

The famous Aerocar III

of Public Works equipment lot before being restored and sent to the museum.

A fairly recent addition is the nation's only full-size simulated air-traffic control tower, where visitors can follow an imaginary flight from Denver to Seattle, listen in on the live chatter between pilots and tower controllers at Boeing Field, or just enjoy the view out the huge windows.

Don't let the shiny things in the Great Gallery keep you from visiting the Red Barn, which traces aviation history from its earliest days through 1938. There's a restored 1917 Curtiss Jenny biplane here, a working replica of the wind tunnel used by the Wright Brothers, a re-created aircraft manufacturing wood shop, and lots of Boeing memorabilia—including some of the bedroom furniture the company produced after World War I, when there was a slump in aircraft production.

The museum offers a wide range of special programs for visitors of all ages. The flight-related programs include themed and family events, films, lectures, symposia, and hands-on workshops.

*Web site: www.museumofflight.org/*
*Hours: Thurs 10am–9pm, Fri–Wed 10am–5pm.*
*Admission charged. Free first Thurs of the month, 5pm–9pm.*
*Directions: From I-5, take exit 158 and follow the signs.*

## ■ Museum of History and Industry
2700 24th Avenue E
Seattle, WA 98112
(206)324-1126

The Museum of History and Industry (MOHAI) collects, preserves, and interprets the history of Seattle and the Pacific Northwest. Special

Fresh-caught salmon

exhibits have covered everything from the Klondike gold rush to the history of the Pacific Northwest Ballet. Permanent exhibits draw visitors into Northwest history with a stroll down a Seattle street circa 1878, complete with storefronts, machines, and tools used by early settlers. In *Seattle Roots,* visitors become a historic character—a Native American fisher, a Scandinavian logger, or an early Seattle-area nurse. And in the *Great Seattle Fire,* early firefighting equipment, computer kiosks, films, and artifacts tell the story of how Seattle burned in 1889—and then went about the task of rebuilding.

The newest permanent exhibit, *Salmon Stakes,* offers the sights and sounds (but not the smells, thank you) of an industry closely identified with the Northwest. Visitors can climb aboard a fishing boat and try their hands at hauling in 20- to 40-pound salmon, step onto a cannery floor and try slicing and canning 60-pound chinooks, and visit a bunkhouse to learn about how the folks who worked in the canning business spent their precious few hours of rest.

MOHAI has a large library and an extensive and nationally renowned photo archive with images dating back to the early 1860s. The museum also hosts special programs practically every weekend: crafts, storytelling, concerts, dance and theater performances, lectures, and more.

*Web site: www.historymuse-nw.org*
*Hours: Tues–Fri 11am–5pm, Sat–Sun 10am–5pm.*
*Admission charged.*

*Directions: The museum is just south of the University of Washington's Husky Stadium. From I-5, take exit 168B (eastbound State Route 520) and get off at Montlake Boulevard E. Go through one stoplight to 24th Avenue E and turn left.*

## ■ Nordic Heritage Museum
3014 NW 67th Street
Seattle, WA 98117
(206)789-5707

As you learn in the *Dream of America* exhibit on the Nordic Heritage Museum's lower level, folks from Denmark, Finland, Iceland, Norway, and Sweden started heading for the United States in the mid–1800s for the same reason folks from many other countries did: Land and jobs were scarce back home, and the New World held out the promise of cheap (or free!) land, good wages, and political freedom.

Once here, many Scandinavians ended up out west, settling into the Pacific Northwest as farmers, loggers, and fishermen. Galleries on the main level of the museum explore these rugged lifestyles, but displayed here too are precious costumes, textiles, tools, crafts, and other items that show the strong links people maintained to Scandinavian culture.

On the third floor, five 1,000-square-foot rooms give each of the Nordic countries a chance to strut its stuff. The Finnish room, for example, has a sauna and picture of a cow that set a world's record for giving milk. There's a replica *badstofa* (sod home) in the Icelandic room, a small bakery in the Danish room, and a tribute to skiing in the Norwegian room.

The museum is housed in a three-story 1907 elementary school building in Ballard, known for years as Seattle's Scandinavian neighborhood. The museum now also serves as something of a Scandinavian community center: the Scandinavian Language Institute is housed here, and the museum offers a Mostly Nordic concert series, films, dances, and

Swedish carved figures

many family-oriented workshops year-round. On the weekend after the Fourth of July, the museum hosts a Tivoli/Viking Days celebration and, on the weekend before Thanksgiving, a Yulefest.

*Hours: Tues–Sat 10am–4pm, Sun noon–4pm.*
*Admission charged. Free first Tues of the month.*
*Directions: From I-5, take exit 169 (NE 45th Street) and travel west to*
*32nd Avenue NW. Turn right and drive to NW 67th Street. The*
*museum is housed in an old school building*

■ **Northwest Seaport Maritime Heritage Center**
1002 Valley Street
Seattle, WA 98109
(206)447-9800

At a distance, the Northwest Seaport Maritime Heritage Center's compound looks like an unlikely collection of outbuildings at the edge of Lake Union. Its treasures are three ships: the 1897 coastal schooner *Wawona*, the 1889 tug *Arthur Foss,* and the 1904 lightship *Swiftsure* (currently moored in Ballard).

The *Wawona* is undergoing major restoration, but you can still walk the decks and duck into the captain's cabin, the cargo hold (originally designed for hauling lumber), the galley, and the fo'c'sle. You might also see (and ask questions of) the volunteers and shipwright at work restoring the planks of this 165-foot vessel, which has fished in Alaska and, during World War II, hauled spruce for the aircraft industry.

Back on shore, be sure to inspect the replica deck section from an 18th-century sailing ship and get a sense of what all those ropes and sails were for. Also take a look at the engine from a World War II U-boat.

*Hours: Memorial Day to before Labor Day: Mon–Sat 10am–5pm, Sun*
*noon-5pm. After Labor Day to before Memorial Day: Mon–Sat*
*10am–4pm, Sun noon-4pm.*
*Admission by donation to board the* Wawona.
*Directions: From I-5, take the Mercer Street exit, head north on Fairview*
*Avenue N, and turn left on Valley Street.*

---

### While You're near Lake Union:

You'll want to stop at the Center for Wooden Boats next door to Northwest Seaport, too. The center is home—or, rather, port—to a collection of more than 100 dazzling wooden boats, including Native American and Polynesian dugout canoes. The center rents out many of its vessels and hosts a Wooden Boat Festival each year on the first weekend in July.

*Center for Wooden Boats, 1010 Valley Street, Seattle, WA 98109; (206)382-BOAT. Hours: Wed–Mon 11am–5pm. Admission by donation. Directions: Same as Northwest Seaport Maritime Heritage Center.*

# ■ Odyssey: The Maritime Discovery Center
Pier 66
2205 Alaskan Way
Seattle, WA 98121
(206)374-4000

There were already several historic maritime museums in the Northwest, so the folks at Odyssey: The Maritime Discovery Center focused their 30,000 square feet of display space on contemporary maritime themes: commercial fishing, shipping, trade, transportation, and marine protection. The center's four galleries feature a pair of giant sculptures and more than 40 hands-on, state-of-the-art exhibits that tell the story of the people who work, play, and travel on the waters in and around Puget Sound.

The soaring Waterlink Gallery lures you into the maritime environment with two dramatic 35-foot-tall sculptures. Then it's on to Sharing the Sound, where the fun begins. Here you might try navigating a freighter through Elliott Bay or gaze out the floor-to-ceiling windows at one of the busiest ports in the country to see how others do it. Other exhibits let you listen in on real-time Coast Guard traffic, view a database of different ships, take a simulated kayak ride, and find out what individuals, companies, and communities are doing to protect the area's waters.

The Harvesting the Sea gallery explores the large commercial fishing industry based in Puget Sound. Here kids can climb aboard a small fishing boat and experience what it's like to fish on the North Pacific seas. Then everyone can get a close-up look at models of 19 different fish that are caught and sold here commercially, and learn how all the fish get processed and prepared for your table, at a Pike Place Market–type exhibit.

Over in the Ocean Trade gallery, visitors can see themselves "on deck" of a container ship or test their skill "loading" 20-ton containers onto a ship or a railcar. This exhibit follows apples, cattle hides, and Ken Griffey Jr.'s baseball glove on the trade route back and forth between Asia and the United States.

*Web site: www.ody.org*
*Hours: Summer: Sun–Wed 10am–9pm, Thurs–Sat 10am–5pm. Rest of year: Daily 10am–5pm.*
*Admission charged.*
*Directions: Odyssey is "docked" at Bell Street Pier (Pier 66), on the northern end of the downtown waterfront along Alaskan Way.*

■ **Pacific Science Center**
Seattle Center
200 Second Avenue N
Seattle, WA 98109
(206)443-2001

When you visit the Pacific Science Center, you don't have to tell the kids it's about science—they'll think it's just fun. And you don't have to be a kid to have fun here. In fact, it's adults who most often have to be told to stop hogging the controls of the hands-on experiments.

The center's Tech Zone offers technology-related exhibits including robotics and computer software that let you play virtual basketball, hang-glide in a virtual city, match wits with a robot, and create your own cartoon. Over in the Kids' Works section is an area with simple science projects and activities for kids under 44 inches tall. For everyone else, there's a Rocket Climb; a clear-plastic-tube city occupied by naked mole rats; and Sound Sensations, a room where you can create music with electronic drums and synthesizers. Note to parents: This room is blissfully soundproof!

In the Body Works section you can learn about your health, test your grip, and find out whether your nose and ears are working correctly. In the outdoor Water Works area you can power a water wheel with your body, play with a water-gun arcade, and try to maneuver a two-ton granite ball on a thin film of water. A Seattle favorite, the High Rail Bike, is out here too.

No matter how much fun you're having with everything else, be sure to visit the family of five moving, roaring robotic dinosaurs in their lush, semitropical Mesozoic land. In residence are a pachycephalosaurus ("thick-headed lizard"), a Tyrannosaurus rex ("tyrant king lizard"), a triceratops ("three-horned face"), a stegosaurus ("plated lizard"), and an apatosaurus ("deceptive lizard").

Other offerings include the Willard W. Smith Planetarium, a laser light show, an IMAX theater, and a wide variety of special classes, workshops, lectures, and events for kids and adults.

*Web site: www.pacsci.org*
*Hours: Mid-June to Labor Day: Daily 10am–6pm. After Labor Day to*
    *mid-June: Mon–Fri 10am–5pm, Sat–Sun and holidays 10am–6pm.*
*Admission charged.*
*Directions: From I-5, take exit 167 (Mercer Street) and follow the signs to*
    *the Seattle Center. The Science Center is on the grounds of the Seattle*
    *Center, under the arches near the Space Needle—another wonder of*
    *science and engineering.*

■ **Seattle Art Museum**
100 University Street
Seattle, WA 98101
(206)625-8900

When it opened in 1931 at Volunteer Park, the Seattle Art Museum focused mainly on Asian art. Since then SAM, as it's now known, has grown into a world-class arts institution; it has a collection of more than 21,000 objects and has expanded into downtown digs designed by noted architect Robert Venturi.

The original Volunteer Park facility is now the Seattle Asian Art Museum (see next listing), featuring exhibitions of Japanese, Chinese, Korean, Indian, Himalayan, and Southeast Asian art. The downtown facility features some Asian art but mostly showcases major touring exhibitions and highlights the permanent collections, particularly African art, Northwest Coast Native American art, modern art, and European painting and decorative arts. Paying the admission charge at one museum grants you admission to the other within a week, so take your time.

You'll no doubt want to spend time wandering about whatever mega-show the museum has in its Special Exhibitions Gallery, but leave

*Pompone II de Bellièvre* (circa 1640–41) by Sir Anthony van Dyke

time to explore the other galleries, which hold treasures from SAM's permanent collections.

Three galleries, curated with the help of an advisory group of Native American elders and advisors, present Northwest Coast Native American objects relating to the spiritual and performance arts, sculptural arts, and fiber and fabric arts. The collection includes sculpture, textiles, decorative and household objects, and more than 200 masks from the Pacific Northwest, British Columbia, and Alaska.

The objects in the three galleries showcasing the African collection are organized according to whether an item was designed to be worn, performed with, or worshipped. Look for sculpture, masks, textiles, basketry, decorative arts, and contemporary African artwork.

Six rooms feature rotating exhibitions of SAM's modern art holdings as well as visiting shows. One gallery is dedicated to work from the 19th century, two to work of the 20th century, two to contemporary Pacific Northwest art, and one to prints and photographs. The collection includes work by Mary Cassatt, Willem de Kooning, Jackson Pollock, Andy Warhol, Jacob Lawrence, Fay Jones, and others.

Six galleries are filled with European paintings, sculpture, and decorative arts arranged chronologically, beginning with art of the ancient world and ending with neoclassical art of the 18th century. The collection includes European paintings, prints and drawings, porcelain from the 18th century, and Greek, Hellenistic, and Etruscan art and coins.

Before you even get to the main galleries housing Asian art, you'll encounter rams, camels, and large-scale stone funerary statues from the Ming and Qing dynasties. Several other galleries feature Chinese jade, an eight-panel Korean screen, and a complete Japanese teahouse where tea ceremonies are held on a regular basis (reservations required).

The museum has a sizable gift shop and a full-service cafe, both of which are accessible without paid admission. SAM also hosts a wide variety of special events and programs, including exhibit tours, gallery talks, lectures, demonstrations, family programs, and performances. Art classes for kids and adults are held in the museum's own art studio. SAM also sponsors a well-crafted film series that often sells out early; call ahead to find out whether tickets are available.

> *Web site: www.seattleartmuseum.org*
> *Hours: Thurs 10am–9pm, Tues–Wed, Fri–Sun 10am–5pm.*
> *Admission charged; includes admission to the Seattle Asian Art Museum within one week. Free first Thurs of the month; seniors free first Fri of the month.*
> *Directions: The museum is in downtown Seattle, on First Avenue and University Street at the top of the Harbor Steps; look for the giant* Hammering Man *sculpture.*

■  **Seattle Asian Art Museum**
Volunteer Park
1400 E Prospect Street
Seattle, WA 98112
(206)625-8900

In 1991, when the Seattle Art Museum moved out of this Volunteer Park building, the structure got a facelift. Now the stately 1931 building, originally constructed to house the Asian art collection of Richard Fuller and his mother, Margaret McTavish Fuller, is home to an Asian art collection that ranks in the top 10 outside Asia. The Seattle Asian Art Museum (SAAM)'s Japanese collection is one of the top five in the United States.

Highlights of the Japanese collection include folk art, screens, ink paintings, calligraphy, Buddhist art, ceramics, and one of the world's greatest collections of 18th- to 20th-century Japanese folk textiles. A lacquered wood statue of a Rakan Buddhist saint from the Edo period is a highlight of the sculpture collection.

The Chinese collection, which extends from the neolithic period through the 19th century, fills five galleries and features jades, snuff bottles, and more than 350 puppets. The first gallery offers burial ceramics emphasizing the importance of clan and ancestor worship. The next gallery presents household objects, military items, ritual pieces, and other

*Exalted Monk (Moment of Enlightenment),*
Chinese sculpture from the Yuan Dynasty

metalwork created from the bronze age to the end of the Tang dynasty. Changes in Buddhist art from the fifth to the 17th century are traced in the third gallery, while ceramics (celadon, Cizhou ware, and porcelain) fill the fourth gallery. The fifth gallery explores the imperial arts of the Qing dynasty and presents artwork made for both public display and private consumption.

Folding screens, early gray stoneware, a mammoth painting titled *Amitabha and 39 Attendants,* and a gilt-bronze Bodhisattva figure from the eighth century are featured Korean artworks, while the South and Southeast Asian collection presents bronze and stone Buddhist and Hindu sculptures, paintings, decorative arts, and Thai ceramics.

The museum has a gift shop, a tearoom, and special programs that include lectures, gallery tours, demonstrations, and tea tastings. On clear days, the front steps offer wonderful views of the city and beyond. And don't forget that your SAAM admission ticket is good for entry within seven days at the downtown Seattle Art Museum.

> *Web site: www.seattleartmuseum.org*
> *Hours: Thurs 10am–9pm, Tues–Wed and Fri–Sun 10am–5pm.*
> *Admission charged; includes admission to the Seattle Art Museum within one week. Free first Thurs and first Sat of the month; seniors free first Fri of the month.*
> *Directions: From northbound I-5, take the Olive Way exit, head east (uphill), turn left on 15th Avenue E, then turn left at E Prospect Street. The entrance to Volunteer Park is at 14th Avenue and E Prospect Street. From southbound I-5, take the Roanoke Street exit, turn left, and cross the freeway overpass to 10th Avenue E. Turn right on 10th, then left on E Boston Street, and continue to the Volunteer Park entrance.*

### ■ Seattle Metropolitan Police Museum
317 Third Avenue S
Seattle, WA 98104
(206)748-9991

The brainchild of longtime Seattle police officer Jim Ritter, the Seattle Metropolitan Police Museum chronicles the development of the city's police department over the past 140 years. Exhibits include weapons, prisoner restraints, communications devices, historical photographs dating back to the mid-1800s, newspaper clippings detailing infamous local crimes, a 1950s-era jail cell, and a wide variety of police tools, such as rifles, pistols, submachine guns, and a leather-wrapped billy club.

Dioramas show police officers at work during various periods in Seattle's history, from the gold rush days and Prohibition to the 1934 longshoremen's strike. A section on police communications details how, before there were two-way radios and computers, the police department relied on whistles, call boxes, and, later, a city-owned radio station, to dispatch officers. In addition to the jail cell, prisoner restraints on display range from vintage handcuffs and leg irons to the Oregon Boot, a serious-looking heavy metal collar that was strapped to an inmate's ankle to discourage escape attempts while the prisoner was in transit or on outside work duty.

Other exhibits include uniforms, "wanted" posters, badges, a mug book from the early 1900s filled with cranky-looking bad guys, and a wide variety of photographs. Look for photos of the city's first officer (appointed in 1861), early horse-drawn and motorized paddy wagons, some of the city's first female officers, and citizens getting deputized so they could help the police department during the 1919 Seattle General Strike.

The museum also has a play area where kids can try on uniforms, turn on a police light, listen in on the operations of a 911 communications center, and use a map to locate crime scenes.

*Hours: Tues–Sat 11am–4pm.*
*Admission charged.*
*Directions: The museum is located in Pioneer Square, about a block*
*north of Amtrak's King Street Station and across the street from*
*Seattle Lighting.*

■ **Vintage Telephone Equipment Museum**
7000 E Marginal Way S
Seattle, WA 98101
(206)767-3012

Telephone switching equipment used to take up entire buildings. Computers and satellites have made much of that old stuff, well, just old stuff. Luckily, some retired telephone workers, members of the wonderfully named Telephone Pioneers of America, have gathered up all sorts of telephone-related equipment for a museum dedicated to the evolution of the phone call, from Alexander's Graham Bell's first communications device to the modern phones so easily taken for granted these days.

Tours of the Vintage Telephone Equipment Museum start on the third floor, which contains a variety of switchboards, historical photographs, and all manner of telephones, including a working picture phone. The second floor is especially fun and kid-friendly. Here you can crank the phones, watch how a step-by-step switch works, play at being a telephone operator, try to stump the "computer," and examine a variety of "slugs" and other objects folks have tried putting in pay phones instead of a quarter. Be sure to visit the Hewitt Room, which houses a collection of vintage telephones, each with a different ringer. The collection belonged to Ted Hewitt, a general plant manager for Pacific Northwest Bell, who for years maintained a central phone office for the imaginary town of Timbuktu in his basement.

On the second floor you'll also encounter the Red Box, a working British call box topped by the crest of Queen Elizabeth II. Don't try tipping this phone booth over; the box weighs in at three-quarters of a ton, without the flooring or the telephone. Another display here is dedicated to the Western Electric Company (WECO), the manufacturing arm of the Bell System that existed prior to 1984. In addition to telephones, WECO made hearing aids, fans, washing machines, sewing machines, radios, and vacuum cleaners.

*Web site: www.scn.org/tech/telmuseum/*
*Hours: Tues 9am–2pm or by appointment.*
*Admission by donation.*
*Directions: From southbound I-5, take the Corson Avenue S exit. Bear*
*    left on Corson Avenue S and continue for one and a half miles to*
*    E Marginal Way S. The museum is across from the Hat and Boots on*
*    E Marginal Way S. The parking lot and museum entrance are behind*
*    the building. Look for the museum's sign on the left of the building as*
*    you face it from the parking lot (if the door is locked, you're at the*
*    wrong door).*

## ■ Wing Luke Asian Museum
407 Seventh Avenue S
Seattle, WA 98104
(206)623-5124

This award-winning, multicultural Asian American museum was created in 1967 to honor Wing Luke, the son of an immigrant laundryman who, in 1962, became the first Asian American to win elective office in the Pacific Northwest when he won a seat on the Seattle City Council. Councilman Luke died in an airplane crash before the end of his first term in office, but his spirit lives on in this warm, inviting museum in a converted auto garage in the heart of the International District.

At first the museum focused primarily on the folk art, culture, and traditions of the Chinese American community, but now it has a more multicultural approach, including Seattle's Japanese, Chinese, Korean, Cambodian, Filipino, Pacific Islander, Southeast Asian, and other immigrant groups in its definition of community.

Representatives of most of these groups worked together to raise money, design, and create the museum's centerpiece, *One Song, Many Voices,* an artifact-filled permanent exhibit that integrates photographs, costumes, musical instruments, tools, costumes, and other items donated by community members to portray the varied experiences of the many cultures represented in the International District. A second permanent exhibit uses photographs, videotaped interviews, and artifacts to relate the history of the International District itself, a neighborhood described as the "only area in the United States where Chinese, Japanese, Filipinos,

Lun Poy Woo in front of the import-export business his granduncle
started in 1884

Vietnamese, and African Americans formed one neighborhood." And
each winter the museum sponsors a show celebrating the Asian New Year.

Plans are under way to move the museum to larger quarters. In the
meantime, every inch of space is being put to good use: There are several
special exhibits throughout the year, and suspended from the rafters are
colorful, whimsical, handpainted kites of bats, turtles, goldfish, and other
animals as well as a delightful 35-foot-long dancing Chinese dragon.

The museum sponsors readings, group tours, lectures, concerts, and
other special events.

*Hours: Tues–Fri 11am–4:30pm, Sat–Sun noon–4pm.*
*Admission charged. Free Thurs.*
*Directions: The museum is in the International District, just south of*
*downtown Seattle. From I-5, take the Dearborn Street exit and head*
*west. Turn right on Seventh Avenue S and follow it for three and a*
*half blocks; the museum is on the left.*

## ■ Ye Olde Curiosity Shop and Museum
Pier 54
1001 Alaskan Way
Seattle, WA 98104
(206)682-5844

Like Marsh's Free Museum in Long Beach (see listing), Ye Olde
Curiosity Shop and Museum is half souvenir shop and half wacky, offbeat museum, mixing the truly curious with the truly tacky. Since 1899,

shoppers have flocked to some version of this store. They continue to come not only to purchase Northwest crafts and souvenirs from around the world, but also to get a good look at the matchstick tugboat, the huge Puget Sound octopus, the record-size geoduck clam, the nine-foot blowgun and the thousands of other odd items that cram the shelves, cover the walls, and hang from the ceiling.

The hands-down favorites are at the back of the shop: nightmare-inducing shrunken heads, taxidermied twin calves, a pickled pig, Sylvia the mummy, and Sylvester, a long-dead prospector who, according to museum notes, was discovered perfectly preserved and dehydrated in the Arizona desert by two cowboys back in 1895.

> *Hours: Summer: Daily 9am–9:30pm. Rest of year: Mon–Fri*
> *9:30am–6pm, Sat–Sun 9:30am–9pm.*
> *Admission free.*
> *Directions: The museum is on Pier 54 on the downtown Seattle waterfront,*
> *near Ivar's Acres of Clams restaurant.*

## SEQUIM

### ■ Museum and Art Center in the Sequim-Dungeness Valley
175 W Cedar (PO Box 1002)
Sequim, WA 98382
(360)683-8110

Back in 1977, Clare and Emanual "Manny" Manis agreed that it would be a good idea to dig a pond on their land for their livestock. Manny got a backhoe and started digging in a low spot. To his great surprise, what he thought were simply some dug-up tree limbs turned out be mastodon tusks.

Archaeologists moved in, kept on digging, and over the next nine years found evidence of four mastodons, several bison, and tools made of stone and wood, all dating back about 12,000 years. Now, thanks to Clare, Manny, and that thirsty herd of livestock, visitors to the Museum and Art Center in the Sequim-Dungeness Valley can touch a real mastodon rib, learn about the history of the dig, and see tusks, ribs, toe bones, and other evidence of what's known as the Manis Mastodon.

While those old bones are certainly a good reason to stop by, you'll also want to explore the other exhibits, which feature historical photographs and artifacts focusing on the Coast Salish Indians, pioneer life, and local dairy-farming traditions. The museum also has a display dedicated to the nearby Dungeness Spit and the 63-foot-high New Dungeness Lighthouse, located at the end of the spit and accessible either by boat or by a hike out the five-mile length of the spit.

> *Hours: Daily 9am–4pm.*
> *Admission by donation.*

*Directions: The museum is one block north of Highway 101, on W Cedar
between N Sequim and Second Avenues.*

## SHELTON

### ■ Mason County Historical Museum
427 W Railroad Avenue (PO Box 1366)
Shelton, WA 98584
(360)426-1020

The Mason County Historical Museum is actually two museums, one
housed in the 1914 town hall and library and another out at the fairgrounds. Both contain exhibits relating the history of Mason County
home life and displaying artifacts from local industries, including logging,
farming, and oystering.

The museum has a collection of Native American baskets from the
Skokomish and Squaxin tribes, every edition of the local *Shelton-Mason
County Journal,* and a large archive of vintage photographs. Kids enjoy the
scale replica of Grisdale, the last live-in logging camp in the United States
and the only one with its own bowling alley. The model, built on a large
slab of Douglas fir, features tiny animals, trees, a logging railroad, and
cabins.

The fairgrounds museum, located at 751 W Fairgrounds Road, is
open only during special events, including the Forest Heritage Festival
(third week of May), the Mason County Fair (the end of July), and Oys-
terfest (first full weekend in October).

*Hours: Tues–Fri noon–5pm, Sat noon–4pm.*
*Admission by donation.*
*Directions: Take northbound Highway 101 from Olympia toward Port
Angeles. Take the second Shelton exit (Matlock interchange) and
follow W Railroad Avenue to Fifth Avenue. The museum is on W
Railroad and Fifth.*

## SHORELINE

### ■ Shoreline Historical Museum
749 N 175th Street (PO Box 7171)
Shoreline, WA 98133
(206)542-7111

Housed in the historic Ronald Elementary School, the Shoreline Historical Museum offers a wide variety of historical and hands-on exhibits
depicting Seattle's Shoreline area, which extends from Puget Sound to
Lake Washington and from 85th Street north to 205th.

On the main floor are a changing-exhibit room and the Shoreline
Arts Council Gallery, presenting quarterly shows of work by local and

Northwest artists. One schoolroom on this floor has been preserved and contains the original school bell, vintage photographs, and wooden benches where you can sit and read aloud from one of the schoolbooks thoughtfully provided on an open bookshelf nearby.

Kids may enjoy the gallery exploring the history of Shoreline through transportation. There's a 1926 Model T roadster, a variety of railroad and gas-station sound effects, and a train whistle that everyone's welcome to pull.

The lower floor contains most of the original Richmond Beach post office, a well-stocked blacksmith shop, and the Tracy Owen Country Store and Farmyard, complete with barnyard sounds and a hands-on old-time toy exhibit.

The Puget Sound Antique Radio Association has filled much of the upper floor with a wonderful display of vintage radios and television sets. While classic radio programs from the 1940s play in the background, you can tap out your name on a telegraph key and follow the history of radio from the earliest days of transmission to the introduction of "picture radio."

Special programs include an all-ages Fun with History workshop on the fourth Saturday of each month and the radio swap meets sponsored by the Antique Radio Association on the third Sunday of each month.

*Hours: Tues–Sat 10am–4pm.*
*Admission by donation.*
*Directions: From I-5, take the N 175th Street exit and head west, crossing Aurora Avenue. The museum is one block west of Aurora.*

## SKAMOKAWA

### ■ River Life Interpretive Center
1394 W State Route 4 (PO Box 67)
Skamokawa, WA 98647
(360)795-3007

Skamokawa (a great word to say out loud) got its name from a Native American word meaning "smoke over the water," referring to the ever-present morning fog at the confluence of Skamokawa Creek and the Columbia River. You can learn more about the town's history at the River Life Interpretive Center, which has one floor of historic photographs, interpretive panels, and maps describing the natural, economic, architectural, and social history of Skamokawa and the lower Columbia River from presettlement times to the present.

The center is housed in the Queen Anne–style Central School, a building that was originally dedicated with a gala picnic and patriotic speeches on July 4, 1894. The structure was later moved and refurbished by the Improved Order of Redmen, a local community service group, and is now known as Redmen Hall. If you visit on a day that's at all clear, and you're feeling hearty, climb the 88 steps to the bell tower. Up there you can stand on pedals that open louvers to reveal a superb view of the lower Columbia River, all the way downstream to Astoria.

> *Hours: Wed–Sat noon–4pm, Sun 1pm–4pm.*
> *Admission charged.*
> *Directions: Skamokawa is seven miles west of Cathlamet. From I-5, take the Longview exit (Ocean Beaches/Long Beach), then follow State Route 4 to Skamokawa; the center is right on the highway.*

## SNOHOMISH

### ■ Old Snohomish Village Museum
Pine Avenue and Second Street
Snohomish, WA 98290
(360)568-5235

Snohomish's original pioneer cemetery is the centerpiece of the Snohomish Historical Society's Old Snohomish Village Museum, a collection of historic cabins and other buildings that have been restored and moved to this site. The village includes a blacksmith shop, a weaver's shop, a Victorian cottage, an 1889 pioneer cabin and outhouse, a fully stocked general store, and the 1875 Kikendall Log Cabin, complete with photos of the cabin's original occupants.

> *Hours: Memorial Day to Labor Day: Daily noon–4pm. Closed rest of year.*
> *Admission charged.*
> *Directions: From Everett, follow Highway 2 east to Snohomish. The village is at the east end of town, behind Pilchuck Landing on Pine Avenue and Second Street.*

---

### While You're in Snohomish:
The Snohomish Historical Society also operates the Blackman Museum, built in 1878 for Hyrcanus Blackman, the first mayor of Snohomish. Restored and furnished to reflect the Victorian period, the home contains Mrs. Ella Blackman's piano, portraits of the Blackman children (Eunice and Clifford), the Blackmans' everyday china, a case of cranberry glass, and a human-hair wreath.

*Blackman Museum, 118 Avenue B, Snohomish, WA 98290; (360)568-5235. Hours: June to Labor Day: Daily noon–4pm. March to May, after Labor Day to Dec: Wed–Sun noon–4pm. Closed rest of year. Admission charged. Directions: From Everett, follow Highway 2 east to Snohomish. The museum is on Avenue B.*

■  **Northwest Railway Museum**
38625 SE King Street (PO Box 459)
Snoqualmie, WA 98065
(425)888-3030

The folks at the Northwest Railway Museum want to be sure no one forgets the excitement of a working railroad or the role railroads had in the development of our region. They also know just how much fun a ride on a classic old train can be.

Located in the 1890 Snoqualmie Depot, the museum owns almost 100 pieces of railroad memorabilia that weigh in at more than a ton. These pieces include steam locomotives built between 1941 and 1951, freight cars, wood- and steel-sided passenger coaches, and the special railway equipment that built and maintained the right-of-way. Most of these huge artifacts are kept locked behind fencing at the museum's storage area three blocks from the depot, but they're easy to see from the nearby pedestrian path.

The exhibits inside the depot feature railroading memorabilia including a coal stove from a railroad work car, a set of dining-car china, and a display of old railway signaling devices.

Several passenger coaches and locomotives are kept next to the depot and are used for the five-mile train rides the museum offers between Snoqualmie and North Bend.

*Hours: May to Labor Day: Daily 10am—5pm. Rest of year: Thurs—Mon
    10am—5pm.*
*Admission free. There's a charge for train rides.*
*Directions: From eastbound I-90, take exit 27 and follow the signs to Sno-
    qualmie. From westbound I-90, take exit 31 and follow State Route
    202 toward Snoqualmie.*

N<u>ORTHWES</u>T

RAILWAY MUSEUM

## SOUTH BEND

### ■ Pacific County Museum
1008 W Robert Bush Drive
South Bend, WA 98586
(360)875-5224

In the early 1900s South Bend promoted itself as the "Baltimore of the Pacific." Both cities were known for activities surrounding the oyster industry, and both were active seaports and industrial centers. Baltimore got famous for plenty of other things, but oystering is still the big thing here.

The Pacific County Museum honors the area's 150-year-old oystering industry with an exhibit describing the three different oyster species grown in the bay. Oyster artifacts on display include a couple of small boats and an unusual pair of 12-foot-long wood and brass oystering tongs used to harvest oysters from natural beds.

The museum also displays Chinook Indian craftwork, five nice ship models, logging tools, fossils, and an exhibit on shoreline erosion, a topic of local concern because the fastest-eroding spot in the United States is nearby North Cove, also called "washaway beach."

Be sure to ask about the story behind the lock and key that South Benders "stole" from the Oysterville courthouse in 1892.

Special programs include workshops, lectures, and demonstrations.

*Hours: Daily 11am–4pm.*
*Admission free.*
*Directions: The museum is on Highway 101 in South Bend, in a building that's also the Tourist Information Center.*

## SPANAWAY

### ■ Prairie Home Museum
812 E 176th Street (PO Box 1238)
Spanaway, WA 98387
(253)536-6655

Located in a restored 1890s gable-and-wing farmhouse, the Prairie Home Museum features a variety of changing exhibits, assorted antiques, and permanent displays on topics ranging from farming to baseball.

You'll find a nice collection of moonstone dishes in the dining room and, in the bedroom, furniture made in Spanaway by the Breseman Furniture Company. The room dedicated to Spanaway schools also displays baseball memorabilia and a nice doll collection. There's a kids' corner supplied with games and dress-up clothes, and a 1940s kitchen where volunteers are often making cookies or soup to share with museum visitors.

Outbuildings include a barn, a well-stocked blacksmith shop, a milk and wash house, and a large covered shed full of carriages, tractors, and other farm equipment.

The museum hosts a Kids' Day each April, but invites kids to stop by anytime to see the two giant Douglas fir trees on museum property that have been hit by lightning.

*Hours: Wed 10am–2pm.*
*Admission by donation.*
*Directions: From I-5, take State Route 512 and then the Parkland/*
*Spanaway exit. Drive south on Pacific Avenue and turn left at E*
*176th Street; the museum is just a few blocks down, on the grounds of*
*the Fir Lane Funeral Home and Memorial Park.*

### SPOKANE

### ■ Carr's One of a Kind in the World Museum
5225 N Freya Street
Spokane, WA 99205
(800)350-6469

This private collection features assorted one-of-a-kind items such as cars that once belonged to John F. Kennedy, Jackie Gleason, and Elvis; a large framed velvet picture of Marilyn Monroe; a half-dozen reverse glass paintings; and what museum organizers claim is the world's largest model of a U.S. destroyer: the USS *Nicholas*, constructed with 27,500 carefully placed matchsticks.

The admission charge here is a bit steep compared with most museums in this book, but then again, you're purchasing the priceless opportunity to have your picture taken with the car Jackie Kennedy used for shopping trips in Palm Beach and to sit in the precise seats once occupied by the likes of JFK, Marilyn, Elvis, and the June Taylor Dancers.

*Hours: Sat–Sun 1pm–4pm.*
*Admission charged.*
*Directions: From eastbound I-90, take the Thor/Freya exit. Turn north on*
*Freya Street and follow it as it turns into Green Street and then*
*Market Street. Turn right on Wellesley Street, and drive two blocks to*
*a four-way stop. Turn left to return to N Freya Street and continue*
*two blocks to the museum.*

### ■ Cheney Cowles Museum
W 2316 First Avenue
Spokane, WA 99204
(509)456-3931

From its perch above the Spokane River on lovely landscaped grounds in the historic Browne's Addition neighborhood, the Cheney Cowles Museum offers a wide variety of permanent and changing exhibitions exploring the history of Eastern Washington, the inland Northwest, Native American cultures, and the visual arts.

While the Fine Arts Gallery presents top-notch changing exhibitions covering a broad range of medias, styles, and periods, it's the Native American collection that holds the rare gems. In 1992, when Spokane's Museum of Native American Cultures closed its doors, thousands of artifacts, books, and photographs were transferred to the Cheney. The combined collection of Native American materials now ranks among the top 10 in the nation, and the museum's Plateau collection (western Montana, northern Idaho, eastern Washington, eastern Oregon, southern British Columbia, and Alberta) is considered the finest in the world.

Artifacts from the collection are used to illustrate themes in the History Galleries, including the history and culture of Plateau Indians, the fur trade, early exploration, and the settlement and growth of Spokane and the inland Northwest. You'll see baskets and flat-twined bags, a stagecoach, an electric car, a Tiffany lamp, and modern-day electric inventions such as curling irons and toasters. Kids especially will enjoy the colorful hands-on and interactive displays, which invite you to run your hands over mink pelts, practice weaving a corn-husk bag, and scrutinize lead and silver from 20 different area mines with a magnifying glass.

Admission to the museum includes a tour of the Campbell House next door. Designed in 1898 by architect Kirtland K. Cutter in the Tudor Revival style, the design and furnishing of the home offer an insight into turn-of-the-century family life, architecture, and decorative arts. Tour guides enjoy pointing out the unusual details of the home and make sure visitors are duly impressed by the home's 11 fireplaces before sharing the

Andy Warhol's *Vote McGovern*

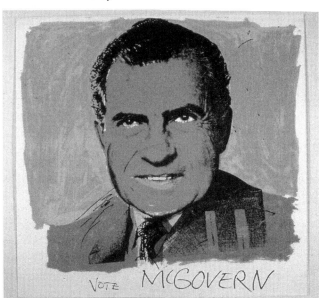

fact that heating the place required the chopping and burning of one cord of wood each 48 hours.

The Cheney Cowles Museum offers a wide range of events related to its exhibits, including a weekly lecture series, FamilyFest Saturdays, tours, workshops, and symposia.

> *Hours: Wed 10am–9pm, Tues and Thurs–Sat 10am–5pm, Sun 1pm–5pm. Admission charged.*
>
> *Directions: The museum is just west of downtown. From I-90, take exit 280A and drive north on Walnut Street, then west on Second Avenue. Watch for signs guiding you to the museum.*

### ■ Crosbyana Room and Crosby Boyhood Home
Gonzaga University
E 502 Boone Avenue (Crosbyana Room)
E 508 Sharp Avenue (Crosby Boyhood Home)
Spokane, WA 99202
(509) 328-4220 ext 4297 (Crosbyana Room)
(509)328-4220 ext 5999 (Crosby Boyhood Home)

Harry Lillis "Bing" Crosby recorded more than 11,000 songs in his long career, acted in more than 100 films, and hosted numerous network radio and TV programs. These days he's best remembered for his crooning voice, for the Road movies he made with his buddy Bob Hope, and for his roles in such classic films as *The Bells of St. Mary's* and *Going My Way*.

Crosby was born in Tacoma and, at age three, moved with his family to Spokane, where he later spent a few semesters at Gonzaga University. Although he dropped out before graduating, he nevertheless became a contributing alumnus and was awarded an honorary doctorate in 1937. Crosby's boyhood home, on the Gonzaga campus, is open for tours; there's a statue on campus featuring a relaxed-looking Crosby complete with jaunty fedora hat and golf clubs; and there's a jam-packed museum called the Crosbyana Room on the first floor of the Crosby Student Center.

The one-room museum features a wide variety of items relating to Crosby's life and career, including gold and platinum records, photographs, trophies, plaques, and numerous Crosby-endorsed items. Highlights of the collection include a colorful Bing Crosby "Call Me Lucky" board game, an (empty) blue-and-white box of Bing Crosby ice cream, a bright yellow hockey puck–size Bing Crosby record cleaner, and a wonderful Bing Crosby coloring book. Sheet music for tunes Crosby made famous, including "White Christmas" and "Moonlight Becomes You," are here, along with Crosby's 1945 Oscar for *Going My Way* and a doughnut-encrusted plaque from the National Dunking Association naming Crosby "the radio star whose face is most conducive to dunking" in honor of National Donut Week in 1949.

Bing Crosby ice cream

With the addition a few years back of almost all the holdings from the Tacoma-based Bing Crosby Historical Society, Gonzaga University now has the largest public Bing Crosby collection in the world. Unfortunately, though, not everything can fit in the single display room. If you ask nicely, the archivists in the library next door are happy to show off some of the items kept in storage.

Crosby's boyhood home now houses the Gonzaga Alumni Association and a variety of Crosby memorabilia.

*Hours: Crosbyana Room: June to Aug: Mon–Fri 7:30am–midnight. Sept to May: Mon–Fri 7:30am–midnight, Sat–Sun 11:30am–midnight. Crosby Home: Mon–Fri 8am–4:30pm.*

*Admission free for both museums.*

*Directions: From I-90, take exit 282 and head north on State Route 290 to Hamilton Street and Gonzaga University. The Bing Crosby Collection is in the Crosby Student Center; watch for the statue of Bing out front. The home is at the southeast corner of the Gonzaga University campus, at the intersection of Addison Street and Sharp Avenue.*

## ■ Jundt Art Museum

Gonzaga University
202 E Cataldo Avenue
Spokane, WA 99202
(509)323-6611

Located on the campus of Gonzaga University, the Jundt Art Museum provides exhibit space for local, regional, national, international, faculty, and student work and houses the university's growing art collection. The holdings include a large number of prints, 29 pieces of glass art by Dale Chihuly, and bronze sculptures by Auguste Rodin as well as paintings, ceramics, photographs, and tapestries. The museum is especially proud of its Chihuly glass collection, which includes the specially commissioned chandelier in the reception lounge made of 800 separate pieces of glass.

Artwork from the permanent collection is periodically rotated from the storage vaults to the exhibition areas. During the school year especially, the museum sponsors art lectures that are open to the public.

> Web site: www.gonzaga.edu/jundt/index.html
> Hours: Mon–Fri 10am–4pm, Sat noon–4pm.
> Admission free.
> Directions: From I-90, take exit 282 and head north on State Route 290 to
>     Hamilton Street and Gonzaga University. The museum is on the
>     southwest corner of the Gonzaga University campus.

## STEILACOOM

### ■ Steilacoom Historical Museum
112 Main Street (PO Box 88016)
Steilacoom, WA 98388
(253)584-4133

Founded in 1854, Steilacoom is Washington's oldest incorporated town, boasting the state's first library, courthouse, and territorial jail. The Steilacoom Historical Museum, on the first floor of the town hall, features some books from that early library as well as vintage photographs and exhibits focusing on early Steilacoom life, from the pioneer period through the first two decades of the 20th century. Displays include a Victorian parlor, a turn-of-the-century kitchen, a back-porch laundry scene, a blacksmith shop, and a Victorian barbershop with a great collection of shaving mugs.

The museum publishes a self-guided walking-tour map of historic buildings and monuments and offers guided tours by special arrangement. An Apple Squeeze, where you can make your own cider "the old-fashioned way" on one of 20 presses, is usually held the second Sunday in October, and a salmon bake on the shores of Puget Sound is held on the last Sunday in July.

> Hours: March to Oct: Tues–Sun 1pm–4pm. Nov, Dec, and Feb: Fri–Sun
>     1pm–4pm. Closed Jan.
> Admission by donation.
> Directions: From I-5, take exit 119 and follow the Dupont-Steilacoom
>     Highway into town. The museum is in the town hall on Main Street.

## ■ Steilacoom Tribal Cultural Center and Museum

1515 Lafayette Street (PO Box 88419)
Steilacoom, WA 98388
(253)584-6308

Located in a restored 1903 church, the Steilacoom Tribal Cultural Center and Museum features three galleries and a snack bar offering Native American foods.

The lower-level gallery explores the prehistory of the Tacoma Basin, the traditional homeland of the Steilacoom tribe. The children's activity center here has a sand-filled container so kids can dig for "artifacts" such as shells and buttons. Nearby is a model showing actual items recovered from an archaeological dig at a Steilacoom village site. Bones and charcoal uncovered there date back to the 1400s, while buttons, trade beads, and nails found on site have been dated to the early 1800s, not long after the tribe's first contact with Europeans.

The upper floor includes a gallery that features touring Native American exhibits and a permanent display of items relating to the history and contemporary lifestyles of the Steilacoom Indians.

> **While You're in Steilacoom:**
> The 1895 Bair Drug and Hardware Store is a living museum displaying early-day post office items, locks, fishhooks, and other hardware, along with pharmacy wares such as Flemex nasal drops. The store also serves breakfast, lunch, and ice cream concoctions from a working 1906 soda fountain.
>
> *Bair Drug and Hardware Store, Wilkes and Lafayette Streets, Steilacoom, WA 98388; (253)588-9668.*
> *Hours: Mon–Fri 9am–4pm, Sat–Sun 8am–4pm. Admission free. Directions: From I-5, take exit 119 and follow the Dupont-Steilacoom Highway into town. Bair Drug and Hardware is on Lafayette Street at the corner of Wilkes Street.*

*Hours: Tues–Sun 10am–4pm.*
*Admission charged.*
*Directions: From I-5, take exit 119 or 129, head west, and turn onto Lafayette Street toward the center of town. The museum is on the corner of Pacific and Lafayette Streets. Look for the sign with carved poles.*

## STEVENSON

## ■ Columbia Gorge Interpretive Center

State Route 14 (PO Box 396)
Stevenson, WA 98648
(800)991-2338

Located on a 10-acre river-view site next to Rock Creek Cove, the grand 23,000-square-foot Columbia Gorge Interpretive Center offers a wide range of exhibits illustrating the cultural and natural history of the people and events that shaped Washington's Skamania County, Oregon, and the Columbia River Gorge.

In the First People Gallery, visitors learn that the Gorge was a large trading center for the Klickitat, Wasco, Wishram, Yakama, and other tribes that lived in the region. Examples of baskets, bowls, walking sticks, and tools used by these earliest residents are on display here, along with a dugout canoe from 1853 and a replica of a pithouse, a subterranean dwelling entered from the top, which took advantage of the fact that seven feet below the surface, the earth is a constant and comfortable 67 degrees.

The soaring Grand Gallery displays a 1921 Mack log truck, a restored Corliss steam engine that once powered a local sawmill, and a 38-foot-tall mechanical fish wheel. The wheel is a replica of the McCord wheel, built in 1882, and is an example of the more than 70 fish wheels that were eventually built on the Columbia River. Powered by the current of the river, the wheel would scoop fish up in a wire mesh and dump them into a barge. (When the wheel is turned for touring groups, soccer balls substitute for chinook salmon.) These fish wheels, which made it possible to take more than 30 million pounds of fish from the river annually, were eventually banned. In sharp contrast with this method of fishing, note the lone Native American dip netter on the molded rock cliffs by the waterfall.

The second-floor galleries explore the coming of hydroelectric power to the region and examine the area's community and spiritual life. A computer station shares the oral histories of a teacher, a logger, a fisherman, a geologist, and a local newspaper editor, while family portraits, artifacts, and other items displayed in a houselike structure offer glimpses into everyday life.

An unusual collection originally housed at the much smaller Skamania County Historical Museum now has a place of honor at the center. The Don Brown Rosary Collection, with more than 4,000 rosaries of every shape and size, is now the centerpiece of an exhibit titled *Spiritual Quest*. There are rosaries made from bone, semiprecious stones, olive pits, nuts, deer antlers, plastic pop-beads, and even Ping-Pong balls (made by a nun in Alaska). They range in size from tiny rosaries that can be stored inside acorns to the largest rosary in the world, one that's more than 16 feet long and made of spray-painted Styrofoam balls for a school play in Massachusetts. The collection also includes a rosary made from lead bullets, a glow-in-the-dark rosary, and one designed to be attached to an automobile's steering wheel so drivers could pray on the road.

When Don Brown was alive, he insisted that people be allowed to touch the rosaries and rub their own rosaries against the museum specimens to transfer the blessing. Surprisingly, some rosaries from the collection disappeared after such rituals. These days the cases remain locked.

*Hours: Daily 10am–5pm.*
*Admission charged.*
*Directions: From eastbound I-84 in Oregon, take exit 44. Cross the Bridge*
*of the Gods and continue east on State Route 14 in Washington for a*
*mile and a half. The museum is on the outskirts of Stevenson.*

## SUNNYSIDE

### ■ Sunnyside Museum
Fourth and Grant Streets (PO Box 789)
Sunnyside, WA 98944
(509)837-6010

Housed in a 1904 building that once served as a mortuary, the Sunnyside Museum displays hand-woven baskets, arrowheads, and artifacts from the Yakama Indians; a nice collection of antique toys and dolls; a pioneer kitchen complete with cookstove and vintage washing machine; and finely furnished "formal rooms," including a turn-of-the-century parlor and dining room.

In addition to photographs and biographies of the folks who settled the lower Yakima Valley (Sunnyside and Bickleton), the museum proudly displays the odds and ends donated over the years, including a human skeleton, a 5,000-year-old mastodon tusk, photographs of people picking hops and asparagus, shots of the old beet factory, and a wide variety of farm tools. No doubt some of those tools were used to help Sunnyside become the Asparagus Capital of the Northwest, an accomplishment now celebrated with an annual Asparagus Festival on the fourth weekend in April.

*Hours: April 1 to the Sun before Christmas: Fri–Sun 1:30pm–4:30pm.*
*Admission by donation.*
*Directions: From I-82, take exit 67 (Port of Sunnyside). Follow S First*
*north, turn right on Lincoln Avenue, and turn left on Fourth Street.*
*The museum is on the corner of Fourth and Grant, across the street*
*from the central park.*

## SUQUAMISH

### ■ Suquamish Museum
15838 Sandy Hook Road (PO Box 498)
Suquamish, WA 98392
(360)598-3311 ext 422

The most famous and honored member of the Suquamish tribe is Chief Seattle, a man remembered for his peacemaking skills and his careful way with words. He's buried in the tribal cemetery behind St. Peter's Catholic Church in Suquamish, in a gravesite marked by two suspended canoes.

You'll learn more about Chief Seattle and the Suquamish people at the Suquamish Museum on the Port Madison reservation. Exhibits feature baskets, canoes, tools and other artifacts, first-person accounts, music, song, and historical photographs. In the exhibit called *The Eyes of Chief Seattle,* visitors are invited to look at the Suquamish as if through the eyes of Chief Seattle himself. The other permanent exhibit offers a glimpse into the tribe's traditional ways of living and into the ancient village site of D'Suq'Wub, "place of the clear salt water."

Before you tour the exhibits, take a moment to watch the two short, well-made videos shown in the museum. In *Come Forth Laughing,* tribal elders give accounts, often humorous, of growing up in the area. *Waterborne: The Gift of the Indian Canoe* uses photographs, music, and the stories of tribal elders to illustrate the importance of water in the lives of Puget Sound Indians and the changes that have occurred in the area over the past 100 years.

A brochure available at the museum will point you toward several intriguing points of interest on the Port Madison reservation, including Chief Seattle's gravesite and a park commemorating the site of Ole Man House, the most well known of a series of longhouses that once existed in the original Suquamish village.

> *Hours: May to Sept: Daily 10am–5pm. Oct to April: Fri–Sun*
> *11am–4pm.*
> *Admission charged.*
> *Directions: From the Bainbridge Island ferry dock, take Highway 305*
> *toward Poulsbo and follow the SUQUAMISH MUSEUM AND TRIBAL*
> *CENTER signs. From the Bremerton ferry dock, take State Route 303*
> *to State Route 3 and then to State Route 305. Look for the*
> *SUQUAMISH MUSEUM AND TRIBAL CENTER signs.*

## TACOMA

### ■ African American Museum
925 Court C
Tacoma, WA 98402
(253)274-1278

Once a "museum without walls," the African American Museum now has a permanent home; not only that, it's the Pacific Northwest's only museum dedicated to the preservation and exhibition of African American history. The museum features several changing exhibits and maintains a permanent exhibit honoring Dr. Martin Luther King Jr., which invites visitors to sit for a moment in a jail cell reminiscent of the one King once occupied in Birmingham, Alabama.

The *Splendor of Africa* exhibit introduces visitors to the culture and traditions of several African countries and includes clothing, weapons, art, and a hands-on Nigerian marketplace section for children complete with dress-up shop and Nigerian currency.

The *Harper's Weekly* exhibit focuses on the lifestyles of African Americans from 1840 to 1885, images of African Americans portrayed in the media, and black-owned Washington state newspapers from 1880 through the 1920s. Kids are invited to develop and take home a copy of their own daily paper, created in the museum's modern-day newspaper office.

Special programs include storytelling, African American doll making, and a wide variety of workshops for kids and their families. Once a month, folks 75 and older are invited to stop by for a Genteel Tea.

*Hours: Wed–Sat 10am–5pm.*
*Admission charged.*
*Directions: From I-5, take exit 133 (City Center) and head north to the A Street exit. Turn left on S Ninth Street, drive uphill, and turn onto Court C, just past the Rialto Theatre's sign.*

## ■ Camp 6 Logging Museum
Point Defiance Park
5400 N Pearl Street (PO Box 340)
Tacoma, WA 98401
(253)752-0047

Modeled after actual logging camps, the Camp 6 Logging Museum celebrates the days when "loggers were boss and steam was king." Exhibits include photographs and equipment gathered from a variety of logging camps that operated during the era of steam power. Items on display include an 1887 Dolbeer donkey, a Lidgerwood TowerSkidder weighing more than 200 tons, and a Pacific Coast Shay steam locomotive.

Camp 6 also offers logging-train rides and, during weekends in December, a special Santa Train.

*Web site: www.camp-6-museum.org*
*Hours: After Memorial Day to Sept: Wed–Fri 10am–5pm, Sat–Sun and holidays 10am–7pm. Oct: Wed–Sun 10am–4pm. Feb to Memorial Day: Wed–Sun and holidays 10am–4pm. Closed Nov to Jan. Outdoor exhibit is open year-round, sunrise to sunset.*
*Admission by donation. There's a charge for train rides.*
*Directions: Camp 6 is in Point Defiance Park, 10 minutes from the junction of I-5 and State Route 16.*

## ■ Children's Museum of Tacoma
936 Broadway
Tacoma, WA 98402
(253)627-6031

The Children's Museum of Tacoma is a hands-on sort of place, where it's possible to have loads of fun while learning about art, science, and culture.

The museum has four main galleries, including Omokunle, a re-created Nigerian village. Omokunle, a contraction of three words that together mean "the house is filled with children," offers kids and parents a chance to experience the culture of Yorubaland by exploring how Yoruba people live, what they wear, what foods they eat, and how they shop. This exhibit also features a Marvelous Maps Table and an interactive computer game that takes you on a virtual mountain-bike tour of Africa.

The contents of two exhibit areas are pretty much determined by the community. A changing display of artwork created by, for, and about kids is displayed in the Kids' Gallery. In the Personal Collections Gallery, local collectors are invited to show off their special collections for three months at a time. Past exhibits have included mass quantities of Star Wars and Star Trek memorabilia, Barbies, and lunch boxes.

Exhibits in the fourth major gallery have explored everything from medieval villages and architecture to the human body and bugs.

In addition to its regular exhibits, the museum offers special programs and workshops.

*Hours: Fri 10am–9pm, Tues–Thurs and Sat 10am–5pm, Sun noon–5pm. Admission charged. Free every Fri night 5pm–9pm.*

*Directions: The museum is in downtown Tacoma, between S 9th and S 11th Streets. From I-5, take exit 133 (City Center) and head north to the A Street exit. Turn left on S 11th Street; at the third light, turn right on Broadway.*

■ **Fort Nisqually Historic Site Museum**
Point Defiance Park
5400 N Pearl Street #11
Tacoma, WA 98407
(253)591-5339

The Fort Nisqually Historic Site Museum is a reconstructed Hudson's Bay Company outpost that has been relocated to Five Mile Drive in Point Defiance Park. Back in 1833, when the fort was first built, it was located near the Nisqually River delta north of Olympia.

The fort offers a glimpse into life at a busy fur-trading and agricultural post of the 1850s. The site includes two original structures (the main house and a granary) and several "new-old" structures that would have been part of the original site, such as storehouses, defense towers, housing for laborers, a kitchen, and a blacksmith shop.

The main house, or factor's dwelling house, includes a small museum that displays musket rifles owned by the last person who lived here under the employ of the Hudson's Bay Company, as well as photographs of the women who lived on site with their husbands, who served as clerks and chief traders. There are beaver pelt hats here, along with a pocket watch, a whale oil lamp, and exhibits devoted to the multicultural crew that worked on site.

Special programs include lectures, living-history days, and reenactments to honor events such as Halloween, Christmas, and Queen Victoria's birthday in May.

*Hours: Both museum and grounds: June to Aug: Daily 11am–6pm. Sept to May: Wed–Sun 11am–4pm.*
*Admission charged.*
*Directions: From I-5, take the Bremerton/State Route 16 exit and head west to the Sixth Avenue/Point Defiance exit. Drive north on N Pearl Street, following the signs to Point Defiance Park. Once you reach the park, signs on Five Mile Drive will direct you to the fort.*

## ■ International Glass Museum
1717 Pacific Avenue (PO Box 1616)
Tacoma, WA 98402
(253)572-9310

For centuries, the craft of glassmaking was a European specialty. But ever since glass artist Dale Chihuly, a Tacoma native, burst on the scene with his fanciful glass creations and cofounded the prestigious Pilchuck Glass School north of Seattle, the Pacific Northwest has rivaled Venice as the world's glassmaking headquarters.

Plans are currently under way to construct a facility called the International Glass Museum, scheduled to open sometime in the summer of 2001, on Tacoma's central downtown waterfront. The museum will recognize the art-glass movement and the more than 5,000 artists around the world who work in this medium. In addition to art-glass exhibitions, plans call for an operating "hot shop" and a 600-foot bridge of Chihuly glass that will link the museum to the city.

Can't wait? While construction proceeds, you can visit an exhibition featuring five installations of Chihuly's work at Tacoma's historic 1911 Union Station, now a courthouse. The largest piece, a huge blue chandelier composed of hundreds of blue glass balloons, hangs in the six-story-tall rotunda. The Monarch Window, across the rotunda to the east, features 25 brilliantly colored glass butterflies.

*Hours: Mon–Fri 8am–5pm.*
*Admission free. There's a charge for group tours.*
*Directions: From I-5, take exit 133 (City Center/I-705). Follow I-705 north toward the city center and take the S 21st Street exit. Stay in the center lane (the Port of Tacoma exit is to your right) and turn right on Pacific Avenue.*

## ■ Karpeles Manuscript Library Museum
407 South G Street
Tacoma, WA 98405
(253)572-6044

In the late 1970s David Karpeles started collecting original manuscripts: things like a copy of the Emancipation Proclamation signed by Abraham Lincoln, Benjamin Franklin's "Taxation without Representation" letter to King George III, and Mozart's score for *The Marriage of Figaro.* The false starts, new directions, doodlings, and crossed-out words on what have turned out to be important primary historical documents, Karpeles realized, offer clues for scholars. These original documents, he also discovered, help turn history into a lively and fascinating subject for students.

Karpeles, a wealthy California real estate investor, now owns more than a million original documents and rotates his collection between seven document museums around the country, including the Karpeles Manuscript Library Museum in Tacoma. Although some Northwest-related documents are housed here permanently, most documents in the collection are stored at Karpeles's main museum in Santa Barbara, California. Themed exhibits drawn from the collection periodically tour the Karpeles museums, staying at each facility for about three months. Each exhibit centers on a particular individual, historical event, or aspect of society. For example, past exhibits have featured Thomas Edison's letters, original music manuscripts, and documents relating to the Civil War.

> *Web site: www.rain.org/~karpeles/taqdir.html*
> *Hours: Tues–Sat 10am–4pm.*
> *Admission free.*
> *Directions: From southbound I-5, take I-705 and then the 15th Street S exit. Drive west (uphill) and turn right on Tacoma Avenue, left on S Sixth Street, and right on South G Street. Continue a block and a half to the museum.*

## ■ McChord Air Force Base Museum
Building 517, Corner of Lincoln and A Streets (Box 4205)
McChord Air Force Base, WA 98438
(253)984-2485

The airplanes lined up outside the McChord Air Force Base Museum are there to tell the story of this base's role in the history of military airpower, beginning with Lieutenant Harold Bromley's attempt at a nonstop transpacific flight in 1929.

Included in the aircraft display are a Douglas B-18 bomber, a Convair F106A fighter, and the pride of the fleet, a Douglas C-124C transport. Displays inside the museum feature vintage uniforms, unit exhibits, armaments, models, and a flight simulator that kids love to sit in even if it doesn't actually work.

> *Hours: Tues–Sun noon–4pm.*
> *Admission free.*
> *Directions: From I-5, take exit 125 and turn east on Bridgeport Way. At McChord Air Force Base in Tacoma, get a visitor's pass from the visitors center at the main gate. You'll need to show a driver's license, car registration or rental agreement, and proof of insurance.*

- **Shanaman Sports Museum of Tacoma–Pierce County**
Tacoma Dome
2727 East D Street
Tacoma, WA 98421
(253)848-1360

Located at the Tacoma Dome, the Shanaman Sports Museum of Tacoma–Pierce County highlights 25 different sports and more than 300 athletes, coaches, referees, and other sports figures who came from, or in some cases just stopped by, this area.

Baseball memorabilia on display celebrates local kids who went on to the majors, including Ron Cey (Los Angeles Dodgers), Mike Blowers (Seattle Mariners), Doug Sisk (New York Mets), Jimmy Mosolf (Chicago Cubs), and Marv Rickert (Boston Braves). The exhibit also includes photos of the 1899 Tacoma Baseball Team, the 1914 Tacoma Tigers, and shots of Babe Ruth when he stopped in Tacoma during a national barnstorming tour in 1924.

From Tacoma's football heritage you'll see vintage pigskins from games won by the Pacific Lutheran College team over Gonzaga in 1940 and the College of the Pacific in 1941. The display also features the cleats of Tahoma graduate Ray Horton, his Dallas Cowboys helmet, and Super Bowl memorabilia from 1993.

Got the score? If you're a fan of basketball, hockey, hydroplane racing, mountain climbing, boxing, wrestling, track and field, figure skating, golf, or even soapbox derby racing, there's bound to be a local connection.

> *Hours: Open during sports events and major shows (boating, RV, and so on) at the Tacoma Dome. In general, the museum is open one hour prior to sports events and until the end of half-times and game intermissions. During state championships, the museum is open for a six- to eight-hour period.*
>
> *Admission free, but you must purchase a ticket to whatever event is at the Dome.*
>
> *Directions: From I-5, take one of the Tacoma Dome exits. The museum is adjacent to the lower A-level doors in the northwest corner of the Dome. It's attached to the front of the Dome, next to the Exhibition Hall.*

- **Tacoma Art Museum**
1123 Pacific Avenue
Tacoma, WA 98402
(253)272-4258

Housed in a former bank building until 2001, when its new digs just north of Union Station are set to be completed, the Tacoma Art Museum hosts popular touring exhibitions and a permanent collection that features paintings and works on paper, with an emphasis on Northwest art.

Detail of the triptych *Body Fires* (1991) by Fay Jones

The museum's special collections also include a selection of French Impressionist paintings by Renoir, Degas, Pissarro, and others, a rare set of Japanese woodblock prints, 19th-century Chinese textiles, and one of the world's largest public collections of glass by Tacoma native Dale Chihuly.

As part of its commitment to collecting and presenting art by Northwest artists, the museum sponsors the 12th Street Series, featuring contemporary exhibitions, performances, and site-specific installations by Northwest artists. Every other summer, the museum hosts the Northwest Biennial, a juried competition for artists in Washington, Oregon, Idaho, and Montana.

If the art on the walls inspires you (or if you've gotten that "Heh, I can do that" feeling), head for the ArtWORKS gallery, full of art supplies that let you create your own exhibition-inspired work. Or come back another day for one of the many scheduled tours, lectures, festivals, and workshops. Special programs include Art on Saturdays, which serves foster children and their caregivers, and Imagine Art, an annual art project involving at-risk youth.

> Web site: www.tamart.org
> Hours: Thurs 10am–8pm, Tues–Sun 10am–5pm.
> Admission charged.
> Directions: From I-5, take exit 133 (City Center). The museum is in the center of downtown Tacoma's cultural district at 12th Street and Pacific Avenue.

■ **Tacoma Pioneer Telephone Museum**
757 Fawcett Avenue S
Tacoma, WA 98402
(253)627-2996

Like the Vintage Telephone Equipment Museum in Seattle (see listing), the Tacoma Pioneer Telephone Museum is run by current and former telephone company workers and filled with vintage telephones, test equipment, tools, and all manner of communication-related parapher-nalia. Much of it still works, and museum volunteers are more than happy to show you how.

The collection includes a variety of early switchboards, teletype machines, phone booths, historical photographs, turn-of-the-century phone directories, and telephones dating from the early crank models to the first cordless phone, exhibited at the 1962 Seattle World's Fair.

> Hours: Thurs 8am–1pm.
> Admission by donation.
> Directions: From I-5, take exit 133 (City Center) to Pacific Avenue in downtown Tacoma. Turn left (uphill) on S Ninth and travel four blocks to Fawcett Avenue S. The museum is at the corner of S Ninth and Fawcett Avenue S.

■ **Washington State History Museum**
1911 Pacific Avenue
Tacoma, WA 98402
(888)BE-THERE or (253)272-WSHS

In 1911 the Washington State Historical Society began showing artifacts and exhibits related to the history of the Evergreen State. That first Wash-ington State History Museum was housed in an ornate building perched on a bluff northwest of Tacoma's city center. The museum had a great view of Commencement Bay and the Olympic Mountains, but there just wasn't enough room inside to tell the state's story properly.

Walk through this reconstructed mining shack

Now, hold on to your wagon wheels! In 1996 the museum moved into bright, airy new digs in downtown Tacoma, in a huge building reminiscent of historic Union Station next door. While the museum may look traditional on the outside, the exhibits inside give visitors a colorful, noisy, high-tech tour through Washington history. Real artifacts—such as Native American baskets and beadwork; logging, mining, and shipbuilding tools; and hundreds of historic photographs—are on display, but you'll have to look hard to find them among the talking mannequins, computer screens, walk-through dioramas, and hands-on displays depicting the people and events that shaped Washington's history and development.

What the museum offers is a theatrical presentation of history: On the main floor, at least 49 interactive exhibits offer something to touch, sit on, listen to, or interact with. For example, not only can you walk inside a traditional Coast Salish plank house, but you can listen to an audio program describing the roles and tasks of each family member. Springs under your seat give you a sense of how uncomfortable a ride in a prairie schooner might have been. A soundtrack supplies vintage radio programs, news bulletins, and music to set the scene for folks who sit down at the 1930s-era "radio" lunch counter. And a computer program called Encyclopedia Washingtonia will test your knowledge of Washington history. For example, question 80 asks, "What U.S. president once grew potatoes in southwest Washington?" (Answer: Ulysses S. Grant, who cultivated spuds while serving in the army at Fort Vancouver in the 1850s).

The permanent exhibits sprawl through the half-acre Hall of Washington History, and this floor can tucker you out. But be sure to go upstairs to see the temporary and traveling exhibits and the impressive world-class HO-scale model railroad being built by the Puget Sound Model Railroad Engineers. Longtime favorites Dave and Dandy are up here too. These are the very same oxen that pulled Ezra Meeker's wagon as he retraced the Oregon Trail in 1906. Meeker donated the oxen to the Washington State Historical Society and later made trips across the trail by car and by plane. The oxen lived in a corral next to the historical society for several years before they passed on and were stuffed for display. When the museum moved to its new site, the oxen spent a year getting freshened up before reappearing as the cornerstone artifact in an exhibit titled *Transportation Time*. (See also the listing for the Meeker Mansion in Puyallup.)

The museum sponsors family activity days, book discussions, lectures, workshops, and other special events throughout the year.

*Web site: www.wshs.org*
*Hours: Thurs 10am–8pm, Tues–Wed and Fri–Sat 10am–5pm, Sun 11am–5pm.*
*Admission charged.*
*Directions: From I-5, take exit 133 (City Center) and then the E 26th Street exit. Turn left on E 26th Street, continue for three blocks, turn right on Pacific Avenue, and continue for five blocks. The museum is on the right.*

## TENINO

### ■ Tenino Depot Museum
399 Park Avenue W
Tenino, WA 98589
(360)264-4321

Housed in a 1914 railroad depot built with local sandstone, the small Tenino Depot Museum contains exhibits describing Tenino's quarries, area logging and agriculture, and the state's first territorial prison. Of special interest are displays containing examples of the wooden dollars Tenino issued during the Great Depression after the local bank failed.

The sandstone depot itself is a local treasure, with the original men's and women's waiting rooms, ticket counter, baggage check area, and railroad vault all still intact.

*Hours: Mid-April to mid-Oct: Fri–Sun noon–4pm. Closed rest of year.*
*Admission by donation.*

*Directions: From Olympia, take Capitol Way (old State Route 99) 17*
*miles south to Tenino. At the main intersection in Tenino, turn right on*
*Sussex Avenue, drive five blocks, and turn left on Olympia Street.*
*Follow it for two blocks to the park entrance and turn right. The*
*museum is just past the quarry house.*

## THORP

### ■ Thorp Grist Mill
11640 Thorp Highway N (PO Box 7)
Thorp, WA 98946
(509)964-9640

The Thorp Grist Mill, built by Oren Hutchinson, ground flour for the people of the Kittitas Valley and meal for their livestock from 1883 until 1946. It began as a buhrstone milling facility but, when the Northern Pacific Railroad made it possible for newer, heavier machinery to be hauled in by train, roller milling equipment was brought to town.

Many local folks remember that as kids they sometimes wore clothing made from the mill's old flour sacks. And while ownership of the mill changed hands many times during its 63 years of operation, the mill's last owner is fondly remembered for his unique customer-relations campaign. In each sack of ground flour, Walter Leonard would include a lollipop for the kids and a single silk stocking for the "lady of the household." Leonard was banking that, in search of that other stocking, women would steer their husbands back to his mill.

The three-story Thorp Mill structure has been restored and opened as a museum with tools of various trades, historical photographs, and at least 15 pieces of milling machinery made of oak and walnut.

*Web site: www.thorp.org*
*Hours: Memorial Day to last weekend in Sept: Wed–Fri and Sun*
*    1pm–4pm, Sat 10am–4pm. Closed rest of year.*
*Admission by donation.*
*Directions: From I-90, take the Thorp exit and go west three miles through*
*    the village of Thorp, past the schools, to the millstream and the mill.*

## TOPPENISH

### ■ American Hop Museum
22 South B Street
Toppenish, WA 98948
(509)865-4677 (865-HOPS)

While the Pacific Northwest has become famous for coffee, it's also famous for microbreweries and brewpubs. Perhaps that has something to do with the fact that the region once grew all of the United States's hop crops and now supplies 25 percent of the world's hops. These days, America's hops culture is centered in Washington's rich Yakima Valley, and the industry's history is celebrated with displays of equipment, artifacts, and historical photos at the American Hop Museum.

Volunteers from area hop families and people from the hop industries have spent years turning the old cement Hop Growers Supply building into a mural-adorned homage to *Humulus lupulus,* the perennial vine whose flowers are used for flavoring beer. The murals, which follow the crop from planting through marketing of the finished product, tell just part of the story. Inside are antique hop presses, a horse-drawn hop duster, tools, scales, old picking baskets, balers, and examples of the stencils that hop companies once plastered on their bags and bales. Look in the yard for giant, rusting hop-picking machinery, and on weekends keep your ears open for the steady stream of retired hop workers who stop by to share memories of the days when the vines were trained to grow on poles 12 to 15 feet high, instead of on the low trellises used today, and when all hop farmers had their own hop storage houses and kilns for curing harvested crops.

And here's something you'll learn at the American Hop Museum that you might not have learned in grade school: According to a museum tour guide, beer has been a staple in the American diet since before the Pilgrims set foot on Plymouth Rock. According to an entry in the logbook of the *Mayflower,* a major reason the ship landed at Plymouth Rock instead of its original destination (New York City, then called New Amsterdam) was that the ship was dangerously low on beer! Crew members wanted to negotiate with local settlers for some suds. The rest, as they say, is hop history.

> *Hours: May to Sept: Daily 11am–4pm. Closed rest of year.*
> *Admission by donation.*
> *Directions: From I-82, take exit 50 into Toppenish (three miles). Turn left*
> *on Asotin Avenue (past the football field), left on Toppenish Avenue,*
> *and then right on South B Street.*

■ **Toppenish Museum**
One S Elm Street
Toppenish, WA 98948
(509)865-4510

Brochures for the Toppenish Museum try to spark curiosity by wondering if you'd know where to find "a portable anvil, a 14-inch oyster shell, a curtain stretcher, or a picture of the town's 1934 kindergarten class." By now you know the first place to look for any (well, usually all) of this sort of stuff is in a community museum. The Toppenish Museum won't let you down.

In addition to all the items mentioned above, the museum has a nice collection of photographs, social club memorabilia, furnishings from old homes and ranches, souvenir plates, and a variety of items relating to the area's earliest settlers. Be sure to ask about the Brand Quilt, patterned with brands used by area ranchers.

The museum sponsors demonstrations of gold panning, lace-making, bullet-making, and fly-tying, and offers classes ranging from storytelling to basket making.

> *Hours: Tues–Thurs 1:30pm–4pm, Fri 2pm–4pm.*
> *Admission charged.*
> *Directions: The museum is on the corner of S Elm Street and Buena Way*
>    *(State Route 22) in Toppenish.*

■ **Yakama Indian Nation Museum**
Highway 97 and Buster Road (PO Box 151)
Toppenish, WA 98948
(509)865-2800

This museum of Native American history is housed inside the large Yakama Nation Cultural Heritage Center, which was designed to be reminiscent of the traditional tule mat–covered longhouse of the Yakama people. Inside the Yakama Indian Nation Museum are a wide variety of artifacts, exhibits, and dioramas relating the history of the Yakama people, which extends back to the beginning of time.

Many exhibits provide information about the sacred places, the local plants, and the many animals that played an important role in Yakama life. For example, the Mount Adams diorama features a hawk, a raccoon, a bear, and other animals native to the region, while the re-creation of Celilo Falls relates how the spot served as an important trading area and was considered to be sacred fishing grounds.

Dwellings re-created include an earthen lodge structure made of willow branches, reeds, grasses, and mud; a tepee made of tule mats; and a sweathouse made of willow branches covered with animal skins. The earthen lodge is an example of the first dwelling used as a permanent homesite by the Columbia Plateau people thousands of years ago, while the tule tepees functioned more as summer homes during the food-gathering seasons. The sweathouse was a spiritual spot, used for a variety of ceremonial purposes.

Elsewhere in the museum are exhibits illustrating how Yakama children learned to gather and store food, hunt, catch wild horses, and otherwise prepare for adulthood. Once married, you'll learn, many women

**While You're in Toppenish:**
Murals adorn the outside walls of many buildings in Toppenish, which calls itself the City of Historical Murals. Look for colorful historical scenes and depictions of pioneer life. For more details, pick up a walking tour brochure from the Mural Society at A-11 S Toppenish Avenue, (509)865-6516.

created and kept a time ball, made of hemp string decorated with beads and knots to create a "diary" or lifelong calendar of memories and events. When the woman died, the time ball was buried with her.

*Web site: www.wolfenet.com/~yingis/spilyay.html*
*Hours: Summer: Daily 9am–6pm. Rest of year: Daily 9am–5pm.*
*Admission charged.*
*Directions: From Highway 97, take the Buster Road exit. The museum is*
*    in the Yakama Nation Cultural Heritage Center, next to the highway.*

■ **Yakima Valley Rail and Steam Museum**
10 S Asotin Avenue (PO Box 889)
Toppenish, WA 98948
(509)865-1911

Constructed in 1911, this old depot was one of three built in the Toppenish area for the Northern Pacific Railroad. Abandoned by the railroad in 1982, the depot was refurbished as the Yakima Valley Rail and Steam Museum in the early 1990s by local rail fans. Now the depot contains antique oak showcases full of railroad memorabilia such as toothpicks, light bulbs, china, and lanterns.

Outside is the big stuff: trackside equipment, such as semaphores and crossing signals, and rolling stock, including coaches, gang cars, and cabooses. Several times each year, association members hook up their old Pennsylvania Railroad coaches to a 65-ton locomotive for excursion rides through scenic Simcoe Valley.

*Hours: May to Nov: Sat–Sun 10am–5pm. Closed rest of year.*
*Admission by donation. There's a charge for train rides.*
*Directions: From I-82, take exit 50 to S Asotin Avenue (the left-hand part*
*    of the Y you'll come to at the railroad tracks).*

## UNION GAP

■ **Central Washington Agricultural Museum**
Fulbright Park
4508 Main Street (PO Box 3008)
Union Gap, WA 98903
(509)457-8735

Central Washington's fertile volcanic soil makes this area one of the most productive agricultural areas in the nation. But even the earliest pioneers couldn't plant or harvest their crops without the help of some sort of farm implements. The Central Washington Agricultural Museum therefore operates as a sort of shrine to agricultural equipment, displaying everything from early horse-drawn plows to modern-day high-tech machinery.

Appropriately enough, the museum is on a 15-acre former farm on the outskirts of what was originally called Yakima City. Twenty buildings filled with farm machinery form a ring around a working windmill. Equipment too big to fit into the buildings is displayed outdoors on terraces along the circular asphalt pathway. What's there? Just about anything that anyone in the area used on a farm: a 10-20 McCormick Deering tractor, a portable hop-picking machine, a pea picker, a wide variety of horse-drawn machinery, and lots more.

Other exhibits include the steam engine that was used to power the Old Naches sawmill, a log cabin (circa 1917) filled with vintage household items, a Burlington Northern boxcar filled with railroad memorabilia, and the Magness Room, containing a former shop teacher's collection of more than 3,000 antique hand tools: carpentry tools, wrenches, cobbler tools, kitchen tools, and just about any other kind of tool you can imagine—all neatly labeled.

If you're in the area in late summer, try to make it to the annual Washington State Pioneer Power Show, held each year during the third weekend in August. The show includes a gala display of vintage farm machinery and equipment, an old-time threshing bee, and a starlight parade featuring a procession of lighted farm machinery down Main Street.

> *Hours: Museum: April to Oct: Mon–Sat 9am–5pm, Sun 1pm–4pm. Nov to March: Thurs–Sun 1pm–4pm. Grounds: Daily till dusk.*
> *Admission by donation.*
> *Directions: From eastbound I-82, take exit 36 (Valley Mall Boulevard) to Main Street. From westbound I-82, take exit 38 to Union Gap. The museum is near the overpass for Highway 97. Look for the FUL-BRIGHT PARK signs.*

## VANCOUVER

### ■ Clark County Historical Museum
1511 Main Street
Vancouver, WA 98660
(360)695-4681

In 1806, Meriwether Lewis wrote that Clark County was the best place for a settlement west of the Rocky Mountains. It had good soil and a great view of Mount St. Helens, the "most notable object in nature."

At the Clark County Historical Museum, you can find out what else Lewis and his team observed during their 10 days in the county. You'll also see Chinook Indian artifacts and turn-of-the-century displays, including a doctor's office filled with medicines, prescription books, and instruments; a well-stocked general store; an old post office; and an early newspaper office complete with cast-iron printing press, type case, and printing tools.

If you have kids with you, don't forget to pop down to the basement for a tour of the railway museum, which features railroad memorabilia from the S. P. & S. Railway, a model train set depicting the north side of Columbia River, a ticket office, and a furnished train compartment. Retired railroaders are often on hand to share stories of their adventures.

*Hours: Tues–Sat 12:30pm–4:30pm.*
*Admission free.*
*Directions: From I-5, take the Mill Plain exit to Main Street and drive*
   *west for three blocks on Main Street. The museum is in a Carnegie*
   *library building on the corner of 16th and Main Streets.*

## ■ Fort Vancouver National Historic Site
612 E Reserve Street
Vancouver, WA 98661
(360) 696-7655 ext 17

Between 1825 and 1849, Fort Vancouver served as the western headquarters of the Hudson's Bay Company fur-trading operations. The fort became the Pacific Northwest center for political, cultural, commercial, and manufacturing activities and was where newly arrived pioneers headed for supplies to begin their Oregon Territory farms during the 1830s and 1840s.

Today visitors to the Fort Vancouver National Historic Site can tour nine major fort buildings, which have been reconstructed and furnished with items appropriate to the time. The visitors center offers a 12-minute introductory video and several museum exhibits, which include beads, archaeological items, ceramics, and other items from the fur-trading era.

In addition to regular tours of the buildings and cultural demonstrations, the site offers special events including a late May celebration of Queen Victoria's birthday, a brigade encampment on the third or fourth weekend in July, a candlelight tour on the first weekend in October, and Christmas at Fort Vancouver on the second or third Sunday in December. The site is also the location of the Pearson Air Museum (see next listing).

*Web site: www.nps.gov/fova/*
*Hours: Early May to late Sept: Daily 9am–5pm. Late Sept to early May:*
   *Daily 9am–4pm.*
*Admission charged early May to late Sept.*
*Directions: From I-5, take exit 1C (Mill Plain Boulevard) and follow the*
   *brown directional signs to the visitors center on Evergreen Boulevard.*

## ■ Pearson Air Museum
1115 E Fifth Street
Vancouver, WA 98661
(360)694-7026

Pearson Field is the oldest continually operating airfield in the United States, dating back to the landing, during Portland's 1905 Lewis and Clark exposition, of a dirigible named the *Gelatin*. Although the *Gelatin* didn't go all that far, taking off from Portland and landing on the polo grounds at Vancouver Barracks, the flight constituted the first aerial crossing of the Columbia River.

Today, Pearson Field is a general aviation center and the site of the Pearson Air Museum, which features a children's hands-on activity center, vintage aircraft, a cockpit simulator, aviation computer software, and loads of vintage photos.

Throughout the year the museum presents historical reenactments and hosts an annual biplane fly-in at the end of August.

*Web site: www.pacifier.com/~pearson/*
*Hours: Tues–Sun 10am–5pm.*
*Admission charged.*
*Directions: The museum is within the Fort Vancouver National Historic Site (see previous listing). From I-5, take exit 1C (Mill Plain Boulevard) and follow the signs through Vancouver Barracks to E Fifth Street.*

Petroglyphs at the museum

**VANTAGE**

- **Ginkgo Petrified Forest State Park Interpretive Center**
  Interstate 90 (PO Box 1203)
  Vantage, WA 98050
  (509)856-2700

Back in the 1930s a rare piece of petrified wood was discovered near Vantage. The wood, from the subtropical ginkgo tree, seemed out of place here and led professor George Beck on a research quest to uncover the mystery of the ginkgo petrified forest.

To learn what Beck and his colleagues discovered, stop by the museum inside the Gingko Petrified Forest State Park Interpretive Center. On display are more than 30 tree species found in this ancient forest and more than 200 examples of both polished and unpolished fossilized wood, including the rare ginkgo that inspired Beck, which was once extinct on this continent but later reintroduced from a species that survived in Asia. The museum has a great display of "picture wood," slices of fossilized wood that contain "natural drawings" that seem to depict such images as landscapes, ducks floating on a pond, Jimmy Durante, a baboon, and Dagwood Bumstead.

Outside are petroglyphs, live ginkgos, and, on the three-quarter-mile Trees of Stone trail, 22 different types of petrified logs in their natural habitat.

*Hours: Mid-June to mid-Sept: Daily 10am–6pm. Call for hours rest of year.*
*Admisson by donation.*
*Directions: The museum is in the interpretive center at Ginkgo Petrified Forest State Park, located where I-90 crosses the Columbia River.*

## WALLA WALLA

### ■ Fort Walla Walla Museum
755 Myra Road
Walla Walla, WA 99362
(509)525-7703

In 1964, retired farmer Carl Penner teamed up with a county extension agent to create an exhibit of farm machinery for the Southeastern Washington Fair. The exhibit stole the show, and work soon began on the 15-acre Fort Walla Walla Museum complex, which now includes 14 historic structures and five exhibit buildings arranged in a broken-wheel design on land adjacent to an 1857 military cemetery.

The historic structures, all filled with family heirlooms, tools, and household items used by early pioneers and settlers, include the Ransom Clark Cabin, Walla Walla County School House No. 26, a general store, and the Babcock Railway Station. The Umapine Cabin, circa 1878, contains a variety of Native American artifacts such as baskets and items collected along the shores of the Columbia and Snake Rivers. One showcase depicts Celilo Falls, a former Native American fishing ground that has been covered by water since the construction of the Dalles Dam on the Columbia River.

The large exhibit buildings contain items showing the pioneer lifestyle and the variety of equipment used during the horse era of farming. Of special interest in Agricultural Building No. 3 is the large sidehill combine pulled by a team of 33 full-size fiberglass mules, all fully harnessed and hooked up to the famous Shandoney hitch, which is driven by just one man. Carl Penner designed the mules, which mimic the animals that pulled hitches in his own wheatfields, and had them made by the same person who made plastic animals for Disneyland. Elsewhere, six fiberglass Clydesdale draft horses are hitched to a double wagon once used to haul threshed grain to the storage sheds.

Special events include a fall harvest festival in September and the Lewis and Clark Festival in October.

*Web site: www.bmi.net/fortw2*
*Hours: April to Oct: Tues–Sun 10am–5pm. Closed rest of year.*

*Admission charged.*
*Directions: From State Route 125, follow the signs north to Fort Walla*
  *Walla, just under a mile from town. From Highway 12, take the Col-*
  *lege Place exit and follow the museum signs on Wallula Road to*
  *Myra Road and Walla Walla Park.*

## ■ Whitman Mission National Historic Site
On Highway 12 (Route 2, Box 247)
Walla Walla, WA 99362
(509)522-6360

In 1836, Marcus and Narcissa Whitman established a Christian mission among the Cayuse Indians at Waiilatpu, which means "place of the people of the ryegrass." During the early days of the Oregon Trail, the mission also served as an important way station for immigrants heading west, but deep cultural differences and a terrible epidemic eventually led to an Indian attack on the mission on November 29, 1847. Many Indians had died of measles despite the efforts of Marcus Whitman, a doctor, to treat them. After the eruption of violence was over, the Whitmans and 11 other mission residents lay dead.

Today the Whitman Mission National Historic Site is a park preserving the mission site, Mill Pond, a short segment of the Oregon Trail, and the victims' gravesites. Visitors can walk along a path past outlines of the buildings' foundations and read panels that provide historical information about the site.

Inside the visitors center, there's a 10-minute slide program and a one-room museum. Exhibits tell the history of the Cayuse people and display artifacts such as stone net sinkers, mortars and pestles, a combination tomahawk and pipe, a Cayuse saddle, and storage bags as big as modern-day grocery bags. The display documenting the mission includes several Spodeware dishes that belonged to Narcissa Whitman and other artifacts excavated from the site in the late 1940s, including silverware, iron tools, square nails, a pick ax, and the iron end of a hoe. In the center of the room is a diorama with mannequins depicting the Whitmans meeting with some of the Cayuse.

Demonstrations of everything from how to make adobe bricks to how to cook over a campfire are offered on summer weekends.

*Web site: www.nps.gov/whmi/*
*Hours: Summer: Daily 8am–6pm. Rest of year: Daily 8am–4:30pm.*
*Admission charged.*
*Directions: From I-84, follow northbound State Route 11 from Pendleton,*
  *Oregon, to Walla Walla. From Walla Walla, drive west for seven miles*
  *on Highway 12.*

## ■ Two Rivers Heritage Museum
One 16th Street (PO Box 204)
Washougal, WA 98671
(360)835-8742

The communities of Camas and Washougal are located at the conver-
gence of the Columbia and Washougal Rivers. In addition to the two
rivers, the towns have in common the shared history that comes with
being mill towns. Camas (originally called LaCamas in honor of the
camas root eaten by the native Chinook Indians) was the site of early-day
sawmills and paper mills. In Washougal a woolen mill served as the main-
stay of the local economy even before 1912, when it was purchased by
Pendleton Woolen Mills.

Today the story of these two communities is told at the Two Rivers
Heritage Museum. Offerings include vintage photographs, Native
American artifacts, dolls, toys, and a variety of changing exhibits
throughout the year.

> *Hours: Tues–Sat 11am–3pm.*
> *Admission charged.*
> *Directions: From Portland, Oregon, via northbound I-5, head east on State
>    Route 14 to the 15th Street/Washougal exit. Turn left and continue to
>    A Street; turn right and then right again. The museum is next to the
>    Pendleton Woolen Mills parking lot.*

## ■ Douglas County Historical Museum
Highway 2, next to Pioneer Park (PO Box 63)
Waterville, WA 98858
(509)745-8435

Originally built to house a local couple's rock collection, the Douglas
County Historical Museum has had to more than double its size to
accommodate all the memorabilia and community artifacts donated by
area folks.

Still, not everything fits indoors; for example, there's a tram car sitting on the front lawn. It's one of two buckets left over from the
Columbia River Tramway, which, from 1902 until 1910, moved wheat
from the plateau west of Waterville to the Columbia River. Large bread
pan–shaped buckets filled with wheat were sent down to steamboats on
the Columbia River and hauled back up filled with lumber, supplies, and
the occasional passenger.

Inside the museum are the 4,500 rocks, fossils, and Native American
artifacts that William and Etta Schulenz donated, along with William's

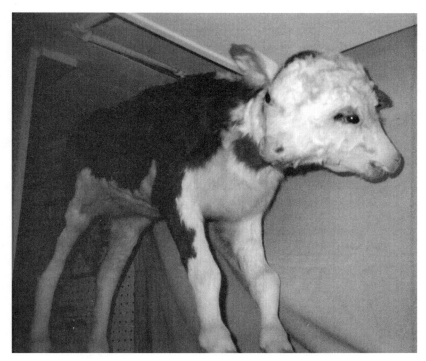

You'll do a double-take when you see this two-headed calf

handwritten collector's diary. The collection includes rocks and minerals that glow in the dark as well as three meteorites. The museum keeps special watch over the 1917 Waterville Meteorite: Found in a farmer's field, the space rock was later lent to a Tacoma museum, which sliced off almost 10 pounds of it and then tried to claim ownership. Legal battles ensued, but in 1963 the meteorite came back home to Waterville.

In addition to all the rocks and meteorites, the museum exhibits a variety of heirlooms from area pioneer families along with some unusual items, including a church made of 3,500 Popsicle sticks (with eight pews inside) and a pair of made-to-order boots given to Vitus Fitzgerald by his uncle back in 1902.

Don't miss the chance to visit the lower level, which boasts a nicely labeled display of 30 types of antique barbed wire and, up on top of a water heater, a taxidermied two-headed calf. Maybe that's why Waterville brochures say the museum is "worth a second look."

*Hours: Memorial Day to mid-Oct: Tues–Sun 11am–5pm. Closed rest of year.*
*Admission free.*
*Directions: The museum is next to Pioneer Park on Highway 2 in Waterville.*

■ **North Central Washington Museum**
127 Mission Street
Wenatchee, WA 98807
(509)664-3340

The North Central Washington Museum is doing its part to make sure no one forgets this area is the Apple Capital. The colorful apple exhibit, designed to resemble the interior of an apple-packing shed, includes the Apple Theater, a wall of apple-box labels (with names such as William Tell and Yum Yum), and vintage but operational equipment, including a unique apple wiper and a catapult-sizing machine. Heads up, everyone, when that catapult sorter goes into action!

**While You're in Wenatchee:**
The sculpture in front of the North Central Washington Museum is titled *Coyote Reading a Candy Wrapper.* Created by Richard Beyer, the piece was chosen by the general public as part of Wenatchee's continuing Art on the Avenues public art project. To see other selections, pick up a walking-tour map at the museum.

The apple lovefest doesn't stop there. The museum also holds the world's record for baking the largest apple pie. Wenatchee's prizewinner filled a 24- by 44-foot pan, had to bake for five hours, and weighed in at 56,000 pounds. (The apples were cored but not peeled.)

Of course, the north-central Washington area is known for more than its apples. The Clovis exhibit describes the discovery, in an east Wenatchee orchard, of a primitive tool kit containing spear points and bone implements. An exhibit of Columbia River petroglyphs lends insights on the culture and lifestyle of the local Native Americans. Pioneer life and the growth of the agricultural and business community are represented by the trading post, the farm shop, the 1910 pioneer home, and the shops along the boardwalk on the "old Main Street" of Wenatchee.

Kids of all ages love the apple catapult, of course, but they'll also enjoy the working 1919 Wurlitzer pipe organ and the coin-operated *Great Northern Railway* exhibit, which illustrates just how challenging an engineering feat it was to move trains across the Cascades.

An engineering feat of a different sort is reflected in the handiwork required to make the items on display from the world-famous Charbneau-Warren miniature collection. Begun in 1900 by 16-year-old apprentice seaman Jules Louis Charbneau, the collection grew to more than 30,000 pieces and was exhibited around the world. Charbneau's daughter, Isabella, inherited the collection and donated 94 pieces to the museum, which displays a selection of 30 or so tiny items at a time. Look for the world's smallest belt, hand-crocheted hats no larger than a bean, and the Japanese kimono painted on a pea.

After inspecting some of the world's tiniest artwork, take a look at the large original murals on the museum walls. Each depicts a scene from early Wenatchee history. The museum also displays changing art exhibits in the Skybridge Gallery and the Fine Arts Gallery.

Special programs include concerts, lectures, silent movies, gallery demonstrations, family days, and a variety of kid-oriented educational programs.

> *Web site: www.televar.com/communityweb/ncwmuseum/index.html*
> *Hours: Mon–Sat 10am–4pm.*
> *Admission charged. Free Mon.*
> *Directions: From southbound Highway 2, take State Route 285 to*
> *downtown Wenatchee. The museum is on the corner of Yakima and*
> *Mission Streets.*

## WESTPORT

### ■ Westport Maritime Museum
2201 Westhaven Drive
Westport, WA 98595
(360)268-0078

The Westport Maritime Museum is housed in an imposing Colonial Revival structure originally built as the Coast Guard's lifeboat station at Grays Harbor. Now the building offers exhibits describing the life-saving work of the Coast Guard on the area's South Beach, local shipwrecks, and daily life in a maritime community. The museum also displays maritime equipment, Native American artifacts, and information about the area's cranberry industry.

What most people remember, though, are the objects relating to whales and whaling, especially the whale skeletons on display in the two Whale Houses right next to the museum. Kids will enjoy getting up close to a gray whale, but they'll espe-

**While You're in Westport:**
The Westport Maritime Museum also offers tours of the Grays Harbor lighthouse, built in 1898. If you make it all the way up to the lantern room, you'll see a rare third-order Fresnel lens, made in Paris in 1895. "Third-order" means the lens is the third most powerful type of lens made. The museum is working on getting a first-order Fresnel lens for display. The first-order lens removed from the Destruction Island lighthouse in 1995 contains more than 1,150 prisms and is valued by the Coast Guard at $6 million.

cially enjoy the discovery room with its "guess-what-you're-touching" drawers and other marine-life activities.

>  *Hours: Summer: Daily 10am–4pm. Rest of year: Wed–Sun noon–4pm. Admission charged.*
>  *Directions: From State Route 105, take the second Westport exit (Forest Street) and continue for three miles to Montesano Street. Turn left (at the Hungry Whale) and watch for the MARITIME MUSEUM signs.*

## WHIDBEY ISLAND (COUPEVILLE)

### ■ Island County Historical Museum
908 NW Alexander Street
Coupeville, WA 98239
(360)678-3310

Located at the foot of Coupeville Wharf in the Ebey's Landing National Historical Reserve, the Island County Historical Museum displays items relating to the Skagit Indians and other tribes of northern Puget Sound, area maritime and agricultural activities, and pioneer lifestyles. In addition to a historical logging exhibit, the museum has an agricultural exhibit that displays the certificates awarded to four Whidbey Island farms in honor of their designation as Centennial Farms—operated by family members for at least 100 years. Most are still in operation, although one farm's property is under consideration as the location for a superstore.

There's a large Native American basketry collection as well as a textile room featuring quilts and a historical loom once owned by Maude Fullerton, a well-known teacher of weaving and crafts during the early 1900s. Washing machines, typewriters, telephones, and other vintage artifacts fill the basement, while the meeting room displays cameras, Native American artifacts, and a flipbook of historical photos.

One of Washington's oldest cities, Coupeville has more than 30 well-preserved historic buildings. Self-guided walking-tour brochures are available at the museum.

>  *Hours: Summer: Daily 10am–5pm. Rest of year: Fri–Mon 10am–4pm. Admission charged.*
>  *Directions: From northbound I-5, drive to Burlington and turn west on State Route 20 toward Anacortes; cross the Deception Pass Bridge and pass through Oak Harbor on your way to Coupeville. Or take the ferry: From northbound I-5, turn onto State Route 525 at exit 182. Take the ferry from Mukilteo to Whidbey Island, and drive north on State Route 525 for about 26 miles to Coupeville. The museum is on the wharf.*

## WINTHROP

■ **Shafer Museum**
Castle Avenue (PO Box 46)
Winthrop, WA 98862
(509)996-2712

Winthrop's downtown has been retrofitted with wooden sidewalks and faded wooden storefronts to give it an Old West feel. By all means, shop and stroll the main street, but visit the Shafer Museum just up the hill for a lesson in how the area's pioneers really lived.

When Guy Waring opened Winthrop's first general store in 1891, miners and ranchers were his clientele. Back then there weren't espresso stands dotting Main Street, so to entice his wife to move out west from Boston, Waring built her a finely crafted log house. Today that house, filled with musical instruments, fine furniture, and a bear rug in front of the fireplace, is known locally as the Castle and is part of the Shafer Museum complex.

In addition to the Waring cabin, the museum grounds include a homesteader's cabin, an assayer's office, a barn housing a buggy and a stagecoach, a millinery shop, a print shop, and a general store. Each building is filled with early Methow Valley relics, including a horsehide coat, an old whiskey still, a early "fire engine" consisting of nothing more than a wagon with a water barrel sitting on top, and the first telephone switchboard used in the nearby town of Twisp. Among the items displayed in the general store is a small section of a tree that grew around an old pistol. According to the notes nearby, a prospector claimed that he found a pile of bones from a man and a bear at the foot of the tree in Alaska. The pistol, apparently "thrown out of the man's hand in a furious fight," lay in one spot so long that the limbs of the tree grew around it.

*Hours: Memorial Day to Sept: Thurs–Mon 10am–5pm. Closed rest of year.*
*Admission by donation.*
*Directions: Take eastbound State Route 20 to Winthrop. The museum is above Winthrop's main street, Riverside Drive. A pedestrian path up the hill begins just over the covered bridge toward the south end of Riverside. Or drive up Bridge Street to Castle Avenue, turn right, and continue for a few blocks to the museum.*

■ **Pomeroy Living History Farm**
20902 NE Lucia Falls Road
Yacolt, WA 98675
(360)686-3537

The Pomeroy Living History Farm is a working museum depicting 1920s farm life in the pre-electrical era of the rural Pacific Northwest. Visitors can experience firsthand what it was like to live and work on a farm by assisting the costumed interpreters as they grind corn and coffee, wash clothes on a scrubboard, feed the animals, pump water, use a crosscut logging saw, and engage in a variety of other "fun" chores. If you have any energy left, you may want to tour the six-bedroom log home built by E. C. Pomeroy and his son, Tom; the herb and vegetable gardens; and the operating blacksmith shop.

Most weekends feature special events such as an herb festival, a pumpkin festival, or a harvest festival.

> *Hours: June to Oct, first full weekend of the month: Sat 11am–4pm, Sun 1pm–4pm. Closed all other weekdays and for the rest of the year. Admission charged.*
> *Directions: From I-5, take exit 9 (Battle Ground) to exit 30 on I-205. Take State Route 503 (122nd Avenue), follow it for about five and a half miles to NE Lucia Falls Road, and turn east.*

YAKIMA

■ **Yakima Electric Railway Museum**
306 W Pine Street (PO Box 649)
Yakima, WA 98907
(509)575-1700

In 1907 local businessmen created the Yakima Valley Transportation Company (YVT) to provide electric railway service for the rapidly growing community of North Yakima. In 1909 the line was taken over and extended by the Union Pacific Railroad, which operated YVT as an interurban passenger railroad and later used the tracks to haul freight. Today the line is operated as a museum of electric railroading and is listed on the National Register of Historic Places.

Visitors can tour electric rail equipment displays in the Yakima Electric Railway Museum's historic one-room 1910 YVT shop building, inspect the belt-driven machinery used to maintain the trolleys and locomotives, and then board a trolley for a two-hour tour of the area.

> *Hours: July to Aug: every day and holidays 10am–4pm (last ride at 7pm). May to June, Sept to Oct: Sat–Sun and holidays 10am–4pm (last ride at 4pm). Closed rest of year.*

*Admission charged for rides.*
*Directions: From I-82, turn west on Yakima Avenue and continue to trolley*
*tracks. Follow the trolley tracks south on N Sixth Street to Pine, then*
*head east on Third. The museum is at Third Avenue and W Pine*
*Street.*

## ■ Yakima Valley Museum
2105 Tieton Drive
Yakima, WA 98902
(509)248-0747

Located adjacent to Franklin Park, the Yakima Valley Museum offers a
wide range of exhibits celebrating the Yakama Indian Nation, the fruit
industry, the area's agricultural and natural history, and the lives of notable
Yakima natives such as Supreme Court Justice William O. Douglas.

The *Dark Times, Bright Visions* exhibit focuses on art, crafts, and artifacts from the indigenous cultures of the plateau region. Yakama Indian
beadwork, basketry, woven bags, and other objects are among the items
that help illustrate the cultural and economic transitions resulting from
the formation of the Confederated Tribes and Bands of the Yakama
Nation and the creation of the Yakama reservation.

Historic tools, household items, orchard equipment, apple crate
labels, and a large collection of wagons, carriages, and motorized vehicles
trace the settlement of the Yakima Valley from the earliest pioneers to the
modern-day farmworkers who help make the area the "fruit bowl of the
nation." An agricultural exhibit focuses on apples and other fruits and
vegetables as well as hops, vineyards, and irrigation.

The Washington, D.C., office of former Supreme Court Justice
William O. Douglas is here too. "Don't let people think it's a replica," a
museum staff member cautioned. "It's actually his reconstructed office,
including the actual desk, chair, books, and other items that were in it."

Kids should head straight for the Children's Underground, a large
hands-on learning center filled with interactive displays, computer programs, games, a well-stocked aquarium and frog habitat, and lots of pullout bins and drawers filled with animal bones and other items perfect
for close-up inspection. Western costumes are provided so kids can be
appropriately dressed for playing in the miner's cabin, general store, and
old wagon.

For a real treat, visit the ground-floor, art deco–style 1930s soda
fountain. Filled with antique equipment once used in Jordan's Drugs (the
last operating soda fountain in Yakima), this fountain serves soda, malts,
root beer floats, assorted phosphates, and ice cream treats from old-
fashioned soda and syrup dispensers, and uses vintage recipes to boot.

Special programs include concerts, lectures, and kid-oriented Saturday Specials.

*Web site: www.wolfe.net/~museum*

*Hours: Museum: Mon–Fri 10am–5pm, Sat–Sun noon–5pm. Children's Underground: Wed–Sun 1pm–5pm.*
*Admission charged.*
*Directions: From downtown Yakima, take Yakima Avenue west to 16th Avenue and turn left. Drive four blocks to the first traffic light, turn right on Tieton Drive, follow it for four blocks, and look for the museum on the right.*

*Bike Rider,* circa 1930s, is part of *Neon Garden,* the museum's exhibit of historic neon

Oregon

## ■ Albany Fire Museum

120 34th Street SE
Albany, OR 97231
(541)917-7700

While you must call ahead to make an appointment to visit the Albany Fire Museum, fire chief Darrel Tedisch promises it will certainly be worth the extra effort. In fact, if a volunteer isn't around to open the museum for you, Chief Tedisch might come on over himself to take you on a guided tour through this three-quarter-size replica of a fire station that once stood in downtown Albany.

The chief is quick to boast that of course there are vintage fire engines here, including a 1927 American LaFrance and a 1925 Seagraves, but the museum also features old alarm boxes, leather helmets, lifesaving nets from the 1930s and 1940s, and fire extinguishers from the early 1900s. Photographs and record books from the days when all the town's firefighters were volunteers are here too. In fact, those early volunteers are the same folks who ended up buying all the town's early firefighting equipment. According to the chief, back in the 1800s roll call was taken after every fire. Volunteers who showed up to help fight the fire paid 25¢ into the fire department coffers. Volunteers who didn't show up were dunned 50¢.

> *Hours: By appointment only.*
> *Admission free.*
> *Directions: From southbound I-5, take the first Albany exit, follow Pacific Boulevard through town toward Linn-Benton Community College, and turn left on 34th Street SE. The museum is about a mile up the road, on the right at Fire Station No. 12.*

## ■ Albany Regional Museum

302 Ferry Street SW
Albany, OR 97321
(541)917-7587

Housed in an old Carnegie library building, the Albany Regional Museum focuses on local Albany and Linn County history and features a wide variety of personal and business-related memorabilia, including advertising signs, stocked mercantile display cases, tools, and costumes. Artifacts rescued from the Blain Clothing store include some colorful outdoor-advertising barn signs, clothing, and photos; before it closed in 1976 after 100 years in business, Blain's was the oldest continually operating clothing store west of the Mississippi River. Special museum collections include the costumes, makeup, stage props, and travel trunk that once belonged to Harlin Talbert, a local resident who was also a vaudeville actor and stage manager.

The museum also has a good many items from Camp Adair, at one time the second-largest city in Oregon. Built in 1942 and torn down in 1947, Camp Adair housed close to 50,000 American soldiers as well as German and Italian prisoners of war, just six miles from Albany. Artifacts on display include uniforms, medals, patches, combat gear, C rations, and war recruiting posters.

*Web site: www.albanyrm.org*
*Hours: Mon–Sat noon–4pm.*
*Admission free.*
*Directions: From I-5, head west on Highway 20 (Santiam Highway) to downtown Albany. The museum is on the corner of Ferry Street SW and SW Fourth Avenue.*

## ASHLAND

### ■ Schneider Museum of Art
Southern Oregon University
1250 Siskiyou Boulevard
Ashland, OR 97520
(541)552-6245

The Schneider Museum of Art is part of Southern Oregon University, the only school within the state university system officially established to emphasize the fine and performing arts. Founded in 1986, the museum is housed in a building designed by Will Martin, who also designed Portland's Pioneer Courthouse Square. Although still young, the museum has already gathered a small but solid permanent collection of more than 500 works of art by mostly 20th-century American artists, including pieces by Alexander Calder, Arthur B. Davies, Charles Heaney (the "Master of the Oregon Scene"), George Innes, and others. Historical materials and other holdings include Renaissance engravings and medieval illuminated manuscripts, 17th- and 18th-century maps, artists' books, collages, and photographs.

At least a dozen exhibitions a year are mounted in the museum's four galleries. Three or four shows are organized from the permanent collection, and the balance are touring or special exhibitions. Throughout the year, the museum also presents lectures by visiting artists, critics, and scholars.

*Hours: Tues–Sat 11am–5pm.*
*Admission by donation.*
*Directions: From I-5, take exit 14 and follow Highway 66 to Siskiyou Boulevard. The museum is on the campus of Southern Oregon University.*

### While You're in Ashland:

From late February though early November, Ashland is home to the tremendously popular Oregon Shakespeare Festival, presenting matinee and evening performances in a downtown complex that includes an outdoor Elizabethan theater and two indoor theaters. The Festival Exhibit Center features costumed mannequins, props from current and past productions, and vintage photographs (see if you can spot some well-known film stars), and they'll even let you dress up in some of the costumes and handle props used onstage. You can take a backstage tour too.

*Oregon Shakespeare Festival Exhibit Center, 15 S Pioneer Street, Ashland, OR 97520; (541)482-4331.*
*Hours: Exhibit Center: Open each performance day; hours vary. Tours: 10am each performance day. Admission charged. Directions: From southbound I-5, take exit 19. Turn right onto Valley View Road and continue to Highway 99; turn left. Continue 2 miles to downtown Ashland. South Pioneer Street is one block east of Main Street.*

## ASTORIA

### ■ Columbia River Maritime Museum
1792 Marine Drive
Astoria, OR 97103
(503)325-2323

The Columbia River Maritime Museum opened its doors, appropriately enough, in 1982, on the 190th anniversary of Captain Robert Gray's 1792 "discovery" of the entrance to the Columbia River. Of course, the area's Native Americans already knew the river well, but Gray took the opportunity to name the "newly found" body of water "Columbia's River" after his ship, the *Columbia*. Modern-day visitors to the museum can retrace Gray's journey, and learn more about the rich maritime heritage of the Columbia River region and the Pacific Northwest, in this huge waterfront building that reminds some visitors of a boat and others of a cresting wave.

The museum's seven topical galleries feature thousands of artifacts, documents, paintings, and photographs that trace maritime history from the days of fur trading and exploration to fishing, whaling, shipping, pleasure boating, and naval activities. The first gallery, for example, describes the exploration of the Columbia River and the Northwest Coast and displays examples of hatchets, knives, nails, liquor, blankets, and other goods that white traders bartered with the local tribes for sea otter, beaver pelts, and salmon.

According to museum notes, almost 2,000 craft—including about

200 major vessels—have been lost in the area. The treacherous bar at the river's mouth claimed many of them, but others simply missed the entrance in fog or storm and were wrecked on the coast. The lost treasures recovered from area shipwrecks include keel timber from the HMS *Raccoon*, silverware, clocks, large pieces of furniture, bells, and tiny cream pitchers. Other major artifacts salvaged from history include periscopes and a torpedo from the submarine USS *Rasher*, an anti-aircraft gun, two operating lighthouse lenses, marine engines, gillnet fishing boats, a pilot boat, and Native American canoes.

Even if you're not a big maritime fan, the museum's worth visiting for the exhibit of beacons and buoys with red, white, and blue flashing warning lights, the panels displaying hundreds of colorful salmon labels from the many canneries that once lined the Astoria riverfront, the shiny array of ship bells and whistles, and the glass floats of all shapes and sizes found washed up on Oregon beaches. These items, along with sailor-made scrimshaw carvings, embroidery, and knotwork, might just as easily be on display in a fine-art or craft museum.

Kids will enjoy climbing into the replica steamboat pilothouse, where they can turn the five-foot-tall helm's wheel, check the compass, and bark orders to the engine room through the voice tube. They'll also enjoy the navigation bridge from the USS *Knapp*, a destroyer active in the Pacific during World War II and the Korean War. When the ship was dismantled for scrap, the museum got the bridge and the pilothouse intact and had them barged to Astoria (the museum had to be erected around them).

The retired U.S. Coast Guard lightship *Columbia*, which once served as a marker for the river's entrance, is moored next to the museum. Now a National Historic Landmark, this was the last floating lighthouse to serve on the West Coast. Visitors are welcome to climb on board for a self-guided tour.

> *Web site: www.crmm.org*
> *Hours: Daily 9:30am–5pm.*
> *Admission charged.*
> *Directions: The museum is on the waterfront side of Highway 30, at the east end of Astoria.*

## ■ Flavel House Museum
441 Eighth Street
Astoria, OR 97103
(503)325-2203

The Clatsop County Historical Society operates the Flavel House Museum as well as the Heritage Museum and the Uppertown Firefighters Museum (see listings), all in Astoria. (Each emphasizes a different aspect of local history, and your admission fee at one admits you to all of them.)

The Flavel House Museum is in a classic Victorian mansion, built in 1885 for pioneer Columbia River bar pilot and entrepreneur Captain George Flavel and his family. The property occupies a full city block and features six fireplaces, three parlors, a library, and five bedrooms. Nineteenth- and early 20th-century toys are on display in one second-floor bedroom, and down in the basement is a museum with early post office boxes, a telephone switchboard, wool and flax spinning wheels, wagons, tools, a horse-drawn sleigh, and a Victorian-era pool table.

The grounds surrounding the house are lovely and include a fishpond, a rare cork elm, a rose garden, and a wide variety of trees planted more than 100 years ago by the Flavel family. Not all the plants are old: Each August, during Regatta Week, Portland's Royal Rosarians stop by for a rose planting ceremony.

*Hours: May to Sept: Daily 10am–5pm. Oct to April: Daily 11am–4pm.*
*Admission charged; includes admission to the Heritage Museum and the*
*Uppertown Firefighters Museum, all operated by the Clatsop County*
*Historical Society.*
*Directions: From Highway 30, drive west through downtown to Eighth*
*Street. Turn left and go uphill for two blocks. From Highways 26 and*
*101, head east into downtown. Go straight on Eighth for two blocks.*
*(The highway turns left on Commercial Street.)*

■ **Fort Clatsop National Memorial**
92343 Fort Clatsop Road
Astoria, OR 97103
(503)861-2471

After completing its journey from the Mississippi River to the Pacific Ocean, the Lewis and Clark expedition spent the winter of 1805 at Fort Clatsop, a log stockade six miles southwest of Astoria, named in honor of the local Clatsop tribe. During their three months here, the expedition members fished and hunted elk and deer for food, made buckskin clothes, traded with the local tribes, worked on maps and journals of their journey west, and prepared for the trip home.

Today the Fort Clatsop National Memorial contains a replica of the fort and, during the summer months, features buckskin-clad rangers demonstrating many of the activities that kept the members of the Lewis and Clark crew busy during their winter here.

Interpretive exhibits at the visitors center feature maps, shopping lists and copies of other documents created in preparation for the trip west, and a display describing the natural history and scientific discoveries the team made and wrote about in their journals along the way.

While most of the items displayed here are replicas, the three-person Makah Indian dugout canoe made at the turn of the century is real. And while the canoe isn't a vessel Lewis or Clark actually rode in, it's the same style as those the explorers saw here and learned how to make for themselves.

Other nearby Lewis and Clark–related sites are the Salt Works site in Seaside; the trail over Tillamook Head to Cannon Beach; the Lewis and Clark campsite in McGowan, Washington; and the Lewis and Clark Interpretive Center at Fort Canby State Park in Ilwaco, Washington (see listing).

*Web site: www.nps.gov/focl/*
*Hours: Mid-June to Labor Day: Daily 8am–6pm. After Labor Day to*
*mid-June: Daily 8am–5pm.*
*Admission charged.*
*Directions: The memorial is six miles southwest of Astoria, just off*
*Highway 101. Look for signs along Highway 101 (and alternate 101).*

## ■ Heritage Museum
1618 Exchange Street
Astoria, OR 97103
(503)325-2203

Housed in Astoria's former city hall, the Heritage Museum does a thorough job of introducing visitors to Clatsop County's rich history. Gallery I deals with the area's natural history and geology, the local Native American tribes, and the pioneers who made their way this far west. Gallery II highlights the logging, lumber, fish-packing, and other industries that once flourished here. Gallery III celebrates the immigrants from more than 25 different ethnic groups that came to Clatsop County to start new lives.

Some of those seeking "new lives" may have contemplated their future while having a shot or two at the vintage bar that is a centerpiece of the exhibit called *Vice and Virtue: Clatsop County, 1890–Prohibition.* Society's tug-of-war between behavior deemed morally upright and activities severely frowned upon clearly played itself out in the streets of Astoria. At one time waterfront saloons lined the Columbia River, and a good deal of prostitution, shanghaiing, and gambling occurred. The exhibit's church pulpit, photos of liquor stills getting busted, and items promoting temperance are reminders of other Astorians' efforts to subdue or eliminate the illicit activity.

*Hours: May to Sept: Daily 10am–5pm. Oct to April: Daily 11am–4pm.*
*Admission charged; includes admission to the Flavel House Museum and*
*the Uppertown Firefighters Museum, all operated by the Clatsop*
*County Historical Society.*
*Directions: From Highway 30, turn south (uphill) on 16th Street and drive*
*one block. From Highways 26 and 101, drive east through downtown*
*Astoria and turn right at 16th Street.*

### ■ Uppertown Firefighters Museum
2986 Marine Drive
Astoria, OR 97103
(503)325-2202

Early Astoria firefighters were a thrifty bunch. They kept almost every truck, hose cart, and piece of firefighting equipment they ever used, and they used every item as long as they could make it last. What they couldn't use, they saved. And that's a good thing, because Astoria's Uppertown Fire Station No. 2 is now the Uppertown Firefighters Museum, full of vintage and rare firefighting memorabilia dating back to 1879.

It's not as if the equipment wasn't used much, either: Astoria was built on timber, and early fires at area lumber mills and wooden cannery buildings took their toll. Then there was the terrible fire that broke out on December 8, 1922, and spread quickly along a wooden viaduct below Astoria's main street. The Astoria Fire Department had purchased a reliable secondhand high-performance Stutz pumper just a few months earlier, but although it pumped a steady stream of water for 22 hours straight, few downtown buildings were saved. That Stutz pumper, now housed in the museum, was also pressed into service after the fire: For a full month, it pumped water from the river for the city's water supply.

Other early fire trucks parked here include a prized 1911 American LaFrance chemical wagon and a 1946 Mack Triple-Combination. The museum also displays hose carts, antique fire extinguishers, the original brass fire pole, a variety of early ladders and hoses, and the Bowder Life Saving Machine—a large, tightly sprung trampoline with a red dot in the middle.

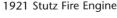

1921 Stutz Fire Engine

Each October, during Fire Prevention Week, fire departments from around the county rush over to the museum to participate in fire prevention programs, show off firefighting equipment, and compete in the annual 4-Alarm Chili Cook-Off.

*Hours: May to Sept: Fri–Sun 10am–5pm. Oct to April: Fri–Sun 11am–4pm.*

*Admission charged; includes admission to the Heritage Museum and the Flavel House Museum, all operated by the Clatsop County Historical Society.*

*Directions: From Highway 30, turn right at the first traffic signal after entering the city limits. From Highways 26 and 101, drive east through downtown Astoria, then head east on Highway 30 and turn left at 30th Street.*

## AURORA

### ■ Old Aurora Colony Museum
Second and Liberty Streets (PO Box 202)
Aurora, OR 97002
(503)678-5754

The hippies of the 1960s weren't the first to experiment with a communal lifestyle. In the 19th century, the communal Shaker, Amana, and Harmony colonies thrived in the eastern United States. Aurora was the only such settlement in the Pacific Northwest.

During the late 1840s, William Keil, a Prussian-born tailor turned preacher, convinced more than 250 folks to follow him in establishing a self-sustaining community in which Christians would share both their labor and their property. The group first moved to Missouri and eventually headed west to settle in Aurora Mills, a place named by Keil to honor both his daughter and the sawmill already on the site.

Through sales of their handmade quilts, woven goods, sausage, and hams, the colony prospered. They amassed 18,000 acres of land by 1870, but Keil's death in 1877 and opportunities luring younger colony members away from home eventually eroded the colony's cooperative spirit. In 1883 the colony dissolved, and all commonly held assets were divided among the remaining society members.

Five original colony buildings now make up the Old Aurora Colony Museum: an ox barn, two homes, a communal wash house, and a farm machinery building. Museum tours start with a slide show describing the colony's history and proceed through exhibits featuring Aurora-made quilts, textiles, and furniture; a variety of farm equipment; and other aspects of daily colony life.

Despite all their hard work, it appears that some colony folks took time out for a little fun. In the main building you'll see (and hear) the instruments used by the Aurora Pioneer Brass Band. Four of the dozen instruments displayed have unusual "back-thrust" or "backfire bells," which were common in civilian marching bands during the Civil War era. The bells "aimed" sound to the rear of the player, making a small band sound much bigger than it was.

The town of Aurora was Oregon's first National Historic District, so after you've toured the museum, grab a walking-tour brochure at the museum and explore the town to see more colony and postcolony historic buildings.

*Hours: Tues–Sat 10am–4pm, Sun noon–4pm.*
*Admission charged.*
*Directions: From I-5, take State Route 99E to Aurora. The museum is on the corner of Second and Liberty Streets, just off 99E, which goes right through the center of town.*

## BAKER CITY

### ■ Baker County Visitor Center and Chamber of Commerce
490 Campbell Street
Baker City, OR 97814
(800)523-1235 or (541)523-3356

In 1861 a gold rush erupted in the Baker Valley, and by 1880 Baker City was known as the Queen City of the Mines. While several booming gold rush towns from that era are now ghost towns, Baker City remains, with more than 135 buildings on the National Register of Historic Places.

The second floor of the Baker County Visitor Center and Chamber of Commerce has a mini-museum displaying early mining and agricultural artifacts, pioneer household goods, and historic photographs that include scenes of early skiing exploits and an open-air meat market.

*Hours: Memorial Day to Labor Day: Mon–Fri 8am–6pm, Sat 8am–4pm. Rest of year: Mon–Fri 8am–5pm.*
*Admission free.*
*Directions: The visitors center is at exit 304 on I-84.*

### ■ National Historic Oregon Trail Interpretive Center
Flagstaff Hill (PO Box 987)
Baker City, OR 97814
(541)523-1843

Maybe explorers Meriwether Lewis and William Clark made it sound like paradise, or maybe it was the lure of adventure and the promise of good land, but over a 40-year period beginning in the mid-1840s, more than 350,000 pioneers made their way west from Missouri to Oregon in what has been called the largest voluntary mass migration of people in world history. While many Northwest museums tell the story of how these folks lived, worked, and played in towns throughout the region, the

National Historic Oregon Trail Interpretive Center focuses on the pioneers' experience on their journey west, across the 2,000 miles of dusty plains, rugged mountains, and dangerous river crossings called the Oregon Trail.

The center perches atop Flagstaff Hill, a spot that offered weary pioneers a glimpse of the forested Blue Mountains and a hint of the lush Willamette Valley beyond. Today the ruts left by thousands of wagon wheels passing through this section of the Oregon Trail can still be seen from the center's scenic overlooks and on five miles of interpretive trails.

Inside the center, life-size interactive displays offer a taste of what it was like to walk along the Oregon Trail in 1843. A group of settlers sets out with a wagonmaster leading four wagons hitched to mules and oxen; a mother and her daughter gaze wistfully back over the trail while a young man pushing his belongings in a large wheelbarrow dreams of gold rush country. Your presence in the gallery activates audiotapes that fill the air with the sound of trail chatter, creaking wagon wheels, clinking chains, and bellowing oxen. For example, a young boy of about seven sits in the back of a wagon and holds out a branch to a billy goat; when he begins "speaking," you hear him wonder what school will be like out west.

The center has gone to great lengths to ensure authenticity in these exhibits. The words "spoken" along the trail come directly from pioneer diaries and journals, and the first oxen sent to the center by the taxidermist were rejected because they were a more modern breed than the oxen that would have been pulling the wagons on the Oregon Trail.

> ### While You're in Baker City:
>
> Ask the folks at the visitors center for information about the 100-mile loop that will take you through Granite, Bourne, Bonanza, Whitney, and other once-bustling mining towns that are now nothing more than ghost towns in the Elkhorn Mountains west of Baker City. Along the way you'll find Sumpter, a revitalized ghost town with a restored narrow-gauge steam train that operates during the summer.
>
> Don't have enough time to travel the full loop? Then be sure to ask for directions to Baker City's US Bank branch, right on Main Street in downtown Baker City. The bank lobby features Oregon's largest display of gold, including the famed 80.4-ounce Armstrong Nugget (Mon–Thurs 9am–5pm, Friday 9am–6pm).

The exhibit at the "end" of the trail contains another authentic touch. A video includes original film footage of 87-year-old Ezra Meeker, who traveled the length of the trail west to east in the early 1900s. Meeker is seen taking the wheels off his wagon and paddling it across a river. (For a look at Meeker's wagon and the oxen, now taxidermied, that accompanied him on his trip, see the listing for the Washington State History Museum in Tacoma.)

Oxen and wagon on the Oregon Trail

On a seasonal basis, volunteers and actors populate an outdoor pioneer encampment and the lode mine, creating living-history exhibits. Special programs throughout the year include films, lectures, craft demonstrations, theater performances, storytelling, and holiday events.

*Hours: April to Oct: Daily 9am–6pm. Nov to March: Daily 9am–4pm. Admission charged. One free day per month; call for a schedule.*
*Directions: Flagstaff Hill and the center are five miles east of Baker City. From I-84, take exit 302 to eastbound State Route 86; the center is five miles east of the junction of I-84 and State Route 86.*

■ **Oregon Trail Regional Museum**
2480 Grove Street (PO Box 214)
Baker City, OR 97814
(541)523-9308

Local Baker City citizens banded together to keep the wrecking ball from destroying the town's brick Natatorium Building, a 35,000-square-foot indoor swimming palace built in 1920. Then they worked even harder to turn the classic site into the Oregon Trail Regional Museum, chock-full of artifacts and exhibits honoring Native American culture, pioneer living, and the region's mining, farming, logging, and ranching.

Look closely among the photographs, vintage buggies, covered wagons, and pioneer artifacts for a charming display of ornate old car-radiator caps, an artfully arranged collection of nails in their sample case, and a wide variety of barbed wire once offered for sale at a local hardware store.

The museum is also home to the Wyatt Family Cabochon Collection of more than 2,000 agate and picture-jasper cabochons, as well as the 15-ton Cavin Collection of rocks and minerals. In the 1930s, Elizabeth Cavin (Warfel) and her sister Mamie became avid rockhounds and began combing the western mountains in search of specimens for their collection. They bought their own rock-cutting equipment and mastered the art of slicing, cutting, and polishing their finds. The sisters and their rocks moved to California in the 1960s, but when Elizabeth died, Mamie sent the collection home to Baker. Now museum visitors can enjoy shelves upon shelves of geodes, jewels, fossils, corals, shells, and a stunning 950-pound Arkansas crystal.

*Hours: May to Oct: Daily 9am–4pm. Closed rest of year.*
*Admission charged.*
*Directions: From I-84, take exit 304. The museum is on the corner of*
*    Campbell and Grove Streets, in the large brick building across from*
*    the city park.*

## BANDON

### ■ Coquille River Museum
270 Fillmore Street (PO Box 737)
Bandon, OR 97411
(541)347-2164

The second structure built after the 1936 fire that leveled most of the seaside town of Bandon was a city hall. Now the "Historic Old City Hall" is home to the Coquille River Museum, which, appropriately enough, includes memorabilia from that 1936 fire.

This volunteer-staffed museum also features collections of Coquille Indian artifacts, an extensive photographic archive of early Bandon, and items representing the work associated with a variety of local industries, including cranberries, logging, and shipping.

Don't be surprised to find a whole section of items from Ireland here. Bandon is named after Bandon, Ireland, and whenever folks from Bandon, Oregon, visit Bandon, Ireland, they bring home a wee souvenir for the museum.

*Hours: Summer: Mon–Sat 10am–4pm, Sun noon–3pm. Rest of year:*
*    Mon–Sat 10am–4pm.*
*Admission charged.*
*Directions: The museum is on the corner of Fillmore Street and Highway*
*    101, three blocks west of the Bandon Cheese Factory.*

## ■ Deschutes County Historical Museum
129 NW Idaho Street (PO Box 5252)
Bend, OR 97708
(541)389-1813

While many folks come here to take advantage of the area's recreational offerings, Bend also offers visitors a chance to catch up on regional history. The Deschutes County Historical Museum, downtown in the solid 1914 Reid School building, is filled with rare and memorable artifacts from the county's colorful past.

The biggest item on display here is a giant boulder. Museum officials had it brought down from a bluff overlooking the Deschutes River when someone noticed the year 1813 and the names of two early trappers carved onto the rock's face. Smaller tools and other artifacts on display are reminders that many Native American tribes lived in the area long before trappers and explorers showed up.

Just about every room of the old schoolhouse is filled with intriguing exhibits. Head upstairs to see radios, cameras, business equipment, branding irons, fine saddles, and an architectural history of Deschutes County. Poke around downstairs for early timber, railroad, and Forest Service memorabilia. And stroll through the Pioneer Room to get a good look at the barbed-wire collection, a snazzy buffalo coat, and the "chair in which the first twins born in central Oregon were rocked."

Older travelers may remember Bend's Pilot Butte Inn, a large Bavarian-style chalet that author Irving S. Cobb once praised as the "finest little hotel in America." The inn is long gone, but the museum rescued a classic wooden sign from the hotel and keys that once opened 150 of the rooms.

*Hours: Tues–Sat 10am–4:30pm.*
*Admission charged.*
*Directions: From Highway 97, take Franklin Avenue west to Bond Street.*
*Turn left on Bond Street and continue to NW Idaho Street. The*
*museum is three blocks from downtown Bend, between Wall and Bond*
*Streets.*

## ■ High Desert Museum
59800 S Highway 97
Bend, OR 97702
(541)382-4754

The constantly expanding High Desert Museum offers an in-depth look at the cultural history and natural resources that exist in the high desert, a region spanning eight western states and the province of British Columbia. The area includes a delicately balanced mix of timberland, rivers, volcanic hot springs, and, yes, high desert.

Don't let the words "desert" and "museum" fool you: This place is a 45-acre oasis of activity featuring live animals in natural habitats, historical reenactments, and a wide variety of indoor and outdoor exhibits on nature, art, science, and history.

Inside, in the Spirit of the West Gallery, are walk-through dioramas on the history of the American West, spanning a period of time from a Native American encampment circa 8000 B.C. to the arrival of fur trappers, miners, and settlers. Audio clips and artifacts are used to create realistic settings, so the pioneer cabin is furnished with a handmade quilt and the kitchen table is strewn with pie-making utensils. And over in the Hall of Exploration and Settlement, you might feel the warmth from a kettle steaming in a cowboy's bunkhouse, hear the clang of a blacksmith's anvil, and find yourself looking around for one of the Northern Paiute Indians, who seem to have just stepped away from their camp.

The main museum complex also offers permanent and changing exhibits with western and wildlife art, crafts, and scenic photography. The Desertarium is here too, showcasing bats, kangaroo rats, burrowing owls, and other small and not-often-seen animals from the region.

Outdoors you'll meet a family of otters headed by Bert and Ernie, porcupines named Thorndyke, Cactus, and Spike, and a host of other wildlife. Meandering through the network of nature trails leads you to a settler's homestead, a working turn-of-the-century sawmill, a sheepherder's wagon, and a forestry exhibit.

The museum offers daily interpretive talks and live-animal demonstrations, living-history demonstrations, and a wide variety of classes,

This collared lizard lives in the museum's Desertarium

workshops, and field excursions for all ages. It also features an extensive gift shop and an eatery called the Rimrock Café. Annual events include an October Bat Day (live bats, not baseball bats), a Ruggers' Rendezvous each July to celebrate the art of rug hooking, and several special weekends when the sawmill is in full operation.

*Web site: www.highdesert.org*
*Hours: Daily 9am–5pm.*
*Admission charged.*
*Directions: The museum is three and a half miles south of Bend on*
   *Highway 97.*

## BROOKS

### ■ Antique Powerland Museum
### Pacific Northwest Truck Museum
3995 Brooklake Road NE (Truck Museum: PO Box 9281)
Brooks, OR 97305
(503)393-2424

If you like old trucks, tractors, threshers, steam engines, and any other sort of antique farm machinery, the Antique Powerland Museum is the place for you. In fact, even if you don't know the difference between the fictional Bambi and a John Deere tractor, you'll be impressed by the variety and sheer number of vintage tractors, trucks, and related equipment amassed and cared for by the team at the museum.

Among the more than 100 tractors displayed, look for a steam model from 1880 (the oldest), a 1909 four-wheel-drive tractor, and a Samson Iron Horse—steered with old-fashioned horse reins, despite the fact that no real horses were needed to pull it.

Also on the grounds of the Antique Powerland Museum is the self-contained Pacific Northwest Truck Museum, featuring lovingly restored antique trucks, truck parts, and truck-related memorabilia. Vehicles on display include a 1915 delivery truck with kerosene-powered running lights, a 1923 Mack log truck, a 1949 Freightliner built in Portland, and a 1920 Doane transfer truck with a label warning owners that "operation at speeds in excess of 20 mph voids the manufacturer's warranty."

If you can, plan your visit to coincide with the museum's annual tractor shows, held on the last weekend of July and the first weekend of August. That's when thousands of people show up for the Great Oregon Steamup, featuring threshing, tractor pulls, and all sorts of tractor and farm machinery exhibitions.

*Web site (Truck Museum): www.teleport.com/~flame/C/Museum/*
*Hours: Antique Powerland: April to Oct: Daily 10am–6pm. Nov to*
   *March: Daily 10am–4pm. Truck Museum: April to Oct: Sat–Sun and*
   *holidays 10am–4:30pm. Closed rest of year.*

*Admission charged. One admission fee grants you access to both museums
(when open).*
*Directions: From I-5, take exit 263, turn west, and drive a quarter-mile.
Look for the antique trolleys.*

## BROWNSVILLE

### ■ Linn County Historical Museum
101 Park Avenue (PO Box 607)
Brownsville, OR 97237
(541)466-3390

This county's resourceful folks turned Brownsville's former railroad
depot into the lobby of the Linn County Historical Museum. Then they
strung together several old Southern Pacific railroad boxcars and a
caboose and filled them with life-size dioramas depicting Linn County
life at the turn of the century. There's a dentist's office, a general store, a
bank, a barbershop, a milliner's shop, and exhibits depicting the area's
early manufacturing, logging, and agricultural activities.

The museum's claim to fame is William Drinkard's covered wagon,
one of the three such wagons that came across the Oregon Trail and are
still in existence. According to Drinkard's descendants, during the Civil
War young William was taken prisoner by the Union army and released
only after taking an oath not to return to Missouri until after the war.
Honoring that commitment, the Drinkard family packed up their wagon
and started their journey west on the Oregon Trail without William,
picking him up in Iowa, three miles over the Missouri border.

*Hours: Mon–Sat 11am–4pm, Sun 1pm–5pm.*
*Admission by donation.*
*Directions: From State Route 228, take Main Street to Park Avenue and
turn right. The museum is on the left.*

### While You're in Brownsville:

The Moyer House, an elegant 1881 mansion built in the Italianate style
with 12-foot ceilings, a white Italian marble fireplace, and curved
walnut banisters, is worth a stop. Now on the National Register of Historic Places, it's open to the public as a museum. You may wish to time
your visit to Brownsville for the third weekend in June, when the Pioneer Picnic takes place. Begun in 1887, this is the oldest continuously-
running annual celebration in the state of Oregon.

*Moyer House, 204 N Main Street, Brownsville, OR 97327; (541)466-3390.
Hours: Sat 11am–4pm, Sun 1pm–5pm. Admission by donation. Directions:
The Moyer House is a short walk from the Linn County Historical Museum, on
N Main Street.*

## BURNS

### ■ Harney County Historical Museum
18 West D Street
Burns, OR 97720
(541)573-5618

Located on Brewery Hill, a site that once sported—what else?—a brewery, a laundry, and, later, a wrecking yard, the two-story Harney County Historical Museum is home to a wealth of dearly loved community treasures that were stored for years in the courthouse basement.

The museum features Native American artifacts, early cowboy photos, woodworking tools, a shed full of old wagons and farming equipment, and a coatrack, safe, photos, and other items from the ranch of well-known cattle baron Peter French. Other exhibits include handmade quilts, a turn-of-the-century kitchen where you can crank the apple peeler and lift the hand irons, clocks, vintage clothing, household items dating back to pioneer days, and dioramas featuring local birds.

Speaking of birds, the museum displays Dr. L. E. Hibbard's collection of more than 200 bird eggs—as well as the portable dental drill and chair the traveling dentist took with him on his rounds. Included in the collection are ostrich eggs, goose eggs, hawk eggs, nests, and eggs from egrets, blackbirds, and swans.

> *Hours: April to Sept: Tues–Sat 9am–5pm. Closed rest of year.*
> *Admission charged.*
> *Directions: The museum is on Highway 20 in Burns, at the north end of*
>     *Main Street, by the Chamber of Commerce.*

## BUTTE FALLS

### ■ Bill Edmondson Memorial Museum
432 Pine Street
Butte Falls, OR 97522
(541)865-3332

For a small town with a population of just 450 people, Butte Falls has lots of slogans, including "Home of Loggers" and "The Biggest Little Town in Oregon." The town also has two museums, the Bill Edmondson Memorial Museum and the Railroad Museum (see sidebar), each with its own personality and spunk.

Each room in the Bill Edmondson Memorial Museum is done up in classic 1950s style, from the dishes, cooking utensils, gadgets, and spices in the kitchen to the 1950s dress on the dressmakers' form in the sewing room.

The building housing the museum was once the home of Dr. Ernest W. Smith and his wife, Lucy. Smith was a photographer, surveyor, historian, and poet, and you'll see enlargements of his black-and-white photos depicting early Butte Falls displayed in the area that was his living room. Another room is set up to look like Smith's workshop, with typewriters, photographic and surveying equipment, and old negatives hanging by wooden clothespins attached to a homemade wooden wheel.

The room dedicated to the late timber faller and wood carver William "Bill" Edmondson displays some of his carvings, along with his awards and drawings. Edmondson's best-known works, though, are outside the museum. He created the roadside signs that welcome visitors to Butte Falls, and carved Paul Bunyan's little brother Ralph, the life-size wooden statue on the Butte Falls town square.

> **While You're in Butte Falls:**
> An 1890s Medco caboose serves as the town's Railroad Museum. Originally built to transport logging crews to and from the woods in the 1930s through the 1950s, the caboose is now filled with local logging memorabilia.
>
> *Railroad Museum, 626 Fir Street, Butte Falls, OR 97522; (541)865-3333.*
> *Hours: Fri and Sun 1pm–4pm, Sat 10am–4pm. Admission by donation. Directions: The museum is a two-block walk from the Bill Edmondson Memorial Museum.*

*Hours: Fri and Sun 1pm–4pm, Sat 10am–4pm.*
*Admission by donation.*
*Directions: Take northbound State Route 62 to Butte Falls Road, turn right, and drive 15 miles to Butte Falls. Turn left on Pine Street; the museum is on the left.*

## CANYON CITY

### ■ Grant County Historical Museum
Highway 395 (PO Box 464)
Canyon City, OR 97820
(541)575-0362

Each year, in the second full weekend in June, Canyon City holds a festival called '62 Days, in honor of the raucous gold rush ignited here by the discovery of gold in Canyon Creek back in 1862.

To learn more about the area's mining history, stop by the Grant County Historical Museum to examine its exhibit of picks, shovels, and other mining tools and to visit with the mannequin depicting the miner whose initial pan of gold started the frenzy. While that first pan of gold netted only $4, more than $20 million worth of the precious stuff was eventually mined from the area.

The museum also houses several rock and fossil collections, Native American artifacts, antique pianos and organs, and items detailing the area's ranching industry. Other exhibits feature guns, washtubs, a Chinese laundry wagon, and (a record) three sets of taxidermied two-headed calves from local farms in the John Day Valley.

Next door to the museum are the Greenhorn Jail and the cabin in which acclaimed Oregon poet Joaquin Miller lived with his family. Inside the museum are photos of Charles W. Brown's Standard Oil service station circa 1935. Many of the same artifacts Brown displayed on his office walls back then are on display in the museum today.

*Hours: June to Sept: Mon–Sat 9:30am–4:30pm, Sun 1pm–5pm. Closed rest of year.*
*Admission charged.*
*Directions: The museum is on Highway 395, just north of the post office in Canyon City.*

### ■ Ox Box Trade Company Museum of Horse-Drawn Vehicles
Highway 395
Canyon City, OR 97820
(541)575-2911

At the south edge of Canyon City, in what was once the town's 11,000-square-foot dance hall, is the Ox Box Trade Company Museum of Horse-Drawn Vehicles: a collection of more than 100 buggies, wagons, carriages, sleighs, surreys, and pretty much every other sort of vintage horse-drawn vehicle ever made. In among the ranch wagons, ice-cutting wagons, and horse-drawn hearses, you'll also find tools from the wheel-wright, blacksmith, woodworker, and harness maker; a goat car treadmill; rope-making equipment; and, here and there, some fishing gear.

*Hours: Call for hours.*
*Admission by donation.*
*Directions: The museum is at the southern edge of Canyon City, on Highway 395. Look for the stagecoach, wheels, and wagons out front.*

## CANYONVILLE

### ■ Pioneer-Indian Museum
421 W Fifth Street
Canyonville, OR 97417
(541)839-4379

Established by a group of pioneer and Cow Creek Indian descendants, Canyonville's Pioneer-Indian Museum traces the history of the South Umpqua Valley, from the days when Native American tribes lived here through the arrival of pioneers lured west by the Donation Land Claim Act and tales of mineral wealth.

Exhibits include cooking utensils, crockery, needlework, and examples of the crude furniture built by early settlers. Early medical instruments and druggists' remedies are displayed along with a well-used butcher block, a cast-iron scalding pot, and other items from an early meat market. Native American items include a large mural painted by local artist Elva Paulson, which re-creates pictographs drawn by the Umpqua tribe several hundred years ago.

In addition to farming, most early settlers tried their luck at mining. The mine display includes a time book, stock certificates, mineral specimens, and an exhibit about the Hanna Nickel Mining and Smelting Company, which after World War II became the only successful nickel operation in the United States, employing up to 700 people at its peak of operation.

*Hours: Sat–Sun, call for hours.*
*Admission by donation.*
*Directions: From northbound I-5, take exit 98, turn left at the bottom of the ramp, and drive through the underpass. From southbound I-5, take exit 98, cross First Street, continue to W Fifth Street, and turn right.*

## CASCADE LOCKS

### ■ Cascade Locks Historical Museum
355 Wanapa Street (PO Box 321)
Cascade Locks, OR 97014
(541)374-8535

In 1805, Meriwether Lewis and William Clark's Corps of Discovery had to portage around the whitewater rapids and dangerous cascades they encountered at this part of the Columbia River. Pioneers traveling the water route of the Oregon Trail 40 years later did the same thing, making their way on foot, by mule-drawn railcars, and, beginning in 1862, on the Oregon Pony, Oregon's first steam locomotive. In 1896, when work on a navigational canal and a series of locks was completed, Cascade Locks was officially in business.

These days, the portion of the lock system that remains above water can be seen at Marine Park, where the former lock tender's house now serves as the home of Cascade Locks Historical Museum. The original Oregon Pony sits out front. Three floors inside the museum contain exhibits full of artifacts, photographs, and information about the journey around the rapids, steamboats that ran on the river, the building of the locks, and the history of the area's logging and fishing industries.

The museum has a large tool collection, featuring some of the tools actually used to build the locks, and a great barbed-wire display. There's also a herd of taxidermied animals and a large replica of the sort of fish wheels once used on the river to efficiently scoop up fish and deposit them in large boxes.

Each year, on the last weekend in June, the museum takes part in the citywide Sternwheeler Days celebration, welcoming home the stern-wheeler *Columbia Gorge* for the summer months.

*Hours: May to Sept: Daily noon–5pm. Closed rest of year.*

*Admission free.*
*Directions: From I-84, take exit 44 to Cascade Locks and follow Wanapa*
   *Street to Marine Park.*

■  **Crater Rock Museum**
   2002 Scenic Avenue
   Central Point, OR 97502
   (541)664-6081

Rockhounds of all ages love Oregon, and they also love the Crater Rock Museum, filled with fossils, geodes, petrified wood, agates, crystal, and just about everything else you can imagine digging up.

The museum has a nice meteorite and amber display and an extensive collection of early Native American artifacts, found mostly in and around the Rogue Valley. The fossils here include vertebrate and invertebrate fossils dating back 500 million years—everything from dinosaur dung to a petrified pinecone.

Be sure to ask about the nest of dinosaur eggs at the museum entrance. They're from China and are estimated to be more than 100 million years old. Examination has revealed that they have some embryonic content inside.

After studying the thousands of neatly labeled specimens on display in the Crater Rock Museum, you may be anxious to go out and find some of your own. The folks from the Roxy Ann Gem and Mineral Society, who run the museum, are happy to point you in the right direction and share tips for successful hunting. They'll also urge you to come by in late March for their annual gem and mineral show.

*Hours: Tues, Thurs, Sat 10am–4pm.*
*Admission free.*
*Directions: From southbound I-5, take exit 35 and follow State Route 99*
   *to the flashing yellow light at Scenic Avenue. Turn left. From north-*
   *bound I-5, take exit 32, turn left, and follow Pine Street through Cen-*
   *tral Point to State Route 99. Turn right and drive about two miles to*
   *the flashing yellow light at Scenic Avenue. Turn right and look for the*
   *museum at the end of the block.*

■  **Collier Memorial State Park Logging Museum**
   46000 Highway 97
   Chiloquin, OR 97624
   (541)783-2471

Settlers arriving in the Pacific Northwest encountered steep mountains covered with dense forests. Those forests were filled with huge trees, many of them already hundreds of years old, hundreds of feet tall, and many feet in diameter. It took skill, plenty of determination, and the right tools to cut down these behemoths and haul away the timber. See how the task got done at the Logging Museum in Collier Memorial State Park, home of one of the most extensive collections of antique logging equipment in the country.

In 1945, as a tribute to their parents, Alfred and Andrew Collier gave the state of Oregon the 146 acres that now constitute Collier Memorial State Park. Two years later, the brothers donated a collection of antique logging equipment so that the evolution of logging, from oxen and axes to logging trucks and chain saws, could be memorialized too. Now a dozen artifact-filled cabins and all sorts of logging tools and machinery are scattered throughout this "logging park," offering something of interest for even the most woods-weary.

Early logging involved oxen and then horses, so blacksmiths were needed in the logging camps. In the blacksmith shed are harnesses, yokes, and a sling designed to help lift the huge animals when shoeing was required. Other sheds display steam donkeys, steam locomotives, and the gas-powered machinery that made it less difficult to get timber out of the woods.

Other equipment on display includes water kegs, log wagons, graders, bunchers, and loaders. The museum offers two areas devoted to sawmills as well as what's reputed to be the largest collection of chain saws in the state.

Not everything in this museum is old. The Beloit tree harvester, for instance, is a piece of modern-day logging machinery that can do on its own what it once took an entire logging crew to accomplish: It can shear a tree at ground level, remove its limbs, and stack it for loading onto a logging truck.

If, after seeing all this logging machinery, you've forgotten just what these loggers were after, take some time to walk through the woods and ponder some big old logs. Near the park entrance are examples of a Douglas fir and a ponderosa pine as well as a slab from the largest Douglas fir ever cut in Oregon.

*Web site: www.prd.state.or.us*
*Hours: Outdoor exhibits: Daily daylight to dusk (the gift shop and infor-*
*mation center are open in summer only).*
*Admission free.*
*Directions: The park and museum are on Highway 97, 30 miles north of*
*Klamath Falls.*

## CLACKAMAS

### ■ Oregon Military Museum
Camp Withycombe
Clackamas, OR 97015
(503)557-5359

Back in 1974, some folks were worried that the tangible evidence of Oregon's military heritage, dating back to militias formed in 1843, was being neglected, lost, and destroyed. So the adjutant general of Oregon got together with the Oregon state legislature and founded the Oregon Military Museum. Now anyone can march themselves out to Camp Withycombe and examine some of the museum's more than 10,000 weapons, uniforms, pieces of equipment, and other military artifacts. The collection also includes military items from other countries, including France, Germany, and Japan.

Objects seem to be categorized by size here. One room has "small" items, such as helmets, bayonets, uniforms, grenades, and military decorations. Another houses bigger equipment, including restored armored vehicles, jeeps, a submarine torpedo, and a depth charge. Tanks, anti-aircraft weapons, and other "big guns" are lined up outside.

Where did all this stuff come from? Well, the museum is the official repository for the 41st (Sunset) Division (the first U.S. division deployed overseas in 1942) and both the 96th (Deadeye) and the 104th (Timberwolf) Divisions, which trained at Oregon's Camp Adair before being deployed overseas for action in World War II.

*Hours: Fri–Sat 9am–5pm.*
*Admission free.*
*Directions: From I-205, take exit 12 from the north, or 12A from the south, and head east to Evelyn Street. Turn left and follow Evelyn to Camp Withycombe. Drive through the gate and proceed straight ahead to the museum, in Building 232.*

## CONDON

### ■ Gilliam County Historical Society Depot Museum Complex
State Route 19 at Burns Park (PO Box 377)
Condon, OR 97823
(503)384-4233

Gilliam County, in north-central Oregon, was named after Colonel Cornelius Gilliam, who commanded the Oregon volunteers during the Cayuse War of 1847 and was later accidentally shot by one of his own men in camp. You'll learn this legend, local history, and the stories behind many local town names at the Gilliam County Historical Society Depot Museum Complex in Condon, a town once known as Summit Springs.

The museum complex's main building is the old Union Pacific depot, which was moved across the tracks and the highway to its present site. The entry room features changing exhibits, but permanent displays in the other areas include a bedroom, parlor, and kitchen furnished in the style of the 1900s, post office boxes and other postal items, Native American and military items, a 1912 buggy, and a complete blacksmith shop and forge.

The settler's cabin (built in 1884), the one-room schoolhouse (circa 1920), and the 1890s frame building were also carefully moved to this site from various points around the county. The schoolhouse has a piano, double-wide student desks, books, charts, maps, a water bucket and dipper, and other period classroom items. The false-front building, which housed a variety of businesses on Condon's Main Street, is now fixed up as a barbershop.

*Hours: May to Oct: Wed–Sun 1pm–5pm. Closed rest of year.*
*Admission by donation.*
*Directions: The museum complex is on State Route 19, next to Burns Park*
*and the fairgrounds, at the north end of Condon.*

---

### While You're in Condon:

Be sure to pick up the detailed "Historic Sites and Driving Tours" brochure for Gilliam County at the Gilliam County Historical Society Depot Museum Complex (see listing). You can travel to all 57 spots or just pick the more interesting ones. For example, in the Mayville Cemetery (no. 42), Henry Beck's gravestone, which reads "Poorly born / Poorly lived / Poorly died / And no one cried," was recognized by the *Ripley's Believe It or Not!* series. Nobel Prize winner Linus Pauling's mom grew up on City Farm (no. 32). And the Last Chance Saloon (no. 57), so named because moonshine was sold there to weary wagon-train travelers, was later cleaned up and restored by the Oregon Trail 4-H Livestock Club.

---

## COOS BAY

■ **Coos Art Museum**
235 Anderson Avenue
Coos Bay, OR 97420
(503)267-3901

Originally housed in the city's old Carnegie library, the Coos Art Museum now occupies the former post office building, an art deco structure with stylish modernistic accents in the lobby frieze, grilles, and stair rails.

The permanent collection is composed mostly of high-quality original graphics, including work by Robert Rauschenberg, Alexander

Calder, Red Grooms, Larry Rivers, and others. Selections from this collection are displayed in the Permanent Collection Gallery, just off the Main Gallery. Other galleries feature changing local, regional, and national touring exhibitions throughout the year.

Upstairs, the Prefontaine Memorial Gallery honors former Olympic runner and Coos Bay native Steve Prefontaine with photographs, trophies, awards, and video footage of races.

Throughout the year the museum offers classes and workshops, family night programs, and guest artist receptions.

*Hours: Tues–Fri 11am–5pm, Sat 1pm–4pm.*
*Admission by donation.*
*Directions: From Highway 101, turn west (away from the bay) on*
*Anderson Avenue.*

### ■ Marshfield Sun Printing Museum
1049 N Front Street (PO Box 783)
Coos Bay, OR 97420
(541)269-0215 (Chamber of Commerce)

Jesse Allen Luse started publishing the weekly newspaper called the *Sun* in 1891. When the presses stopped in 1944, the paper was the oldest Oregon newspaper continuously published by one editor. Today the Marshfield Sun Printing Museum preserves the newspaper's printing office in its original layout, with its original printing presses, 200 type cases and fonts of type, a large paper cutter, and other tools of the printing trade.

Upstairs from the print shop, on the second floor, are exhibits on the history of printing and American newspapers as well as photographs of early Marshfield (now Coos Bay) and early river transportation.

*Hours: By appointment only (call the Chamber of Commerce).*
*Admission by donation.*
*Directions: The museum is between the Central Dock and the Timber Inn*
*on N Front Street.*

### CORVALLIS

### ■ Benton County History Center
110 NW Third Street
Corvallis, OR 97330
(541)758-3550

The Benton County History Center, a small "storefront museum" in downtown Corvallis, serves as both an exhibition annex and a teaser for the much larger Benton County Historical Museum just down the road in Philomath (see listing). The center offers changing exhibits that might feature vintage quilts, clothing and textiles, science and technology, fossils, rocks and minerals, or Native American basketry, culture, and history. The permanent exhibit is an annotated photographic timeline detailing the history of Corvallis and Benton County. The timeline begins with the Kalapuyans, the earliest residents of the Willamette Valley, and continues with the pioneers' arrival and settlement in the 1880s, the arrival and impact of the railroad, and the development of commercial industries through the 1920s.

*Hours: Tues–Sat 10am–5pm.*
*Admission free.*
*Directions: From I-5, take exit 228 (State Route 34) and drive 11 miles west to downtown Corvallis. The museum is on NW Third Street.*

## COTTAGE GROVE

### ■ Cottage Grove Museum
North H Street and W Birch Avenue (PO Box 142)
Cottage Grove, OR 97424
(503)942-3963

Sometimes it's the case that unusual personal mementos, generously shared with a museum, can creatively link a small town with a larger world event, turning an out-of-the-way museum into a must-see. That's the story at the Cottage Grove Museum.

Long before the blockbuster film *Titanic* hit movie theaters, Cottage Grove had caught a bit of "Titanic fever," because John and Isabelle Woolcott had generously shared their *Titanic* mementos with the town. John's mother, Marion Wright, was a survivor of the doomed vessel, and the maroon woolen overcoat she wore to clamber into a lifeboat and the letters she wrote home to her dad after being rescued are some of the more unusual items that have been drawing *Titanic* buffs to Cottage Grove.

Items with more direct local connections include 62 sketches of covered bridges drawn by a local artist, a collection of chrome-plated horseshoes artfully arranged by the grandson of the town's former black-smith, a sewing machine that came "around the Horn," and specimens from a local resident's extensive rock collection.

During the area's gold-mining heyday, heavy stamp mills like the one in the museum's yard were hauled up into the mountains and set up wherever water power or a steam engine was available to operate them. This allowed miners to separate valuable gold from quartz as quickly as possible. To see how the contraption worked, go inside, switch on the small working model, and watch how heavy "stamps" would be lifted up and dropped down on the mined ore, pulverizing and preparing it for a water process that separated the gold from the ore.

The octagonal building housing the museum was built in 1897 as a Roman Catholic church and features Italian stained-glass windows. It is supposedly the only octagonal building in the Northwest.

*Hours: June 15 to Labor Day: Wed–Sun 1pm–4pm. After Labor Day to June 14: Sat–Sun 1pm–4pm.*
*Admission free.*
*Directions: From State Route 99, head west on W Main Street and continue to North H Street, where you turn right. The museum is at the intersection of North H Street and W Birch Avenue.*

## CRESWELL

### ■ Creswell Historical Museum
55 N Fifth Street (PO Box 577)
Creswell, OR 97426
(541)895-5161

Located in a restored 1889 Methodist-Episcopal church, the Creswell Historical Museum offers a trip into the town's past, from the original telephone switchboard to an Astroturfed mini–town square complete with park benches, light poles, and trees.

Displays include the original teller's cage from the Creswell Fruit Growers Bank and Depository, vintage clothing, an Oregon Trail exhibit, and re-creations of a local schoolroom, a mercantile store, an early bedroom, a period kitchen, and a living room complete with a wood-burning stove. The museum also has a children's room and a replica of the Creswell Arch, which stood at the town's entrance between 1909 and 1920, advertising the town's crops (apples, peaches, prunes, berries, dairy, and poultry) and luring visitors with the hard-to-resist message "Stop! Creswell Is the Place."

*Hours: May to Sept: Mon and Wed noon–4pm; Tues and Thurs noon–4pm, 7pm–9pm; Fri 1pm–3pm; Sat–Sun 1pm–4pm. Oct to April: Mon–Thurs noon–4pm, Fri 1pm–3pm, Sat–Sun 1pm–4pm.*
*Admission by donation.*
*Directions: From I-5, take exit 182 (Creswell) and drive six blocks west to the museum, in the church building on the corner of Oregon Avenue and N Fifth Street.*

## CROW

### ■ Applegate Pioneer Museum
Territorial Road
Crow, OR 97487
(541)935-1836

The tiny Applegate Pioneer Museum is housed in a relocated one-room schoolhouse and contains an assortment of tools, farm implements, kitchen items, wood-burning stoves, and other household furniture used by area pioneers. The collection also includes transcriptions of oral history interviews conducted with many local residents.

*Hours: Summer: Second and fourth Sun of the month 1pm–4pm. Rest of*
*year: Second Sun of the month 1pm–4pm.*
*Admission by donation.*
*Call for directions.*

## ECHO

■ **Chinese House Railroad Museum**
210 W Main Street
Echo, OR 97826
(541)376-8411

The Chinese House Railroad Museum is a circa 1883–86 bunkhouse
used first by Chinese laborers and then by section crews. Two interpretive panels outside the building tell a bit about the early history of both
the railroad and the Echo community, but to get inside, you'll need to
check in at Echo City Hall. What's inside? Early railroad tools, historical
photos of Echo's early days, and artifacts excavated from nearby railroad
sites, including bottles, opium tins, and shards of pottery and jugs.

*Hours: May to Oct: Mon–Fri 8am–4:30pm. Nov to April: Mon–Wed*
*1pm–4pm.*
*Admission by donation.*
*Directions: Echo is 2 miles off I-84 at intersection 183. For further directions*
*and to enter the museum, stop at the Echo City Hall, 110 Bonanza*
*Street.*

■ **Echo Historical Museum**
230 W Main Street
Echo, OR 97286
(541)376-8150

Housed in an old bank building abounding with marble, the Echo Historical Museum features a large collection of Native American artifacts,
including beaded clothing and baskets. Other displays include pioneer
artifacts, glassware, vintage photographs and newspaper clippings, and a
wide variety of miscellaneous community memorabilia, including a set of
Dionne Quintuplets dolls, leather postcards mailed in 1907, and a child's
swing that's more than 100 years old.

*Hours: Sat–Sun 1pm–4pm.*
*Admission by donation.*
*Directions: Echo is 2 miles off I-84 at intersection 183. The museum is on*
*the corner of W Main and Bonanza Streets, in the old bank building.*

## ■ Lane County Historical Museum
740 W 13th Avenue
Eugene, OR 97402
(541)682-4239

In 1826, Scottish naturalist David Douglas joined a group of Hudson Bay trappers on a visit to the upper McKenzie River in Lane County to study area vegetation; later, the Douglas fir was named after him. Of course, in those days it wasn't just naturalists and trappers heading west. Over three decades beginning in 1853, more than 300,000 people traveled along the Oregon Trail into the Oregon Territory, and Lane County was a popular destination.

The Lane County Historical Museum has an extensive Oregon Trail exhibition featuring one of only three covered wagons that crossed the Oregon Trail and are still in existence today. The well-preserved "prairie schooner" was owned by the Calvin Reed family, who arrived in Lane County in 1850. Other displays include 19th- and early 20th-century tools, household items, clothing, toys, cameras, and blacksmithing artifacts. Period rooms include a pioneer kitchen and a Victorian parlor.

For most of the 20th century, Lane County led the nation in timber production. The *Logging in Lane County* exhibit features logging equipment, photographs, and taped interviews with loggers.

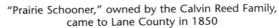

"Prairie Schooner," owned by the Calvin Reed Family,
came to Lane County in 1850

Other ongoing displays include historic vehicles, a children's exhibit, and *Jazz & Spats,* focusing on the 1920s and 1930s. The museum hosts a quilt exhibition each year during the third week of April.

*Hours: Wed–Fri 10am–4pm, Sat noon–4pm.*
*Admission charged.*
*Directions: From I-5, take exit 105 west and follow the signs to the Lane County Fairgrounds. The museum is next to the fairgrounds at W 13th Avenue and Monroe Street.*

## ■ Oregon Air and Space Museum
90377 Boeing Drive
Eugene, OR 97402
(541)461-1101

Located at the south end of the Eugene airport, the Oregon Air and Space Museum displays a wide variety of aircraft and artifacts depicting the history of aviation and space technology. Exhibits include a detailed space exploration timeline, one man's collection of more than 600 scale models showing the development of aviation from the Wright Brothers to the Stealth fighter, aircraft armaments, philatelic airmail covers, and lots more.

Aircraft on display include a McDonnell F-4 Phantom used in Vietnam, a North American F-86 Sabre flown in Korea, and a Grumman A-6E Intruder jet bomber flown in Vietnam and the Persian Gulf. Nonwar aircraft featured here include a single-seat open-cockpit helicopter powered by a Triumph motorcycle engine, and the Taylor 2100 Bullet, Molt (Aerocar) Taylor's experimental two-seat pusher powered by a VW engine.

Special aviation programs at the museum include "fly-ins," dinner speakers, and open house air-fairs.

*Hours: Thurs–Sun noon–4pm.*
*Admission charged.*
*Directions: From I-5 southbound, take exit 195B to Beltline Road; follow Beltline Road five miles west to Highway 99 and then head north one and a half miles to Airport Road. Turn left onto Airport Road and continue on it to Boeing Drive, onto which you turn right. The museum is at the south end of the Eugene airport.*

## ■ University of Oregon Museum of Art
University of Oregon
1430 Johnson Lane
Eugene, OR 97403
(541)346-3027

Comprising four floors of galleries, the University of Oregon Museum of Art is the largest art museum between Portland and Sacramento. The museum presents gallery talks, concerts, family days, and an annual MFA exhibition, and draws on its collection of more than 14,000 items to supplement up to eight changing exhibitions each year.

The permanent holdings include a strong Pacific Northwest collection featuring works by Mark Tobey and David McCosh as well as more than 500 items by Morris Graves. The collection also features photography, Russian icons, Persian miniatures, and European art. The renowned Asian art collection of Japanese, Chinese, and Korean artifacts includes a massive jade pagoda, ancient Buddhist sculptures, samurai armor, and other religious, court, and folk treasures. Of special note are the Throne Room, which features a significant portion of the museum's Chinese art, and the Japanese Galleries, presenting fine Japanese prints and printed books, ceramics, lacquerware and metalwork, hanging scrolls, painted screens, textiles, and several unusual Japanese dolls.

The museum, designed by architect Ellis Lawrence and completed in 1932, is listed on the National Register of Historic Places and features a nice gift shop and a lovely, cloistered interior courtyard complete with sculptures and a pond.

*Web site: uoma.uoregon.edu*
*Hours: Wed noon–8pm, Thurs–Sun noon–5pm.*
*Admission charged. Free Wed 5pm–8pm during MusEvenings!, when the museum usually offers a special lecture or event relating to the current exhibition.*
*Directions: The museum is on the University of Oregon campus, next to the Knight Library, near E 14th Avenue and Kincaid Street on Johnson Lane.*

Rest your feet in the courtyard of the museum, designed by Ellis Lawrence

## ■ University of Oregon Museum of Natural History

University of Oregon
1680 E 15th Avenue
Eugene, OR 97403
(541)346-3024

Think you might have the world's oldest shoes hanging around the back
of your closet? Not even close. The University of Oregon Museum of
Natural History has a pair of sagebrush bark sandals found in Fort Rock
Cave in 1938 by archaeologist Luther Cressman. Radiocarbon dating
showed that the shoes were at least 9,000 years old and helped prove
Cressman's theory that people had been living in Oregon much longer
than most researchers had believed.

These "vintage" sandals and other "worn and discarded" items from
the cave—along with ceremonial axes obtained by Sir Henry Morton

Left: Beaded leather
Métis mittens
Below: 9,000-year-old
sagebrush bark sandals

Stanley on his expeditions to Africa's Congo Basin, million-year-old fossils, and an Eskimo basket made out of whale baleen—are just some of the unusual treasures here.

The museum also houses the Oregon State Museum of Anthropology, the official caretaker for anthropological materials found on Oregon state lands. In addition to those items, the collection includes western Indian baskets made before 1900, Southwestern pottery, costumes from Eastern Europe, archaeological items from Alaska, and textiles and artifacts from Africa, Asia, and almost every corner of the world.

While the museum's specialty is officially anthropology, it also houses major paleontological and zoological collections, including more than 1,000 fossil specimens (collected by Thomas Condon from the fossil beds of Oregon in the mid-1800s) and an extensive collection of mammals and birds, including more than 1,000 egg sets and 250 nests.

Long-term exhibits generally explore the archaeological and fossil history of Oregon, while changing displays explore animals, plants, environmental topics, and traditional human culture.

Special programs include family-day events (called Saturday Safaris), lectures, workshops, field trips, and an annual Identification Day for artifacts and specimens.

> *Web site: natural-history.uoregon.edu*
> *Hours: Wed–Sun noon–5pm.*
> *Admission by donation.*
> *Directions: The museum is on the east side of the University of Oregon campus, at the intersection of E 15th Avenue and Agate Street.*

### ■ Willamette Science and Technology Center
2300 Leo Harris Parkway
Eugene, OR 97401
(541)682-3619

The Willamette Science and Technology Center (WISTEC) features periodically changing displays designed to give kids hands-on educational encounters with the "wonders of the universe ranging from the transcendent nature of atomic particles to what keeps bridges from falling down." That's a pretty tall order, but WISTEC succeeds with entertaining math and science exhibits that turn topics such as the body, visual perception, lasers, and those ever-popular dinosaurs into pure fun. In addition to its changing exhibits, the center features a computer lab, a telementoring project, field trips, and workshops.

> *Web site: www.efn.org/~wistec*
> *Hours: Wed–Fri noon–5pm, Sat–Sun 11am–5pm.*
> *Admission charged.*
> *Directions: The center is off Centennial Boulevard, across from the University of Oregon's Autzen Stadium.*

FLORENCE

■ **Dolly Wares Doll Museum**
3620 Highway 101
Florence, OR 97439
(541)997-3391

If you're lucky, curator Sharon Smith will be able to take a moment from her emergency duties in the "doll hospital" to chat with you about her favorite friends among the more than 2,500 dolls at the Dolly Wares Doll Museum. That way you'll be sure not to miss the oldest doll in the collection, a four-and-a-half-inch-tall pre-Columbian man made of clay, or the elaborately carved Roman wooden soldier (circa 1604) wearing his original outfit.

The far-ranging collection includes one-of-a-kind modern-day "art" dolls, vinyl and plastic store-bought dolls, and dolls from the 1700s and 1800s made of papier-mâché, wood, wax, china, cloth, porcelain, and other materials. Many wear their orig-

Morimura Bros. designed this hunter on his horse sometime between the two World Wars

inal clothing; others are dressed in the style in vogue when they were new. Ethnic dolls represent almost every country in the world, while puppets and other dolls depict political figures, royalty, comic-strip characters, television and radio personalities, and advertising icons.

*Hours: Tues–Sun 10am–5pm.*
*Admission charged.*
*Directions: The museum is in a long pink building on the northeast corner of 36th Street and Highway 101.*

■ **Siuslaw Pioneer Museum**
85294 Highway 101 (PO Box 2637)
Florence, OR 97439
(541)997-7884

The volunteers at the Siuslaw Pioneer Museum take their jobs seriously: They dress in period clothing and all but demand that visitors watch a narrated slide-tape about the area's history before wandering among the thousands of items displayed in the cavernous churchlike structure built from two make-your-own-barn mail-order kits.

Do what they say. The 12-minute slide-tape provides a good introduction to the area's local Native American tribe (the Siuslaw) and the accomplishments of early pioneer settlers. It also describes the role of the river in the town's history and how a single piece of flotsam from an ocean shipwreck caused the town to give up its Indian name, "Oceola, " in favor of "Florence." Because just about every piece of community flotsam on display has been similarly well researched and documented, it's easy to learn the story behind the rare dugout canoe found at the mouth of the Siuslaw River in the early 1900s, the blacksmith's giant forge bellows, or the petrified walrus tusk that Elmer Peterson and his wife discovered while walking on the beach in the early 1970s.

For many years the area's local economy relied on logging and salmon fishing. The tools, workday items, and photographs documenting these industries are on display, along with vintage clothing, kitchen and household items, toys, games, and pretty much anything anyone used in days gone by.

> *Web site: winfinity.com/orgs/spm/spm.htm*
> *Hours: Tues–Sun 10am–4pm.*
> *Admission by donation.*
> *Directions: The museum is on Highway 101, one mile south of the bridge over the Siuslaw River, which is the northern boundary of the Oregon Dunes National Recreation Area.*

## FORT KLAMATH

■ **Fort Klamath Museum and Park**
State Route 62
Fort Klamath, OR 97626
(541)381-2230

Fort Klamath was a frontier military post established in 1863. The Fort Klamath Museum, in the fort's original guardhouse, contains a miniature model of the fort and exhibits depicting the events of the 1872 Modoc Indian War, essentially a four-month siege by the U.S. Cavalry. Display cases contain military medals, medical instruments, cannonballs, and guns dug up on site, as well as personal items that belonged to the soldiers stationed here, including razors, hair clippers, and eating utensils. The graves of Modoc leader Captain Jack and three of his warriors, all of whom were captured and hanged by the army, are on the park grounds.

Several times each summer, history buffs gather on the grounds to stage a reenactment complete with costumes, guns, and cannons.

> *Hours: June to Labor Day: Thurs–Mon 10am–6pm. Closed rest of year.*
> *Admission by donation.*
> *Directions: The museum is one mile south of Fort Klamath, on State Route 62.*

## FORT ROCK

■ **Fort Rock Valley Homestead Village Museum**
(PO Box 84)
Fort Rock, OR 97735
(541)576-2251

"We're a back-to-basics museum," say the community volunteers who run the Fort Rock Valley Homestead Village Museum, "showing the hardship of homesteading in the high desert." How do they show it? By finding homesteading-era structures, relocating them to the museum grounds just west of Fort Rock, and restoring them. Many members of the local historical society are descendants of the area's original home-steading families, and it may be their inherited grit that enables them to organize the complicated process of getting volunteers to pick up and move fragile old buildings.

How are they doing? Well, starting back in 1988 they successfully transported the 1915 Webster cabin and a doctor's office dating back to 1907. Since then they've fanned out and brought to the museum the 1918 St. Rose Catholic Church, the Bodenheimer House (built in 1911), the Menkenmaier cabin, a school, and several other buildings.

> *Hours: Memorial Day through Labor Day: Fri–Sun 10am–4pm. Closed rest of year.*
> *Admission by donation.*
> *Directions: From State Route 31, turn east at Fort Rock Junction onto County Road 510 and drive seven miles.*

## FOSSIL

■ **Fossil Museum**
First Street
Fossil, OR 97830
(541)763-4481 (for information)

Named in honor of the fossils found on a local ranch in 1867, this town has public fossil-digging beds (always open!) behind the high school and a city museum that houses pioneer and Native American artifacts, historical photographs, tape-recorded interviews with early town residents, and exhibits about sheep ranching in the area. The Fossil Museum also displays the orig-inal window from the Fossil post office on Hoover Creek, school desks

**While You're in Fossil:**
At the Fossil Museum, pick up a "Wheeler County Driving Tours" brochure, designed and printed by a Wheeler High School computer class. Tour 1 includes a stop at the Oregon Museum of Science and Industry (OMSI) Hancock Field Station, where you can see fossils and geologic exhibits. Tour 2 leads to the Sheep Rock Unit of the John Day Fossil Beds National Monu-ment, where you'll find a small fossil museum (see listing in Kimberly).

and church pews from the ghost town of Richmond, and memorabilia from the logging company town of Kinzua.

*Hours: Memorial Day to Oct: Daily 10am–5pm. Closed rest of year. Admission by donation.*

*Directions: Fossil is 50 miles south of Arlington. From Highway 19, turn at the big WELCOME TO FOSSIL sign and follow First Street to Washington Street and the museum.*

## GOLD BEACH

### ■ Curry County Historical Museum
920 S Ellensburg Highway (Highway 101)
Gold Beach, OR 97444
(541)247-6113

Located at the county fairgrounds, the Curry County Historical Museum documents the days when the area just north of Gold Beach had the largest black sand gold mine in the United States. When prospectors flocked to the area, many of them no doubt lived like "Herman the Miner." He's the fellow in the museum's spartan one-room cabin, which is furnished with assay equipment, a cookstove, a bed, and the hides of a cougar and a bear tacked proudly on the wall.

In addition to Herman's cabin, the museum boasts a well-stocked general store, examples of tools and machinery used for logging, fishing, farming, and woodworking, and a maritime exhibit featuring information about area lighthouses and coastal shipwrecks. The Native American artifact collection includes a canoe, baskets, tools, arrowheads, and petroglyphs. Almost all the photographs displayed come from the museum's archive of more than 20,000 photographic negatives.

From September through May, the museum sponsors free monthly historical programs.

*Hours: June to Sept: Tues–Sat noon–4pm. Oct to May: Sat noon–4pm. Admission by donation.*

*Directions: The museum is at the Curry County Fairgrounds, on Highway 101 (also known as the Ellensburg Highway).*

## GOLD HILL

### ■ House of Mystery at the Oregon Vortex
4303 Sardine Creek Road
Gold Hill, OR 97525
(541)855-1543

Scientists have painstakingly uncovered the answers to many of the world's big mysteries. But Mother Nature, thank goodness, still keeps some secrets. The puzzle of the Oregon Vortex is one of them—or so generations of tourists have been led to believe.

Originally an assay office for a gold-mining company, the House of Mystery is at the center of an "area of disturbance" where, it appears, balls roll uphill, visitors are unable to stand upright, and (pipsqueaks rejoice!) short people seem to get taller.

How can this be? A courteous guide will tell you that engineer John Litster studied the mysterious phenomena on-site in the early 1940s. In 1943, after conducting more than 14,000 experiments, Litster concluded that the strange doings could be explained only by the existence of the Oregon Vortex, "a whirlpool of invisible energy" where everyday physical facts are reversed. While this may not be a scientifically satisfactory answer for everyone, the Oregon Vortex is a fun place to snap some photos and test your powers of perception.

*Hours: June to Aug: Daily 9am–6pm. March to May, Sept 1 to Oct 15:*
  *Daily 9am–5pm. Closed rest of year.*
*Admission charged.*
*Directions: The house is between Medford and Grants Pass, four miles off*
  *I-5. Take the Gold Hill exit and watch for the signs.*

## GRANTS PASS

■ **Grants Pass Museum of Art**
  229 Southwest G Street
  Grants Pass, OR 97526
  (541)479-3290

Relocated in 1999 from its spot in Riverside Park, the Grants Pass Museum of Art presents up to a dozen changing exhibits each year featuring work by contemporary regional and national artists. Shows feature work by individual artists, group shows, and shows organized around themes such as Women's History Month, local artists, or a personal collection.

*Hours: Tues–Sat noon–4pm.*
*Admission free.*
*Directions: From I-5, take exit 55. Head east on Highway 199; once you*
  *cross the bridge, turn right on SE Park Street and continue until you*
  *see the museum.*

## GRESHAM

■ **Gresham Pioneer Museum**
  410 N Main Avenue (PO Box 65)
  Gresham, OR 97030
  (503)661-0347

Housed in a Carnegie library building, the Gresham Pioneer Museum presents exhibits focusing on Gresham's agricultural and industrial heritage. The core exhibit includes historical photographs, clothing, and artifacts relating to local history from the 1850s to the 1960s. Most other exhibits, however, are temporary and designed around a specific theme, such as "Photography of the Old West" or "The Sporting Life," organized in honor of the town's role as host of the Nike World Games in the summer of 1998.

Special programs include walking tours, bus trips to historic sites, and presentations on local history.

*Hours: Tues, Thurs–Sat 10am–4pm, Wed 1pm–4pm.*
*Admission by donation.*
*Directions: From eastbound Highway 26, head north on N Main Avenue.*
*The museum is on the corner of Fourth Street and N Main Avenue in historic downtown Gresham.*

## HAINES

### ■ Eastern Oregon Museum
Third and School Streets
Haines, OR 98833
(503)856-3233

If you had attended Haines's annual Elkhorn Grange 908 Hobby Show in 1953, you'd likely recognize many of the items at the Eastern Oregon Museum. It was the 1953 show, museum volunteers say, that made folks realize that pretty much everyone in town had cherished historical documents, unusual collections, or interesting relics up in their attics or out in their barns that could help tell the story of the spirited men and women who developed this part of Eastern Oregon.

In 1959 the town's old gymnasium was retired, providing a new home for the museum. Since then, so much memorabilia has been donated that the former gym's two basketball backdrops now sport elk heads and the bleacher seats display cooking utensils, old telephones, vintage clothing, carved stone artifacts, and other collectibles.

Exhibits include a collection of 500 bells, a wide assortment of hen-related items, and a case of doorknobs. A turn-of-the-century kitchen and sitting room are re-created using furniture and appliances from local families; the refurbished Bourne Bar, complete with bartender and spittoons, spent years as a chicken roost before finding a home at the museum. The town's original switchboard is here, along with a huge kerosene popcorn popper, a big round rock found after the 1917 Rock Creek flood, and an old electric permanent-wave machine that bears a note explaining how the contraption worked: "The victim was hooked directly to the current, but there were no reported electrocutions."

When the Union Pacific Railroad eliminated Haines as a stop, the town inherited the depot and dragged it across the tracks near the museum. Now it displays early farming and railroading items, including an old brewery wagon, threshing machines, hay balers, and several manure spreaders. An old fire barrel is kept filled with water—perhaps in case someone fires up that old permanent-wave machine.

*Hours: April 15 to Oct 25: Daily 9am–5pm. Rest of year by appointment.*
*Admission by donation.*
*Directions: Haines is between Baker City and North Powder. The museum*
*    is four blocks east of Highway 30, on Third Street.*

## HEPPNER

■ **Morrow County Museum**
440 N Main Street
Heppner, OR 97836
(541)676-5524

Pioneers headed west on the Oregon Trail passed right through Morrow County, but their hearts were so set on land that was green and inviting that few settlers put down roots in the desolate Eastern Oregon country. Twenty years later, when the cities started getting crowded, some of these same folks started back east along the trail to lay claim to wide-open land and settled here.

The Morrow County Museum has hundreds of photographs documenting the social, economic, and technological development of the area, as well as a wide variety of exhibits ranging from agricultural history to an exploration of the Native American presence here. Objects on display include fine wedding dresses, a set of Haviland china and a silver service that came across the Oregon Trail, kitchenware, cookstoves, quilts, and unusual early medical instruments.

Most intriguing is the exhibit documenting the Heppner Flood, which occurred on June 14, 1903, at about 5pm. According to museum records, on that day a cloudburst overloaded area creeks and sent water rushing toward town. The water picked up debris from the farms along the way. At the south end of town, the water and the debris got dammed up for a while behind a laundry building.

When the water broke free, it hit Heppner with amazing force. Some people simply disappeared, so the death toll for the tragedy had to be listed at "approximately 250," or about one-quarter of the town's population. Objects rescued from the floodwaters and now on display tell a tragic story of loss. There's a family Bible, a porcelain doll (although the doll survived, her young owner did not), and a quilt that rode out the flood in a watertight trunk. Embroidered on the quilt are the words "in the Heppner Flood."

*Web site: ourworld.compuserve.com/homepages/MCMuseum/*
*    homepage.htm*
*Hours: Tues–Sat 1pm–5pm.*
*Admission by donation.*
*Directions: State Route 207 becomes Main Street in Heppner. The museum*
*    is on N Main Street, next to the city park.*

## HILLSBORO

### ■ Rice Northwest Museum of Rocks and Minerals
26385 NW Groveland Drive
Hillsboro, OR 97124
(503)647-2418

Richard and Helen Rice were Hillsboro rockhounds who started collecting agates together along the Oregon beaches in the late 1930s. Over the years their collection grew to include more than 3,400 rocks and minerals and is now considered to be among the finest in the Pacific Northwest.

During their lifetimes the Rices shared their home with the collection and shared the collection with just about anyone interested enough to stop by. They taught classes, they cut and polished their own stones, and in their wills they requested that their collection, their home, and the 23 acres surrounding it be set aside as a museum open to the public.

Minerals on display at the Rice Northwest Museum of Rocks and Minerals include world-class specimens of common quartz and gypsum, emerald and ruby gem crystals, and one of the two finest red rhodochrosite specimens in the world. The collection also includes large polished sections of petrified wood, fossil palms, Oregon thundereggs, and, of course, those agates the Rices collected from the United States, Mexico, and South America.

*Web site: www.ricenwmuseum.org/*
*Hours: Wed–Sun 1pm–5pm.*
*Admission charged.*
*Directions: From westbound Highway 26, take exit 61N and then take the first turn west onto NW Groveland Drive.*

## HOOD RIVER

### ■ Hood River County Historical Museum
Port Marina Park (PO Box 781)
Hood River, OR 97031
(503)386-6772

While many folks are drawn to the Hood River region these days for the abundant wind and great sailboarding conditions, the area's history is tied tightly to lumber and fruit, two industries well documented at the Hood River County Historical Museum.

Items on display from the apple industry include a wall full of colorful framed apple box labels, an apple polisher, apple-picking buckets, and tools that did everything from making apple boxes to checking that the lids were securely attached. Timber industry items include photographs from area mills, handsaws, and other small tools. Judging from the whiskey still that was "donated" by the local sheriff, it seems moonshine might well have been an unofficial local industry at one time too.

Look on the main floor for Native American baskets, stone fishing weights, that old still, period clothing, pioneer-day objects such as quilts and washboards, and items representing the area's Finnish, Japanese, and Hispanic communities.

On the balcony are dolls, toys, a jeweler's workbench, and other memorabilia. Outside, look for a buoy, an orchard duster, a slab from an ancient oak tree, and steamship relics such as the paddle wheel from the SS *Henderson* and a lifeboat from the SS *Georgia Burton*.

> *Hours: April to Aug: Mon–Sat 10am–4pm, Sun noon–4pm. Sept to Oct:*
> *Daily noon–4pm. Closed rest of year.*
> *Admission free.*
> *Directions: From I-84, take exit 64 and follow the signs to Port Marina*
> *Park.*

## INDEPENDENCE

### ■ Heritage Museum
112 S Third Street (PO Box 7)
Independence, OR 97351
(503)838-4989

Established in 1874, the town of Independence is in the Willamette Valley, just 12 miles southwest of the state capital of Salem. By the turn of the century, Independence was surrounded by thousands of acres of hops. In fact, the hop crop became so popular and lucrative that, until the mid-1940s, the town was known as the Hop Capital of the World. To find out just how important hops were to Polk County—and why Washington's Yakima Valley now claims the title of Hop Capital—stop by the Heritage Museum.

Housed in an 1888 former Baptist church in the historic district, the museum displays items pertaining to hop cultivation and coopers' tools along with logging equipment, local Native American artifacts, historical photographs, an 1890s-style parlor, a blacksmith shop, and a covered wagon.

The museum hosts at least two chautauqua programs a year and serves as the starting point for the annual Independence Historic Home Tour, held each year on the second Saturday in August.

> *Web site: www.open.org/herimusm*
> *Hours: Wed and Sat 1pm–5pm, Thurs–Fri 1pm–4pm.*
> *Admission free.*
> *Directions: From State Route 99W, turn east on Monmouth Street, then*
> *north on Third Street. The museum is in a church building in the*
> *downtown historic district, at S Third and B Streets.*

## ■ Children's Museum
206 N Fifth Street
Jacksonville, OR 97530
(541)773-6536

If your kids haven't had enough fun at the Jacksonville Museum of Southern Oregon History (see next listing), in the courthouse right next door, hustle them over to the Children's Museum. Located in the former 1910 Jackson County Jail, the museum has two floors full of hands-on exhibits, including displays depicting the daily life of Native Americans and early settlers, the 1890s I. M. Sellin' General Store (get it?), and an interactive HO-scale model train diorama.

Kids can work the register in the general store, sit in a replica of a Takelma Indian lodge, or climb into a covered wagon and don pioneer clothes. There's also a barn filled with farming tools, an 1890s kitchen with a water pump and woodstove, a children's bedroom with games, and miniature versions of an old-fashioned school, a jail, the Beekman Bank, a Chinese laundry, and a church complete with a working pump organ. In the Peter Britt portrait studio, kids can learn about this famous local photographer and horticulturist, pose for pictures, and look through the lens of a re-created Britt camera.

*Web site: www.sohs.org*
*Hours: Memorial Day to Labor Day: Daily 10am–5pm. After Labor Day*
*to before Memorial Day: Wed–Sat 10am–5pm, Sun noon–5pm.*
*Admission charged. Jackson County residents free.*
*Directions: From I-5, take exit 27 and head west on Barnett Road, turn*
*north on Riverside Avenue, and turn west on Main Street (Jack-*
*sonville Highway). Continue on W Main and follow the signs to*
*Jacksonville. The museum is on the corner of N Fifth and D Streets,*
*next to the Jacksonville Museum of Southern Oregon History.*

## ■ Jacksonville Museum of Southern Oregon History
206 N Fifth Street
Jacksonville, OR 97530
(541)773-6536

The entire town of Jacksonville, founded amid the frenzy of the gold rush in 1851, has been declared a National Historic Landmark, so you'll want to pick up a walking-tour map and explore. But first take a little time to learn about the local history at the Jacksonville Museum of Southern Oregon History, and you'll have a better understanding of what makes the town so unusual.

Located in an 1883 building that formerly housed the Jackson County Courthouse, the museum presents changing and permanent exhibits about the town's history, the area's Native Americans, the development and growth of the Rogue Valley, and the impact of the industrial revolution on the settlement of southern Oregon.

Artifacts in the downstairs local history area include scrip from early gold rush jubilees, the hand bell Jane McCully used to call her students to class in 1862, and a roomful of rifles, shotguns, pistols, and swords. Upstairs, in the hands-on *Miner, Baker, Furniture Maker* exhibit, visitors can pan for gold, weigh their finds at the assayer's office, "relax" in a miner's cabin, and run the lathe over at the cabinet shop. Artifacts sprinkled throughout the exhibit include mining and blacksmith tools, locally made and imported furniture, more rifles and pistols, and a wonderful collection of musical instruments. Local artisans are often featured at work in the museum, demonstrating how they use traditional methods and materials.

**While You're in Jacksonville:** The local historical society operates several other historic sites in town, including the Children's Museum next door (see listing); the Beekman House, where costumed interpreters let you "meet the Beekmans"; and the turn-of-the-century Beekman Bank, the second bank established in Oregon. Pick up a walking-tour map from the information center at the Rogue River Valley Railway depot (on Oregon and C Streets), and see how many of the 85 historic homes and buildings you can spot.

The local historical society presents a wide variety of workshops, family days, lectures, and demonstrations throughout the year as well as annual events, including the Family Heritage Fair in the spring, an old-fashioned ice cream social in the summer, and a Victorian Christmas in December.

> *Web site: www.sohs.org*
> *Hours: Memorial Day to Labor Day: Daily 10am–5pm. After Labor Day to before Memorial Day: Wed–Sat 10am–5pm, Sun noon–5pm.*
> *Admission charged. Jackson County residents free.*
> *Directions: From I-5 take exit 27 and head west on Barnett Road. From Barnett, turn north on Riverside Avenue and then west onto W Main Street (Jacksonville Highway). Continue on W Main Street and follow signs to Jacksonville. The museum is in the old courthouse building on the corner of N Fifth and C Streets, next to the Children's Museum.*

## JOHN DAY

■ **Kam Wah Chung & Co. Museum**
NW Canton/City Park
John Day, OR 97845
(541)575-0028

By the mid-1850s, overpopulation, famine, and the promise of easy fortunes to be made in the American West had lured thousands of Chinese people from their home country to the gold fields of California and the Pacific Northwest. The 1879 census, for example, shows that Chinese miners in Eastern Oregon outnumbered white miners by almost three-to-one.

In 1887 two Chinese immigrants, Ing "Doc" Hay and Lung On, set up their home and their business in a small building in John Day. The former trading post became a general store, pharmacy, doctor's office, and Chinese temple. Now it's the Kam Wah Chung & Co. Museum, full of artifacts representing the unique blending of Chinese and Western culture in Eastern Oregon.

Doc Hay and Lung On began their business by selling mining supplies and foodstuffs to the area's Chinese and white miners. As the community grew, the shop became a fully stocked general store featuring canned goods, notions, tobacco, bootleg whiskey, and many teas and foodstuffs imported from China. The museum contains hundreds of examples of the goods sold during those early days, as well as more than 1,000 Chinese herbs and Western medicines used by Doc Hay in his medical office, which was also housed in the building. Doc Hay was a master of "pulse diagnosis" and could, more often than not, detect an illness through light pressure at the wrist and prescribe an herbal treatment that worked.

Not only did the Kam Wah Chung & Co. building serve as a home, general store, and herbal medicine office, but it was also the social and religious headquarters for the Chinese community. Look for the Buddhist shrine and other religious objects blackened by years of incense smoke. Notice the bunk beds and the mix of cooking utensils in the kitchen, which served as a gathering spot for drinking, gambling, and sorting out business.

*Hours: May to Oct: Mon–Thurs 9am–5pm (closed noon–1pm), Sat–Sun 1pm–5pm. Closed rest of year.*
*Admission charged.*
*Directions: The museum is one block north of State Route 26, adjacent to the city park.*

### JOSEPH

### ■ Manuel Museum
400 N Main Street (PO Box 905)
Joseph, OR 97846
(541)432-7235

Founded by David Manuel, the state of Oregon's official sculptor for the Oregon Trail Celebration, the Manuel Museum houses one of the country's largest collections of Native American artifacts: war bonnets and peace pipes, battle shirts and coup-sticks, beaded bags, dresses and moccasins, more than 4,000 arrowheads, and other items honoring Chief Joseph and the Nez Perce Indians. Other museum offerings include an extensive wagon collection, a children's museum (where kids can dress in costumes and reenact history through play), Civil War memorabilia, John Wayne mementos, sleighs, coaches, a miniature western town, and numerous examples of the bronze sculptures that Manuel has become well known for creating.

Special programs include art demonstrations, foundry tours, and daily showings of a movie called *The Story of the Oregon Trail*.

*Hours: Daily 9am–dusk.*
*Admission charged.*
*Directions: The museum is on State Route 82 (N Main Street), one mile north of Wallowa Lake.*

## ■ Wallowa County Museum
110 S Main Street (PO Box 430)
Joseph, OR 97846
(541)432-6095

The Wallowa County Museum is housed in an ornate 1888 bank building that has done duty as a school, a private hospital, a newspaper office, a city hall, a library, and a social hall. Lovingly restored down to the intricately carved hinges on the outside door, the museum features artifacts from Wallowa County's past, including items related to early pioneers, settlers, and the Nez Perce people who originally lived here.

At 1pm each Wednesday during summer, the museum stages a reenactment of the Great Joseph Bank Robbery of October 1, 1896. Extra "holdups" occur on weekends when the city is hosting a celebration, such as the Chief Joseph Days Rodeo in July or the Rattlesnake and Bear Feed in September.

*Hours: Memorial Day to late Sept: Daily 10am–5pm. Closed rest of year.*
*Admission by donation.*
*Directions: The museum is on State Route 82 (S Main Street), one mile north of Wallowa Lake.*

## KERBY

## ■ Kerbyville Museum
24195 Redwood Highway (PO Box 34)
Kerby, OR 97531
(541)592-5252

If you're heading for the Oregon Caves down the road, it's tempting to pass right by the Kerbyville Museum. But if you do, you'll miss all seven of the jam-packed exhibit buildings.

The main building displays an impressive Native American artifact collection, toys, dolls, a wide assortment of musical instruments, and a case full of items donated by the sheriff, including an "Oregon boot" used in transporting prisoners and the brass knuckles taken from the Black Jacket Gang, a group of "very tough characters in Grants Pass." Back in the Ye Olde Country Store section are pottery jugs, miner's tools, cooking utensils, and a large selection from Bill Chanon's bottle opener collection.

Museum volunteers will gently remind you that there's "way more to see" in the other museum buildings. Believe them. Otherwise you'll miss the rock shop, the print shop, the tool shed, the miner's cabin, the schoolroom, the farm and logging equipment display, and beautiful hair wreath on the wall of the furnished 1873 Stith Naucke House.

*Hours: Daily 10am–5pm.*
*Admission charged.*
*Directions: The museum is right on Highway 199 (Redwood Highway) in Kerby.*

**KIMBERLY**

■ **John Day Fossil Beds National Monument Fossil Museum**
Eight miles west of Dayville (HCR 82, Box 126)
Kimberly, OR 97848
(541)987-2333

In the 1860s frontier minister Thomas Condon recognized the fossil beds at John Day, with their well-preserved record of plants and animals, as a "scientific treasure." Condon later became Oregon's first state geologist, and the north-central Oregon beds became a national monument. Today the John Day Fossil Beds National Monument is a 14,000-acre park made up of three units: the Sheep Rock Unit, the Painted Hills Unit, and the Clarno Unit.

Buried fossils are not commonly seen along the trails to the fossil beds, and visitors are limited to the trails within protected areas. So to be sure you get to see these amazing relics, head for this museum at the Sheep Rock Unit in Kimberly. The Fossil Museum, at the Sheep Rock Unit visitors center, offers indoor geological and paleontological exhibits and a variety of plant and animal fossils collected from the John Day River basin.

*Web site: www.nps.gov/joda*
*Hours: Memorial Day to Labor Day: Daily 9am–6pm. After Labor Day to Thanksgiving: Daily 9am–5pm. After Thanksgiving to Feb: Mon–Fri 9am–5pm. Closed rest of year.*
*Admission free.*
*Directions: The Sheep Rock Unit is at the intersection of State Routes 26 and 19, eight miles west of Dayville.*

## KLAMATH FALLS

■ **Favell Museum of Western Art and Indian Artifacts**
125 W Main Street (PO Box 165)
Klamath Falls, OR 97601
(541)882-9996

Now here's a place where they take western art and artifacts seriously.
The Native American artifact collection in the Favell Museum includes
more than 1,200 woven baskets, paintings, and pieces of pottery from
the Southwest; beautiful beading and quill work; and stone tools, carvings, ceremonial knives, and other early weapons. This section of the
museum also features more than 60,000 mounted arrowheads, including
the "world famous" fire opal arrowhead (found in the Nevada desert
back in 1912) and Monte Sherman's silver treasure from an abandoned
wagon train.

If all those neatly arranged artifacts don't wow you, mosey on over to
the western art section, which features the work of more than 300 artists,
including John Clymer, Charles Russell, and Ray Anderson. There are
more than 800 pieces in the collection: paintings, wood carvings, bronze
sculptures, photography, miniature dioramas, and that ever-popular
western specialty, taxidermy.

Don't forget to look in the walk-in vault, where you'll find a display
of more than 135 miniature working firearms, ranging from Gatling
guns to inch-long Colt .45s.

The museum sponsors an art show each year on the last weekend
in April.

*Hours: Mon–Sat 9:30am–5:30pm.*
*Admission charged.*
*Directions: The museum is at the south end of Klamath Falls, at the*
*Highway 97 interchange. Signs direct you to the museum from*
*the freeway.*

■ **Klamath County Museum**
1451 Main Street
Klamath Falls, OR 97601
(541)883-4209

If your trip includes a visit to both the Klamath County Museum and
the Fort Klamath Museum and Park (see listing), 42 miles north in Fort
Klamath, try to stop here first. The maps, photos, and artifacts in this
museum's Modoc Indian War exhibit provide a great overview of the
period between 1863 and 1890, when white settlers and U.S. government troops clashed repeatedly with the Modoc Indians.

Other exhibits focus on area's geology, logging, and agricultural
crops; the culture of the Klamath Indians; and the experiences of area

pioneers. Wildlife displays show a variety of birds, including pelicans (the county mascot), eagles, and owls, as well as a coyote and a rare albino porcupine in their natural habitats.

The museum features a crime corner complete with a jail cell, a slot machine, a moonshine still, and a photo from the 1920s showing the sheriff arresting some moonshiners with a still that looks much like the one displayed here.

You might be surprised to learn that the Klamath County Museum, along with many of the city's schools, homes, and downtown buildings, is heated by geothermally warmed water that gets piped around town. The free BTUs aren't a modern-day discovery: Local Native Americans and early pioneers used the hot springs for preparing food, for bathing and medicinal purposes, and for staying warm.

*Hours: June to Sept: Mon–Sat 9am–5:30pm. Oct to May: Mon–Sat 8am–4:30pm.*
*Admission charged. County residents free.*

*Directions: From northbound Highway 97, take the downtown exit and follow Klamath Avenue in the right lane to the end. Turn left and you'll see the museum on the left. From southbound Highway 97, follow 97 Business Route to the second full working traffic signal, turn right, drive under the overpass, and turn left at Spring Street. The museum is on the corner of Spring and Main Streets.*

## While You're in Klamath Falls:

The four-story Baldwin Hotel Museum contains original Victorian-era furniture. Many rooms in the 1906 building have been refurbished to depict or display items from old-time area businesses, including a general store, a wedding chapel, a theater, a sporting goods shop, the Crater Lake Creamery, and the photography studio of Maude Baldwin, whose dad was a state senator and the original owner of the hotel.

*Baldwin Hotel Museum, 31 Main Street, Klamath Falls, OR 97601; (541)883-4208. Hours: June to Sept: Tues–Sat 10am–4pm. Closed rest of year. Admission charged. Directions: From northbound Highway 97, take the downtown Klamath Falls exit and stay to the left. Turn left onto Second Street then left onto Main Street.*

## LAKEVIEW

### ■ Schminck Memorial Museum
128 South E Street
Lakeview, OR 97630
(541)947-3134

Dalph and Lula Schminck (with names like that, don't you love them already?) were descendants of prominent pioneer families and a great collecting pair. They filled their Lakeview bungalow with pioneer artifacts, antique furniture, farm tools, toys, dolls, and just about any other treasure a family or community member brought over. When they died in the 1960s, their home, already an official museum, was left in care of the local chapter of the Daughters of the American Revolution, which expanded and cared for the collection. Stop by the Schminck Memorial Museum to see handmade quilts and rugs, bustles, bows, parasols and other Victorian fashions, Native American baskets, saddles, hundreds of dolls, a barbed-wire display, and more than 150 examples of pressed-glass goblets.

*Hours: Feb to Nov: Tues–Sat 1pm–5pm. Closed rest of year. Admission charged. Directions: The museum is one block east of Highway 395 in Lakeview.*

## While You're in Lakeview:

Located in Lakeview, one of the highest-altitude towns in Oregon, the Lake County Museum features an eclectic collection of historical photographs, household items, old school desks, organs, arrowheads, moccasins, and other Native American artifacts, as well as typewriters, saddles, and assorted pioneer memorabilia.

*Lake County Museum, 118 South E Street, Lakeview, OR 97630; (541)947-2220. Hours: Mon–Fri 1pm–4:30pm, Sat 1pm–4pm. Admission charged. Directions: The museum is one block east of Highway 395 in Lakeview.*

## LINCOLN CITY

### ■ North Lincoln County Historical Museum
4907 SW Highway 101
Lincoln City, OR 97367
(541)996-6614

Lincoln City not only is home to the world's shortest river (the D River, about 120 feet long, depending on the tides) and Oregon's oldest covered bridge (the Upper Drift Creek Bridge), but it also is the site of the first Oregon honeymoon. As the story goes, missionaries Jason Lee and Cyrus Shepard, along with their brides of one month and a guide, came over the Old Elk Trail (now State Route 18) and camped for one week. The honeymooners "cured themselves of malaria and evangelized the Salmon River Indians." Sounds romantic, doesn't it?

The folks at the North Lincoln County Historical Museum can point you to a plaque commemorating that historic honeymoon. They'll also share their knowledge and gossip about the county's Native American population, pioneer settlements, and timber industry. Items on display include a deactivated Japanese horned mine that washed up on the beach in 1949, a model of a schooner like the one that was shipwrecked on the sands of Siletz Bay sometime in the mid–1800s, and lovely Native American basketry. The photography collection includes a 1916 picture showing Dovie Odom (the mother of former U.S. senator Mark Hatfield) walking across a suspension bridge to prove to her students that it was safe.

> *Hours: Tues–Sun noon–4pm.*
> *Admission free.*
> *Directions: From Highway 101, drive south just beyond Lincoln City to Taft. When you enter Taft, look for an IGA store on the right. The museum is next to the store.*

## MADRAS

### ■ Jefferson County Historical Society Museum
34 Southeast D Street
Madras, OR 97741
(541)475-3808

The Jefferson County Historical Society Museum is on the second floor of the old Madras city hall, built in 1917. On the first floor is the Jefferson County Extension Service, and out back is the old county jail, so you can learn a great deal about gardening, farming, and regional history all in one place.

As in many community museums, the collection here is somewhat eclectic. There are artifacts that came over the Oregon Trail, a variety of early toys and dolls, well-worn tools used in the area for ranching, farming, and mining, and fine clothing, furniture, and quilts from the turn of the century.

Sheriff Ham Perkins was kind enough to pass along to the museum a few slot machines "donated" to his department during an unannounced raid. Dr. Howard Turner, a Madras pioneer instrumental in the early days of the potato industry, contributed a buffalo rug and the complete furnishings of Dr. Victor Howard's optometry office. And local resident Doug McGoon was somehow persuaded that he should part with the cute Buster Brown outfit he wore as a five-year-old in 1909.

If you have time for a brief historical walking tour, ask for the flyer "A Walk Through Old Madras," which leads you past the first home in town to have indoor plumbing and running water. The home's owner led the petition to incorporate Madras, the flyer tells us, mostly to ensure the quality of the water supply to his home.

> *Hours: June to Sept: Tues–Fri 1pm–5pm.*
> *Admission free.*
> *Directions: From Highways 26 or 97 through Madras, head east on Southeast D Street. The museum is on the left in the old city hall building.*

## MEDFORD

■ **Southern Oregon History Center**
106 N Central Avenue
Medford, OR 97501
(541)773-6536

After the folks in Jacksonville refused to pay the Oregon & California
Railroad a $25,000 "bonus" so the train tracks would go through their
town, the railroad bypassed Jacksonville entirely and instead set up a station in Middle Ford, about 10 miles away. The name Middle Ford eventually got shortened to Medford, and today this is the largest city in
southern Oregon.

Given the city's beginnings, it seems appropriate that the theme of
the permanent exhibit at the Southern Oregon History Center is transportation. *Going Places* presents an interactive journey through the history and development of transportation in the Rogue Valley from 1826
to 1996. Along the way, you'll hear chirping birds in the wilderness area,
train sounds in the train tunnel, highway sounds along the interstate, and
first-person commentary about each portion of the exhibit. Visitors are
also welcome to climb aboard a covered wagon and sit inside a 1960s
Volkswagen Love Bug.

The travel timeline begins with the routes used by Native Americans, fur trappers, government explorers, and packers and includes major
artifacts such as a woven Indian basket and a replica of a trapper's camp,
complete with tools and skins. Stop at the Applegate Trail section to see
some of the Applegate family's personal belongings. Pull over in the Pioneer Period area to inspect its full-size, furnished prairie schooner replica,
stagecoach, blacksmith shop, and Studebaker horse-drawn carriage. Or
simply walk along the tracks of Tunnel 13 in the Railroad section.

The center is also the home of the Southern Oregon Historical
Society's research library, which contains historical photographs portraying subjects ranging from railroading to gold mining and street scenes
to studio portraits. The collection includes 10,000 glass plate negatives
and prints produced by noted pioneer photographer Peter Britt, best
known for taking the first photographs of Crater Lake National Park in
1874. Britt documented more than half a century of changing lifestyles
and landscapes in southwestern Oregon, and the changing exhibits on
the mezzanine level almost always include some of his photographs.

The center's special programs include a variety of family days, craft
demonstrations, and lectures.

> *Web site: www.sohs.org*
> *Hours: Mon–Fri 9am–5pm, Sat 1–5pm.*
> *Admission charged. Jackson County residents free.*
> *Directions: From I-5, take exit 27 and head west on Barnett Road. Turn*
> *north on Riverside Avenue, then west (SW) on Sixth Street. The*

*center is on the corner of Sixth Street and N Central Avenue, in the former J. C. Penney department store building.*

## MILL CITY

### ■ Canyon Life Museum
143 Wall Street
Mill City, OR 97360
(503)897-4088

The Canyon Life Museum's exhibits describe life in the dense forests of the North Santiam Canyon from the late 1800s through the mid-1950s. According to the museum's 10-foot-long topographic map, those thick forests and steep canyon walls kept out all but the most determined homesteaders until the railroad showed up in 1888, enabling loggers, miners, and even farmers to move into canyon areas that were once home solely to wildlife and the Santiam band of the Kalapuya Indians.

Most of the exhibits portray the lives of loggers and their families. There's a huge stump with springboard holes, a forest floor littered with loggers' equipment, and a replica of a logging-camp home, with a mannequin of a logger's wife looking out the window at the cookhouse, the bachelor quarters, and stumps of Douglas fir trees. Outside the building is logging equipment ("iron") that's too big to fit inside.

*Web site: www.wvi.com/~sherryp/santiam.htm*
*Hours: June to Aug: Wed–Sun 1pm–5pm. Closed rest of year.*
*Admission by donation.*
*Directions: Take State Route 22 from Bend or Salem to Mill City. Turn south at the CITY CENTER sign and turn left on Wall Street, just before the bridge.*

## MILWAUKIE

### ■ Milwaukie Museum
3737 SE Adams Street
Milwaukie, OR 97222
(503)659-5780

The small Milwaukie Museum was once the George Wise family farmhouse, built in 1865. United Grocers Inc. purchased the property and donated the home to the Milwaukie Historical Society, which then had the farmhouse moved to this site.

Inside are artifacts belonging to early settlers as well as a wide variety of family heirlooms, including a big rope bed that came across the country on a covered wagon, spinning wheels, woodworking tools, desks, lamps, and toys. The museum also displays two interesting doll collections. One handmade set is dressed in costumes from around the world, while the other features more than two dozen dolls made of dried avocado pits.

Outside the museum is "Old No. 3," the only surviving horse-drawn streetcar of the type originally used in Portland around 1872.

*Hours: Sat–Sun 11am–3pm.*
*Admission free.*
*Directions: From Highway 224 (the Milwaukie Expressway), turn north*
*    on 37th Street, then turn right on SE Adams Street.*

## MOLALLA

### ■ Molalla Museum Complex
616 S Molalla Avenue
Molalla, OR 97038
(503)266-5571

There are two very different historic houses in the Molalla Museum Complex. The 1859 Dibble House, the oldest home in town, is a finely crafted New England saltbox with fir and cedar. The Vonder Ahe House, relocated to the complex in 1972, is an early farmhouse that served as both a home and a stagecoach stopover point in the Carus District, halfway between Oregon City and Molalla. Collections on display in the houses include quilts, vintage photos and fashions, farm machinery, Native American artifacts, toys, households furnishings, pottery, and carefully preserved Oregon linen.

Special events include an annual quilt show that begins on Mother's Day and an apple festival held on the second Saturday in October.

*Hours: March to Dec: Sun 1pm–3pm. Closed rest of year.*
*Admission by donation.*
*Directions: From the intersection of Highways 213 and 211, head east on*
*    Highway 211 (Main Street), then south on Molalla Avenue. The*
*    museum is about six blocks south of the intersection of Main Street*
*    and Molalla Avenue.*

## MONMOUTH

### ■ Jensen Arctic Museum
Western Oregon State College
590 W Church Street
Monmouth, OR 97361
(503)838-8468

The Jensen Arctic Museum invites visitors to "visit the Arctic in Oregon." Is this a unique cold spot on the Oregon landscape? No, it's simply where Dr. Paul Jensen, dubbed Angyalik ("captain of the ship") by an Eskimo council of elders, lived—and where he decided to share his enthusiasm and knowledge of the Arctic people from Alaska, Canada, and Europe.

A taxidermied polar bear at the Jensen Arctic Museum

Jensen first learned about Eskimo culture in 1919, when he was in grade school in Denmark. The friendships he made with the six Eskimo children in his class sparked a lifelong interest in the Arctic experience. As an adult, he spent more than 25 years living and working with Eskimo people in Alaska, Canada, and Greenland. Along the way he amassed more than 4,000 objects relating to Arctic wildlife and the Arctic cultural experience, everything from soapstone sculpture to a taxidermied 1,500-pound Kodiak bear. In 1985, when his collection became too large to display at home, Jensen established this museum on the campus of Western Oregon State College, where he taught educational psychology.

"You'd simply mention an item in the museum," says museum director Mariana Mace, "and 'Dr. Paul,' as his friends called him, would tell you a wonderful story about the person who gave him that object or explain how an Eskimo person might use that item in daily life." Jensen died in 1994, but by then the museum had grown to encompass the Arctic collections of more than 65 other people. Now the museum's volunteers are the ones who'll tell you that the four-foot food trays on display were used to hold big, messy chunks of fatty *muktuk* (blubber) and the berry combs were used each fall to gather cranberries, salmonberries, and blueberries, as they speculate about what it might be like to ride in a 27-foot walrus-skin boat.

To explain how people get around in the ice and snow of the North, the museum recently created a transportation exhibit featuring boats of the north (umiaks and kayaks) along with sleds and snowshoes and a rare ice crampon made from walrus ivory. Other exhibits feature ivory artwork, more than 500 objects made from walrus tusks, and taxidermied examples of arctic wildlife, including wolves, elk, foxes, and Jensen's dear old friend, "Henry" the musk ox.

Each summer the museum sponsors an art exhibit featuring Alaska Native artwork and celebrates the museum's birthday with a week of special events.

*Hours: Wed–Sat 10am–4pm.*
*Admission by donation.*
*Directions: The museum is on the corner of W Church and Stadium*
*Streets, a half-mile off Highway 99 W, on the campus of Western*
*Oregon State College.*

### MORO

■ **Sherman County Historical Museum**
200 Dewey Street (PO Box 173)
Moro, OR 97039
(541)565-3232

North-central Oregon's Sherman County is bounded by four rivers: the Columbia to the north, the John Day to the east, the Deschutes on the west, and Buck Hollow Creek on the south. This "land between the rivers" was originally called Fulton, after the pioneer Fulton family, but was later renamed Sherman in honor of General William Tecumseh Sherman of Civil War fame.

The Sherman County Historical Museum owns more than 12,000 artifacts that tell the story of the area's settlement and growth. Featured exhibits include artifacts from the Tenino Indians, farm equipment, household furnishings, toys, clothes, and memorabilia belonging to the county's early white settlers.

The *Oregon Trails, Rails, and Roads* exhibit uses Native American artifacts, photographs, and objects from the settlement period to illustrate how the local Tenino Indians traveled through the area and how explorers and settlers made their way to the area. This exhibit offers kids a chance to make rubbings of early petroglyphs, dress up in early pioneer clothing, and climb on a wooden pony named Goldie. Wheat, Sherman County's major crop, is celebrated with an exhibit that includes ancient carbonized wheat kernels from Turkey, scientific tools and equipment from the local research station where crop varieties are developed, and a data transmission monitor that lets visitors download information about crop prices and weather conditions.

Other items on display include military items from the Civil War through the Vietnam War, an 1860s stagecoach, a well-stocked blacksmith shop, and needlework from the turn of the century.

Special programs include annual in-county tours along historic trails and roads, guest lectures, and demonstrations.

*Hours: May to Oct: Daily 10am–5pm. Closed rest of year.*
*Admission charged.*
*Directions: Take I-84 to Highway 97 and head south for 18 miles from*
*Biggs to Moro. The museum is next to the city park.*

## MOUNT ANGEL

### ■ Mount Angel Abbey Museum
1 Abbey Drive
St. Benedict, OR 97373
(503)845-3030

The grounds of the century-old Mount Angel Abbey and Seminary at St. Benedict offer great views of the Willamette Valley and the Cascade foothills. Display cases in the rare-book room at the library, designed by the well-known Finnish architect Alvar Aalto, offer a glimpse into the monastery's extensive book collection—but for views of a quite different nature, head for the "collectabilia" (as one monk calls it) at the Mount Angel Abbey Museum.

Until recently, all the church-related artifacts were displayed unceremoniously cheek by jowl with the five taxidermied bears, the bison, the deer, the raccoon, and the many other stuffed specimens left over from the abbey's natural science classes. Now the museum is a bit more orderly, with the prayer books, religious garments, and crown of thorns separated from the military memorabilia and the 11-inch ear of corn grown on the abbey farm in 1950.

Where did it all come from? "Some people leave us stuff in their wills," one monk said, "because they know monasteries have staying power. In fact, the abbey's "mother house" in Europe is 800 years old, and it has a museum too. So that's how the museum came to own a cross-section of a piece of underwater electric cable, a bullet found on the battlefield "just days" after Custer's famous last battle, and a model of a sailing ship that won first prize at the 1939 World's Fair.

But then there's the really strange stuff, like the taxidermied eight-legged calf born in Tillamook, Oregon, in 1932. While shocking to see, the calves aren't so unusual. During a 10-year period, the monastery respectfully turned down donations of at least three sets of two-headed calves and numerous taxidermied house cats.

What makes this museum a favorite, though, is the collection of vintage hairballs. One cardboard box holds five large, brown, smooth hairballs the size of baseballs, each taken from the stomach of a different cow. Nearby is a hairy yam-shaped thing that weighs in at two and a half pounds, an awesome hairball found in the stomach of a 300-pound hog killed at a Portland meatpacking plant on September 19, 1941. The meat inspector on duty declared it to be the largest hairball ever found. It's kept here, one monk admitted, "because it's another example of God's creations." Amen—and I'll pass on the pork chops.

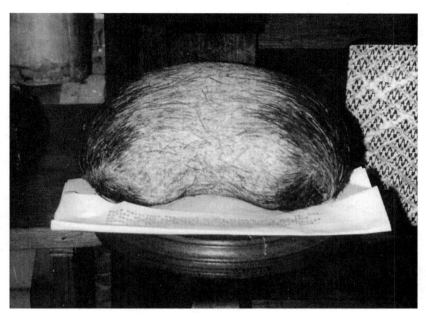

This giant hairball was found in the stomach of a 300-pound hog

*Hours: Daily 10am–11:30am and 1pm–5pm.*
*Admission by donation.*
*Directions: From I-5, take the Woodburn-Silverton exit and drive through*
*Woodburn on Route 214 to Mount Angel. Follow the signs to the*
*abbey.*

## MYRTLE POINT

### ■ Coos County Logging Museum
705 Maple Street
Myrtle Point, OR 97458
(541)572-1014

Would you know a "nose bag" or a "soogan" if you saw one? You'll learn
that a "nose bag" is a logger's lunch pail and a "soogan" a bedroll if you
visit the Coos County Logging Museum, whose mission is the preservation of logging lingo, lifestyle, and tools and artifacts. Look for the log
brands, the "woman's power saw," and the display dedicated to the oxen
and horses that hauled timber in the days before trucks, tractors, and hel-
icopters took over.

Housed in a 1910 building that's a scaled-down replica of the
Mormon Tabernacle, the museum features more than 100 photographs
depicting early logging camp life, logging trains, and the assorted
methods loggers used to move the huge trees around (and out of) the
woods. A recent addition to the museum is the Alexander Benjamin

Warnock Collection: nine large reliefs, carved in myrtlewood, depicting various logging scenes.

In addition to logging memorabilia, the museum displays early blacksmith tools, cookhouse crockery, branding tools, and other community artifacts, including a huge bear trap made by pioneer blacksmith Henry Hermann.

> *Hours: Memorial Day to Labor Day: Mon–Sat 10am–4pm, Sun*
>    *1pm–4pm. Closed rest of year.*
> *Admission by donation.*
> *Directions: The museum is on the corner of Seventh and Maple Streets.*
>    *Look for it from State Route 42.*

## NEWBERG

### ■ Hoover-Minthorn House Museum
115 S River Street
Newberg, OR 97132
(503)538-6629

Herbert Hoover served as the 31st president of the United States, but from 1885 to 1889 "Bertie," as his friends called him, was just a kid hanging around Newberg, Oregon. In 1885 the 11-year-old Hoover was living with relatives in Iowa following the death of both his parents when his uncle, Dr. Henry Minthorn, invited him out west to become part of the Minthorn family. Young Hoover came west by train, enrolled in grammar school, and was raised according to the Quaker faith. (When Minthorn moved the family to Salem in 1889, Hoover went along, ending his stay in Newberg.)

The Minthorns' house is now the oldest house still standing in Newberg, and on August 10, 1955, Herbert Hoover came "home" to dedicate the building as the Hoover-Minthorn House Museum. It was his 81st birthday. Inside the museum, his boyhood room is furnished with the actual bedroom set he used as a child. Other rooms contain both original furniture from the Minthorn home and period items gathered from homes in and around Newberg.

The land surrounding the museum is now called Hoover Park. The front lawn is used for an ice cream social and craft show during Newberg's annual Old Fashioned Festival each July, and a quilt show is held here each May.

> *Hours: March to Nov: Wed–Sun 1pm–4pm. Dec and Feb: Sat–Sun*
>    *1pm–4pm. Closed rest of year.*
> *Admission charged.*
> *Directions: From Highway 99W (which is one way), turn left on S River*
>    *Street.*

# NEWPORT

## ■ Oregon Coast History Center
545 SW Ninth Street
Newport, OR 97365
(541)265-7509

The collections of the Oregon Coast History Center are spread between two buildings: the Log Cabin Museum and the 1895 Victorian-style Burrows House next door.

The Log Cabin Museum features maritime, forestry, and agricultural items, as well as artifacts from the Siletz Indians, including baby cradles, a

Lulu Miller (Nye) was crowned Miss Electricity in 1891

rare whalebone adze, and an unusual beaded dance skirt with a fringe of thimbles along the bottom that did double-duty as decoration and bells. Maritime memorabilia includes items salvaged from the *Blue Magpie* (the last major ship to go down in the area), the wheel from the steam-powered ferry *Newport,* and an ingenious foghorn made from an old tuba and a set of leather bellows.

A highlight of the informative *Bridges of Lincoln County* display includes a toothpick model of the Yaquina Bay Bridge. Completed in 1936, the bridge (not the toothpick model) was the last link on the Oregon Coast Highway and took more than two years to build. Joining forces, local civic groups built the toothpick model in (only) 142 hours. Their design, adapted from blueprints provided by the Oregon State Highway Division, used six boxes of toothpicks and a quart of glue. (Total out-of-pocket cost: $5.)

Exhibits in the Burrows House change quite a bit, but mostly they explore the area's rise as a tourism mecca and celebrate some of the more notable local citizens. One favorite was Lulu Miller (Nye), selected as Miss Electricity in 1891. In her formal portrait, she's draped in a string of light bulbs and also sports bulbs on her crown and scepter. She was a par-ticularly big hit one evening when electric lights were being used at an opera house in Independence, Oregon, for the first time. "Copper plates on the stage and in the soles of Miss Miller's shoes," the local newspaper reported, "caused the electric current to flash through the wires con-cealed in the folds of her clothing. It was a beautiful sight."

*Hours: Summer: Tues–Sun 10am–5pm. Rest of year: Tues–Sun 11am–4pm.*

*Admission by donation.*

*Directions: From southbound Highway 101, turn left on Fall Street (just past the Chamber of Commerce), then left on SW Ninth Street. The museum is on the right.*

### ■ Ripley's Believe It or Not! Museum
250 SW Bay Boulevard
Newport, OR 97365
(541)265-2206

Robert L. Ripley began collecting and promoting the strange and unusual back in the 1920s. Now there are hokey but oddly entertaining Ripley's Believe It or Not! Museums in dozens of cities throughout the world.

Newport's version invites visitors to "witness" water poured from a gourd that no one is holding, marvel at a fountain where water goes up but never comes down, and "experience" the wonders of nature that fill the Odditorium. For the truly brave of heart, there's a chance to chat with a ghost, experience an earthquake, and come face to face with a "real" shrunken head.

There's lots more—Believe It or Not!

*Hours: June 15 to Labor Day: Daily 9am–8pm. After Labor Day to June
14: Daily 10am–5pm.*
*Admission charged.*
*Directions: The museum is just off Highway 101 in Mariner Square, on
Newport's historic bayfront.*

## ■ Wax Works
250 SW Bay Boulevard
Newport, OR 97365
(541)265-2206

Calling itself a living museum, the Wax Works features a wide variety of
static and animated wax figures, including historical figures, celebrities
from the entertainment world, Bigfoot, and a wide variety of freaks,
monsters, and space creatures. A bit out of place, but interesting on its
own, is the short film about the eruption of Mount St. Helens.

*Hours: June 15 to Labor Day: Daily 9am–8pm. After Labor Day to June
14: Daily 10am–5pm.*
*Admission charged.*
*Directions: The Wax Works is just off Highway 101 in Mariner Square, on
Newport's historic bayfront, near the Ripley's Believe It or Not!
Museum.*

## NORTH BEND

## ■ Coos County Historical Society Museum
1220 Sherman Avenue
North Bend, OR 97459
(541)756-6320

You'll know you've reached the Coos County Historical Society
Museum when you see the big locomotive parked out front. To be precise, it's Locomotive 104, built for the Coos Bay Lumber Company in
the early 1920s. To hear how this mighty engine sounded when it was
pulling a train of cars loaded with fresh-cut logs, push the button on the
information panel and stand back.

Inside the museum are several changing exhibits and displays on
local history, including items relating to Native American culture, early
pioneer experiences, logging, and mining.

*Hours: Summer: Mon–Sat 10am–4pm. Rest of year: Tues–Sat
10am–4pm.*
*Admission charged.*
*Directions: From southbound Highway 101, the museum is on Highway
101 (Sherman Avenue), just past the entrance to the north end of
North Bend, in Simpson Park.*

## NYSSA

### ■ Oregon Trail Agricultural Museum
117 Good Street
Nyssa, OR 97913
(541)372-5069

Early farm and ranch equipment used in Treasure Valley is displayed at the Oregon Trail Agricultural Museum, along with restored sheep wagons, historical photographs of farms in Nyssa and the surrounding area, and an assortment of items related to the Oregon Trail. Of special interest is the large rock marked with an R that you'll most likely find propped in an old metal tin near a worn wagon wheel. The stone was one of the crude route markers set out along the Oregon Trail in the 1840s.

The museum is housed in a building that once served as a farmer's feed, seed, and mill business. Other local historic buildings open for tours include the Green Lantern Saloon, which has its original carved wooden back bar (which came around the Horn by ship to San Francisco, and across land by wagon to Nyssa), the Hotel Western, and the blacksmith shop.

*Hours: Summer: Fri–Sat 10am–5pm, Sun 1pm–5pm. Closed rest of year. Admission charged.*
*Directions: Westbound Highways 26 and 20 turn into Main Street in Nyssa. Drive through Nyssa on Main; turn right on First Street. The museum is on the corner of Good and Second Streets.*

## OAKLAND

### ■ Oakland Museum
130 Locust Street
Oakland, OR 97462
(541)459-4531 (Oakland City Hall)

In the 1870s, after the Oregon & California Railroad was built through Oakland, the town became a thriving agricultural and shipping center for prunes, hops, turkeys, hogs, sheep, cattle, and other products. Today the two-block business district contains many 1890s brick buildings as well as the Oakland Museum, which displays a wide variety of artifacts from the area's past. Exhibits feature household furniture, a fully stocked general store, a post office, toys, medical instruments, vintage clothing, farm tools, photographs, and displays about the local railroad and logging activities.

*Hours: Daily 1pm–4pm.*
*Admission by donation.*

**While You're in Oakland:**
At the Oakland Museum, pick up a walking-tour brochure and get directions to the two historic cemeteries. The Old Town and Masonic Cemetery is one mile north of town, while the Cedar Hill Cemetery is one mile west.

*Directions: From southbound I-5, take the Oakland exit. Follow Old
Highway 99 into town and turn left on Locust Street.*

ONTARIO

■ **Four Rivers Cultural Center Museum**
676 SW Fifth Avenue
Ontario, OR 97914
(888)211-1222 or (541)889-8191

Located on the campus of Treasure Valley Community College, the Four
Rivers Cultural Center was conceived as a memorial to the Japanese
Americans interned during World War II and to the Japanese American
soldiers who served throughout the war. The project soon broadened sig-
nificantly to include tributes to the Northern Paiute Indians, Basques,
Hispanics, and other ethnic groups that settled in the western part of
Treasure Valley. Now the facility comprises a conference center, a per-
forming arts theater, a Japanese garden, and a museum.

The Four Rivers Cultural Center Museum presents the history of
the Snake, Owyhee, Malheur, and Payette River region, from the earliest
inhabitants to the present day. Exhibits feature films, photographs, artifacts, full-scale dioramas including an authentic sheepherder's camp, and
hands-on activities.

The exhibit in Gallery I, *The People, the Land, the Water,* presents the
story of several generations of people who have lived on the land. The
exhibit begins with a full-scale diorama of a Northern Paiute camp and
proceeds with displays that describe the arrival of cattlemen and settlers,
the history of irrigation in the area, and the experiences of Japanese
Americans in World War II internment camps. Along the way visitors can
inspect an early mail coach, examine a working water wheel, or stroll
through an irrigation pipe.

Gallery II's exhibit, *Community and Culture,* presents vignettes from
the lives of Native Americans, European Americans, Japanese Americans,
Hispanic and Basque Americans to illustrate various themes. A diorama
of a Hispanic family moving their belongings in their pickup truck illu-
minates the theme of origins. A re-created barracks from a Japanese
American internment camp explores the theme of confronting and over-
coming barriers, while the theme of community is represented by a
Basque boardinghouse.

In addition to its permanent exhibits, the museum has a gallery that
features changing history, science, and art exhibitions.

*Web site: www.4rcc.com*
*Hours: Mon–Sat 10am–6pm, Sun noon–6pm.*
*Admission charged.*
*Directions: The museum is on the campus of Treasure Valley Community
College in downtown Ontario, just across the Snake River from*

*Idaho. From I-84, take the Ontario exit and head west on Idaho Avenue. Turn left on Oregon Avenue, right on SW Fourth Avenue, and left on Fifth Street. The center is at the intersection of SW Fifth Avenue and Fifth Street.*

## OREGON CITY

### ■ Clackamas County Museum of History
211 Tumwater Drive
Oregon City, OR 97045
(503)655-5574

In 1843, Clackamas County was a very big place: From south of Oregon City, it extended north to Alaska, west to the Willamette River, and east to the crest of the Rocky Mountains. Today the county's boundaries are a bit narrower, but that doesn't put a damper on the breadth of history documented in the Clackamas County Museum of History, a large three-story building overlooking Willamette Falls in Oregon City.

Exhibits feature Native American artifacts, medical and surgical tools, a variety of alarming pre-patent medicines (some include strychnine among their ingredients!) in a fully stocked pharmacy, and a wagon that came over the Oregon Trail "clear full," according to one museum volunteer, "with all types of things folks tried to bring out here." The museum also features displays describing electricity and how the falls just outside the museum were used to generate power for local industries.

Be sure to visit the nine-foot statue of Lady Justice that now stands in the museum, balancing the scales of justice. During the 1890s she perched atop the county courthouse; after the courthouse burned, she was rescued and later restored. Admission to the museum includes entrance to the 1908 Stevens Crawford Museum (at 603 Sixth Street, a historic home featuring period furniture, dresses, dolls, china, and kitchen items).

*Hours: Mon–Fri 10am–4pm, Sat–Sun and holidays 1–5pm.*
*Admission charged; includes admission to the Stevens Crawford Museum.*
*Directions: The museum is a half-mile south of Highway 99E, right above Willamette Falls.*

### ■ End of the Oregon Trail Interpretive Center
1726 Washington Street
Oregon City, OR 97045
(503)657-9336

As you approach from the highway, it looks as if there's a wagon train up ahead, but those big wagons are actually the three cleverly disguised main buildings of the End of the Oregon Trail Interpretive Center. Inside, artifacts, displays, and live demonstrations recall the arduous journey undertaken by hundreds of thousands of people intent on reaching Oregon City, the end of the Oregon Trail.

Visiting the museum is as close as you can get to experiencing a journey on the Oregon Trail. "Trail guides" dressed in period clothes welcome "travelers" to the Missouri Provisioners Depot, help them prepare for their journey, and say final good-byes. Then it's off to the Cascade Theater, where a multimedia presentation, complete with surround-sound and special effects, re-creates elements of the trip west. The final stop: the Oregon City Gallery, with artifacts that include a Barlow Road toll booth, clothing, tools, and household items as well as a variety of changing exhibits.

The center's large Willamette Trades and Craft Workshop has a wide variety of hands-on heritage activities. You can grind grain and coffee, leaf through old "teaching technique" books, or play with wooden toys from the 1800s. Or you can spend a few moments watching a demonstration of a 19th-century trade or craft.

Outdoors, you can follow the Luelling Trail to the heritage gardens, filled with heirloom vegetation such as flax, pioneer cosmos, antique roses, vegetables, fruits, and herbs. Trail guides stationed in the gardens describe how settlers and pioneers planted, cultivated, and harvested these plants to use in cooking, dyeing, and concocting home remedies. The guides also point out the historic markers in the gardens acknowledging the end of the Oregon Trail.

In addition to the regular living-history demonstrations, the center presents two changing exhibits each month: the *Pioneer Family of the Month* exhibit and the *Quilt of the Month* display, which presents an heirloom quilt that, in some cases, was sewn by someone who crossed the Oregon Trail.

Special programs and events include pioneer encampments and a summer-long outdoor historical pageant featuring music, dance, and drama. During the winter holiday season, St. Nicholas arrives on—what else?—a covered wagon.

*Web site: www.teleport.com/~eotic*
*Hours: Mon–Sat 9am–5pm, Sun 10am–5pm.*
*Admission charged.*
*Directions: Take eastbound I-84 to southbound I-205; then take exit 10 and look for the giant covered wagons. Or take southbound I-5 to northbound I-205; then take exit 10 and look for the wagons.*

## PARKDALE

### ■ Hutson Museum
4967 Baseline Road (PO Box 501)
Parkdale, OR 97041
(541)352-6808

Jesse Hutson's house burned down in the 1950s. He rebuilt it and, with his wife Winifred, began filling the basement with arrowheads, rocks,

Native American artifacts, and pretty much any odd thing his neighbors brought over.

Now everything from the Hutsons' basement is in the Hutson Museum, from vintage street lamps and Civil War memorabilia to rare Native American hunting and fishing tools made from obsidian, agate, and local basalt. The rock collection is the main attraction, though: thousands of cabochons, fossils, geodes, mineral specimens, and polished pieces of petrified wood, displayed in dozens of showcases and old watch racks.

Hutson had more than 1,500 arrowheads—as well as a good sense of humor. He arranged many of his arrowheads in framed scenes depicting images such as Mount Hood, a Conestoga wagon, and a big bug. Hutson also set a table with a full-course meal made entirely of rocks and minerals cooked up from his collection. The meatballs are lava and the coffee cup is filled with sun stones and obsidian taken from an anthill.

The Hutson Museum sponsors a summer festival each July and is part of a two-acre historical complex at the end of the 22-mile Mount Hood Railroad line, one of the few remaining U.S. railroads operating on a switchback. The museum was constructed in the style of the nearby Ries-Thompson House, which was built around 1900 and is the oldest remaining home in Parkdale. The property is surrounded by a boardwalk and orchards and offers a breathtaking view of Mount Hood. The U.S. Forest Service has built a small amphitheater here for lectures and demonstrations.

*Hours: April to June, Sept to Oct: Wed–Fri 11am–4pm, Sat–Sun*
  *11:30am–5:30pm. July to Aug: Tues–Fri 11am–4pm, Sat–Sun*
  *11:30am–5:30pm. Closed rest of year.*
*Admission charged.*
*Directions: From Hood River, take southbound State Route 35 (the*
  *Mountain Loop Highway). Turn right onto Cooper Spur Road and*
  *then right onto Baseline Road. The museum is on Baseline Road in*
  *Parkdale.*

## PENDLETON

### ■ Pendleton Round-Up Hall of Fame
1205 SW Court Street (PO Box 609)
Pendleton, OR 97801
(541)278-0815

Each year, in the second full week of September, the folks in Pendleton put on the classic Pendleton Round-Up. It's a first-class rodeo featuring wild-horse races, wild-cow milking, and baton races in addition to the steer roping, bull riding, and other traditional cowboy competitions.

Begun by local farmers and ranchers back in 1910 and now the second-oldest rodeo in the country, the Round-Up has its own colorful history, traditions, and lore. To the delight of cowboys and city slickers alike, the Round-Up's heritage is well documented at the Pendleton Round-Up Hall of Fame, a museum tucked under the arena grandstand.

Inside the museum, almost every inch of space is covered with Round-Up memorabilia. You'll see angora riding chaps, rodeo clown outfits, bullwhips, silver-encrusted prize saddles, and pictures of every single rodeo queen and court since 1910. Without a doubt, though, almost everyone's favorite display is smack-dab in the middle of the room. The fierce-looking animal with his teeth bared and his legs kicked up in the air is Warpaint, a horse that rodeo contestants claim was one of the toughest to ride. To get an idea what kind of damage a bucking horse can do, examine the photos in the *Rodeo Wrecks* photo display of arena accidents that, years later, can still make cowboys and cowgirls wince and limp.

Hall of Fame inductees honored here include local ranchers, community volunteers, and rodeo circuit riders who've performed over the years at the Round-Up, including Monty Montana, a trick rider who went on to Hollywood and donated his sparkling red show outfit to the museum. In addition to the accomplished cowboys, the Hall of Fame acknowledges cowgirls who rode at Pendleton until 1929, when Round-Up officials banned women contestants after one unlucky cowgirl, Bonnie McCarroll, was killed in a fall from a bucking horse.

Like many community museums, the Round-Up Hall of Fame is run by volunteers. Don't be shy with your questions; many volunteers are old-timers who've never missed a Round-Up in their lives and have great stories to share.

*Hours: Memorial Day to Sept 30: Daily 10am–4pm. Closed rest of year. Admission by donation.*
*Directions: From I-84, take exit 207 and follow the signs to the rodeo grounds. The Hall of Fame is under the arena grandstand.*

■ **Tamastslikt Cultural Institute Museum**
72789 Highway 331 (PO Box 638)
Pendleton, OR 97801
(541)966-9748

At the same time a proposal for a casino/museum/lodging facility next to I-84 was being considered by the Confederated Tribes of the Umatilla Indian Reservation, the state of Oregon began planning a series of interpretive centers to commemorate the sesquicentennial of the Oregon Trail. The Umatilla reservation was one proposed site. While some thought it ironic that the Confederated Tribes would build a monument to an event that proved devastating to their culture, others realized that tribal control of the center would ensure that the Native American perspective on the Oregon Trail story would finally be conveyed.

Three plateau huckleberry baskets from the Institute's collection

Now the Tamastslikt Cultural Institute Museum (*tamastslikt,* pronounced "ta-MUST-ah-luck," means "interpret" in the Walla Walla language) includes a changing gallery space, the Coyote Theater, and permanent exhibits that employ ambient sound, voices, historical photographs, and video footage to tell the history of the Cayuse, Umatilla, and Walla Walla tribes along the Oregon Trail. Set back (though visible) from the highway, the location of the 45,000-square-foot redwood and basalt building was chosen to maximize the views of the Umatilla River and the Blue Mountains.

The museum's three galleries are organized around the themes "We Were," "We Are," and "We Will Be." In "We Were," illustrations, artifacts, and sounds depict the seasonal lifestyle typical of the tribes who had lived on the Columbia Plateau for centuries. One exhibit features full-size horses and riders in a panoramic scene celebrating the horse-oriented culture of the Cayuse, Umatilla, and Walla Walla people. Several other exhibits tell the story of the Oregon Trail from the Native American perspective, discussing the tribes' first interaction with emigrants, new religions, forced education, and the loss of their native language.

The "We Are" gallery tells the story of contemporary Native life and present-day challenges, addressing such issues as the importance of veterans and the warrior tradition, the extensive efforts to restore the salmon population, modern multicultural lifestyles, the development of a tribal economy, and participation in events such as the Pendleton Round-Up.

Exhibits in the "We Will Be" gallery highlight the tribes' renewal of culture and projects that allow contemporary Native Americans to live between two worlds.

The museum's artifact collection, carefully assembled over the past five years, contains more than 300 Native American pieces, including early tools, children's games, fine beadwork, bonnets, horse regalia, and a rare painted buffalo robe featuring the figures of 23 horses and riders in blues, reds, and greens.

*Web site: www.ucinet.com/~umatribe/tamust.html*
*Hours: Daily 9am–5pm.*
*Admission charged.*
*Directions: The museum is four miles east of Pendleton. From I-84, take exit 216 and drive north on Highway 331 for four miles.*

### ■ Umatilla County Historical Society Museum
108 SW Frazier Avenue
Pendleton, OR 97801
(541)276-0012

Housed in a refurbished 1909 railway depot, the Umatilla County Historical Society Museum traces the history of the county from the days when the Cayuse, Nez Perce, Umatilla, and Walla Walla Indians lived here to the days of sheepherding, farming, and cattle ranches. Artifacts commemorating the days when the Oregon Trail passed through the county are displayed, along with photographs, pioneer items, and an exhibit on the area's sheep industry and the success of the Pendleton Woolen Mills. A 10-foot-long marble shoeshine stand with related memorabilia from early merchants has been installed in the depot, along with a working railroad telegraph system. Permanent exhibits are supplemented with changing shows throughout the year.

*Hours: Tues–Sat 10am–4pm.*
*Admission free.*
*Directions: From I-84, take exit 210 and drive north toward Pendleton's city center. Turn left at Isaac Avenue and right on Main Street. Cross the railroad tracks and turn left into the museum parking lot.*

### PHILOMATH

### ■ Benton County Historical Museum
1101 Main Street
Philomath, OR 97370
(541)929-6230

From 1867 until 1929, the imposing Georgian-style brick building that houses the Benton County Historical Museum was home to Philomath College. Even though college classes no longer meet here, it's still a great place to learn about local logging and agricultural history and the story of the Kalapuya Indians, who once lived in the area. In addition, the museum's art gallery features monthly shows by Oregon artists.

This spice box, circa 1865, was used to carry spices across the Oregon Trail

Historical items permanently on display include Ella and Andrew Kershaw's extensive collection of Native American artifacts, delicate inkwells, antique typesetting and printing equipment, a wonderful collection of quilts, dozens of vintage state license plates, and 40 carefully selected items from Cecil Hayden's horseshoe, bit, and spur collection. Logging artifacts range from classic photos to a giant circular-saw blade almost five feet in diameter.

The museum also has an exhibit detailing the history and impact of Camp Adair, the training site established by the U.S. War Department during World War II on 50,000 acres north of Corvallis. The facility became the second-largest city in Oregon, uprooting families, relocating cemeteries, rerouting train tracks, and completely erasing the town of Wells.

*Hours: Tues–Sat 10am–4:30pm.*
*Admission free.*
*Directions: From downtown Corvallis, take westbound Highway 34 to Philomath. The museum is one and a half blocks past Philomath's second traffic light, on the right.*

## PORTLAND

### ■ American Advertising Museum
5035 SE 24th Avenue
Portland, OR 97202
(503)226-0000

Marshall McLuhan predicted that "historians and archaeologists will one day discover that the ads of our time are the richest and most faithful reflections that any society ever made of its entire range of activities." Some folks involved with the advertising industry in Portland have already figured this out. To help the rest of us see how advertising reflects—and sometimes changes—American culture, the Portland Advertising Federation created the American Advertising Museum and stuffed it full of wonderful examples of ads from the early 1700s through today.

The museum houses the industry's most comprehensive collection of advertising and business artifacts, everything from a neon Pegasus, the flying red horse that represented Mobil gasoline, to an original set of those dancing California Raisins made famous by Portland Claymation artist Will Vinton. Notable ads from the museum's archives are featured in an advertising timeline covering nearly 300 years of American social history. It includes the first documented American ad, which ran in 1741 in Ben Franklin's *General Magazine,* and far more modern pitches for products such as Kellogg's Corn Flakes and Volkswagens. Exhibits also illustrate the early practice of celebrities lending their names and faces to product promotions, and the techniques advertisers used to make even the plainest objects seem sexy.

Radio fans will enjoy listening to a tape tracing the history of radio advertising, and TV fans will love the reel of classic commercials dating back to the 1940s. And just about everyone will have fun getting reacquainted with the ads featured in the *All-Time Best Advertising Campaigns* display.

*Hours: Sat noon–5pm or by appointment.*
*Admission charged.*
*Directions: From SE Holgate Boulevard, turn south on SE 26th Avenue.*
    *Drive about five blocks, turn right on SE Raymond Street, follow it*

The famous California Raisins, created by Portland
Claymation artist Will Vinton, strut their stuff

*for two blocks to SE 24th Avenue, and turn left. The museum is in the
gray building on the right. Enter through the silver door at the far end
of the parking lot (Building 2).*

## ■ Children's Museum
3037 SW Second Avenue
Portland, OR 97201
(503)823-2227

The Children's Museum, part of the Portland Parks and Recreation
Department, has been around for almost 50 years, offering kids of all ages
a bright, friendly place to explore and learn about the world they live in.
In the old days the museum was pretty traditional: It sponsored craft
classes, kid-oriented shows, and displays featuring taxidermied animals,
old toys, and Native American artifacts. Back then the exhibits were
behind glass. Now the place is a totally hands-on experience: Kids can
perform delicate "operations" on each other in the medical center, shop
for groceries and ring them up at the market checkout stand, respond to
a raging blaze in a fire truck, or just have a good time in one of the
museum's other pretend worlds. Maybe they just want to whip up a
magical meal in the make-believe bistro: "Will that be extra chocolate in
your double mocha, sir? And a triple order of chocolate-chip cookies?
Good choice!"

Currently the museum fills two buildings in Portland's Lair Hill
Park, just south of downtown Portland, but there's just not enough room
for all the special programs, school groups, and families who want to play.
So in the future, perhaps by the year 2001, the museum will move to the
old OMSI (Oregon Museum of Science and Industry) building in Washington Park, near the Oregon Zoo, the World Forestry Center (see
listing), and Hoyt Arboretum. What more could a kid want?

*Hours: Daily 9am–5pm. The museum is closed to groups on Monday and
    Thursday, making these days less crowded—and quieter.*
*Admission charged.*
*Directions: The museum is just off SW Barbur Boulevard, four blocks
    south of downtown Portland.*

## ■ Kidd's Toy Museum
1301 SE Grand Avenue (inside Parts Distributing; PO Box 14828)
Portland, OR 97212
(503)233-7807

Although Frank Kidd grew up helping run his family's car parts business,
he got interested in toy cars only after he'd already put together a collection of full-size antique autos. Today, Kidd has a toy collection any kid—
and most adults—will envy, but you have to go to his auto parts store to
see it. He used to keep his collection at home, but it grew so large he
began storing it on spare shelves at the store. Now the walls in the busy

Dolls of various occupations at Kidd's Toy Museum

front sales area are filled with toys, and so are the two first-floor offices, an upstairs storage area, and a second storefront across the street—almost 8,000 toys all together. It used to be that only truck drivers, salespeople, and do-it-yourselfers stumbled upon the collection, but now that it's formally incorporated as a museum, Kidd and his staff are handing out bright yellow brochures and booking group tours of Kidd's Toy Museum.

Not surprisingly, the collection features lots of little vehicles: passenger cars, delivery trucks, fire trucks, and several hundred toy motorcycles and dolls dressed in gas station uniforms. But Kidd's toy fascination also includes character toys, police badges from Oregon and Washington, toy ray guns and cap guns, bicycle badges, railroad memorabilia, and more. At the heart of the museum is an exemplary collection of mechanical cast-iron banks, including a model featuring a girl who skips rope when a penny is deposited as well as others shaped like Santa, frogs, dogs, and a large black, red, and yellow Ferris wheel. Kidd hasn't stopped with toys, either; his growing collection now includes several hundred railroad padlocks and an assortment of Portland-area memorabilia.

> *Hours: Mon–Fri 8am–5:30pm, Sat 8am–1pm.*
> *Admission free.*
> *Directions: From downtown Portland, cross the Hawthorne Bridge and turn left on SE Grand Avenue (which is one way). The museum is on the first block with buildings, between SE Madison and SE Main Streets.*

### ■ Lilah Callen Holden Elephant Museum

Oregon Zoo
4001 SW Canyon Road
Portland, OR 97221
(503)226-1561

A museum in a zoo? You bet. These days, zoos care for the planet as well as for living animals; increasingly, their exhibits help visitors understand the connections between the wild animals they're gawking at and the need to protect and preserve the animals' natural habitats. For example, not only does the Oregon Zoo boast the largest breeding herd of Asian elephants outside their native jungles, but it's also home to the only elephant museum in the country.

The Lilah Callen Holden Elephant Museum, right next door to the zoo's elephant house, explains that while today's children most often associate elephants only with the circus, for thousands of years elephants held an important and often revered role in African, Asian, and European cultures. They've served as work animals, as sure-footed transportation, and as main characters in fiction and mythology. Sadly, elephants have also been hunted, almost to extinction, for the ivory from their tusks.

The museum is filled with art, artifacts, and historical displays highlighting the elephant's role both as worker and as cultural icon. There's a circus elephant's giant red tricycle, a large howdah (saddle), and a wide variety of artwork with an elephant theme, including Salvador Dali prints, paintings, and cartoons, and African masks made from beads, cloth, and wood. Jewelry and other items made from ivory tusks are displayed as part of an exhibit on how the now-banned practice of harvesting ivory has affected the worldwide elephant population.

Just one of the stamps in the museum's elephant stamp collection

On a lighter note, the museum has a book containing every elephant stamp ever issued, photographs of the museum's elephant family, and a pile of "Packy Paraphernalia." Born at the zoo in April 1962, Packy was the first elephant to be born in the Americas in almost 50 years, and was featured in *Life* magazine and in enough newspaper articles to fill a big blue scrapbook.

> *Web site: www.zooregon.org*
> *Hours: May 23 to Sept 7: Daily 9am–6pm. Sept 8 to Oct 25 and April 5 to May 22: Daily 9:30am–5pm. Oct 26 to April 4: Daily 9:30am–4pm.*
> *Admission charged.*
> *Directions: The zoo is three miles west of downtown Portland on Highway 26.*

## ■ Oregon History Center
1200 SW Park Avenue
Portland, OR 97205
(503)222-1741

Did you know that had a coin toss ended differently, the "clearing" along the Willamette River now known as Portland would have been named Boston? Back in 1845, the two men with joint claim on the clearing had different opinions about what to name it. Asa Lovejoy, a lawyer from

Oregon Trail covered wagon

Local women taking advantage of one of Portland's Benson bubblers

Massachusetts, thought Boston would be just fine, while Francis W. Pettygrove preferred Portland, in honor of the largest city in his home state of Maine. To settle the debate, they flipped a copper penny. Pettygrove won, and thus Portland was born. The original Portland Penny is now on permanent display in the Oregon History Center's *Portland!* exhibition, which also uses hands-on activities, multimedia displays, and interactive computer stations to explore the city's history, from the arrival of settlers in covered wagons on the Oregon Trail to the way people get around the city now, using light rail and other newfangled modes of transportation.

Another permanent exhibition, in the Hayes Maritime Gallery, features finely crafted models of historic sailing ships, paintings, and artifacts, including memorabilia from the USS *Oregon* battleship. A copy of Oregon Public Broadcasting's video *Exploration by Sea* provides an overview of Oregon's maritime history.

In addition to these permanent exhibitions, the museum offers a wide variety of changing shows that make wonderful use of the 2.5 million items in its photographic archives (prints are available for purchase) and the more than 85,000 items in its artifact collection, which includes everything from a set of 63 handmade miniature historic wagons to a 12,000-year-old sandal and 16th-century maps. Also the headquarters of the Oregon Historical Society, the center houses a library and bookstore on the premises, each stocked with loads of information about state and local history.

Even the two trompe l'oeil murals by Richard Haas on the outside walls of the center's administrative building (the historic nine-story Sovereign Hotel) offer a lesson in Oregon history: One depicts Sacajawea, York, and other members of Meriwether Lewis and William Clark's Corps of Discovery, while the other relates the story of Oregon's early development.

Special programs include workshops for all ages, lectures, concerts, the Wintering-In Harvest Festival on the last weekend in September, and a Northwest authors' party in early December. From mid-July to mid-August, free noontime concerts are presented each Friday on the plaza outside the center.

*Web site: www.ohs.org*
*Hours: Tues–Sat 10am–5pm, Sun noon–5pm.*
*Admission charged. Seniors free Thurs.*
*Directions: The center is on downtown Portland's South Park Blocks, between SW Jefferson and SW Main Streets.*

■  **Oregon Jewish Museum**
2701 NW Vaughn Street,
Suite 715
Portland, OR 97210
(503)226-3600

Founded more than 10 years ago by a local rabbi, the Oregon Jewish Museum didn't secure office space of its own until 1998. Now museum officials are working on cataloging the archives of the Jewish Historical Society of Oregon. Among the hundreds of books in the collection is an account book full of annotated deposits made to Portland's First Hebrew Benevolent Association dating back to October 1882, so it's clear there's more than a century's worth of Oregon Jewish history for this museum to explore.

In addition to the historical society archives, the museum will present traveling exhibits of Jewish art and artifacts from museums across the United States as well as locally generated exhibits focusing on the Jewish experience in Oregon.

**While You're in Portland:**

Out on Sauvie Island, within the 93-acre Howell Territorial Park, the Oregon Historical Society maintains the historic 1858 Bybee House and an Agricultural Museum, adjacent to the Pioneer Orchard, which displays horse-drawn farming equipment and other items donated by area farmers.

*Bybee House/Agricultural Museum, 13901 NW Howell Park Road, Portland, OR 97231; (503)621-3344.*
*Hours: June to Labor Day: Sat–Sun noon–5pm. Closed rest of year. Admission charged. Directions: From Portland, head north on State Route 30, then east over the Sauvie Island Bridge. Follow signs to Howell Territorial Park.*

*Hours: By appointment only.*
*Admission by donation.*
*Directions: From Highway 405, take exit 3 and follow NW Vaughn Street*
   *to NW 27th Avenue. Turn right into the Montgomery Park building.*
   *The museum is on the seventh floor.*

## ■ Oregon Maritime Center and Museum

113 SW Naito Parkway
Portland, OR 97204
(503)224-7724

Berthed on Portland's historic waterfront, the two-story Oregon Maritime Center and Museum explores the city's rich maritime history.
Highlights include a plethora of marine artifacts, photographs, navigational instruments, and ship models from merchant ships and military
vessels to riverboats. Museum librarian Charles Cardinell is (not surprisingly) most proud of the library, which includes a wide variety of photographs portraying maritime life in the Portland area from 1935 to 1975.
How many photographs? Well, more than you'd imagine: The photography collection includes 10,000 packets of negatives taken by Larry
Barber during his stint as a newspaper photographer assigned to the
waterfront.

Beyond the library, Cardinell says many visitors enjoy the working
model of a 1920s–era ship engine; and just about everyone, especially
children, enjoys the unusual collection of ships in bottles. He's more than
happy to explain how the ships get past those narrow bottle necks, but
you'll have to visit the museum to ask him yourself.

While the displays inside this maritime museum are well done, the
seafaring life becomes a bit more real if you cross the street and climb
aboard the outdoor exhibits, which include a Columbia River fishing
boat and the refurbished sternwheeler *Portland,* one of the last operative
steam-powered sternwheeler tugboats in the United States. Visitors can
wander through the *Portland's* main deck (where the cabins were),
through the captain and pilot's quarters, and then up to the pilothouse for
a great view 32 feet above the water.

If you enjoy the sternwheeler tour, you may want to come back and
actually go for a ride on this historic vessel. The museum fires up the
*Portland* and takes passengers out on the water four or five times a year.

*Web site: www.teleport.com/~omcm/*
*Hours: May to Sept: Wed–Sun 11am–4pm. Oct to April: Fri–Sun*
   *11am–4pm.*
*Admission charged; includes admission to sternwheeler.*
*Directions: The museum is on SW Naito Parkway, in Portland's down-*
   *town waterfront area, between the Morrison and Burnside Bridges.*

■ **Oregon Museum of Science and Industry (OMSI)**
1945 SE Water Avenue
Portland, OR 97214
(503)797-4000

When civil engineer Dr. John C. Stevens founded this science museum in 1944, the exhibits filled a house. Now the Oregon Museum of Science and Industry (OMSI) occupies an 18.5-acre site at the east end of the Hawthorne Bridge and encompasses the historic Portland General Electric Turbine Hall, which once generated power for downtown Portland.

On a busy day, enough energy to light all of Portland is likely generated by kids and their parents excitedly exploring the hundreds of interactive exhibits in OMSI's six enormous halls, the OMNIMAX theater, the planetarium, and the naval submarine docked next door. Folks who live in the Portland area will no doubt want to return several times, but out-of-town visitors should pace themselves for a long, exhilarating day. OMSI focuses on five permanent scientific themes.

Physical science and space science are grouped in the Turbine hall. You can build a boat, determine just what kind of structures withstand earthquakes, and create hydropower. Or climb inside an actual space capsule, check your weight on Mars, and visit the Hab Lab, a replica of an astronaut's working and living environments.

Head to the Earth Science section to discover how geology, weather, biology, and other earthly forces work together as a single system. Then inspect the wild, Rube Goldberg–style Recyclotron, a mechanical contraption of chutes and pathways that demonstrates the global impact of everyday decisions about garbage.

Science appeals to visitors of all shapes, sizes, and ages at OMSI

The Life Science hall invites visitors to ponder the wonders of life, from prenatal development to the impact of technology on life-and-death health care choices. At the Chick Hatchery, baby chicks work their way out of their shells. In the Breaking Down Barriers section, able-bodied visitors experience daily tasks from the perspective of folks with physical challenges. And don't overlook two wonders of nature: the two-headed, two-tailed lamb and the ever-popular transparent woman.

The rapidly advancing world of communications technology is tackled in the Information Science area with computers, fax machines, satellite relays, and cellular phones. Explore the Internet at one of the computer workstations, build a simple electronic device in the lab, or send a message to outer space.

There are supervised labs attached to each hall, so if you want to learn more than an exhibit has to offer, you can get a problem-solving kit from the lab.

But wait, there's more! OMSI is home to a five-story OMNIMAX theater; the Murdock Sky Theater, offering multimedia astronomy and laser light shows; and a 219-foot submarine, the USS *Blueback*. There's also a riverfront cafe, a museum store, and a wide range of camps, classes, and field trips, including Submarine Camp-Ins and Creepy Crawly Halloween Camp-Ins.

> *Web site: www.omsi.edu*
> *Hours: Memorial Day to Labor Day: Fri–Wed 9:30am–7pm, Thurs 9:30am–8pm. After Labor Day to before Memorial Day: Fri–Wed 9:30am–5:30pm, Thurs 9:30am–8pm. Closed Mon except for school and national holidays.*
> *Admission charged. There's an extra charge for the OMNIMAX theater and a tour of the USS Blueback.*
> *Directions: From downtown Portland, cross the Morrison or Hawthorne Bridge. Stay in the right lane. Turn right on SE Seventh Avenue, right on SE Clay Street, and left on SE Water Avenue. The museum is straight ahead.*

### ■ Portland Art Museum
1219 SW Park Avenue
Portland, OR 97205
(503)226-2811

Founded in 1892, the Portland Art Museum (PAM) is the oldest fine-art museum in the Pacific Northwest. Designed by the late architect Pietro Belluschi, the museum building comprises three wings and boasts a permanent collection of more than 32,000 works spanning more than 35 centuries of world art, history, and culture. Holdings include sculpture, prints, drawings, photographs, and ethnographic materials.

Be sure to check the current exhibition schedule, because a decade-long program of facility upgrades and expansions has made it possible for

PAM to host the sort of blockbuster traveling exhibitions that in the past often bypassed the Northwest. Almost any exhibition culled from the permanent collection is sure to be a crowd pleaser too.

Highlights of the permanent collection include paintings and sculptures of the Italian Renaissance, European paintings from the first half of the 20th century, and significant European and American paintings and sculpture from the 17th to the 20th century, including works by Monet, Renoir, Degas, Rodin, and Picasso. The museum also has a collection of artworks on paper that documents the history of Western printmaking from the 15th to the 20th century. The works include 19th- and 20th-century British prints from Hogarth to Hockney, French prints from Pissarro to Braque, Mexican prints from Posado to Rivera, and 20th-century American prints from Hartwell to Motherwell. Hundreds of prints from France, Germany, Japan, Scandinavia, and the former Yugoslavia and Czechoslovakia round out the collection.

The Native American collection includes 3,500 works of art by more than 200 indigenous groups and contains a wide range of objects such as masks, drums, rattles, tools, hunting and fishing gear, and elaborate ceremonial costumes and religious items. The museum also has a significant amount of pre-Columbian art and a rich Asian collection that includes Chinese and Japanese art as well as a growing number of Korean

Above: *Le Petit Patisserie* (circa 1922) by Chaim Soutine. Right: *Helen with apples* (1981) by George Segal

artworks. As part of a major renovation and expansion campaign (called Project for the Millennium), PAM has received significant paintings and sculptures by a variety of Northwest artists and a collection of contemporary glass art by Dale Chihuly and others.

In addition to docent-led and audio tours of special exhibitions, the museum offers a wide range of public programs that include lectures, demonstrations, symposia, and special dance and theater performances. Hands-on programs and Family Sundays are popular with both adults and children. And while PAM and the Pacific Northwest College of Art recently severed their formal relationship, the museum continues its association with the Northwest Film Center, which offers classes, workshops, an annual film festival, and film screenings five nights a week. PAM has a nice gift shop and a cafe, and hosts a popular Museum After Hours evening (with great music and food) every Wednesday from 5:30 to 7pm.

> *Web site www.pam.org/*
> *Hours: May to Sept: Tues–Sat 10am–5pm, first Thurs of the month*
>     *10am–9pm. Oct to April: Tues, Thurs–Sat 10am–5pm, Wed*
>     *10am–9pm, first Thurs of the month 10am–9pm.*
> *Admission charged. Two-for-one Thurs 4pm–9pm.*
> *Directions: The museum is on the South Park Blocks downtown, between*
>     *SW Jefferson and SW Main Streets.*

### ■ Portland Police Historical Museum
Justice Center
1111 SW Second Avenue, Room 1682
Portland, OR 97205
(503)796-3019

Real jails and real police stations are often too scary and too busy these days to open their doors to visitors, so the local police historical society sponsors the Portland Police Historical Museum on an upper floor of the Justice Center, the downtown building that also houses several floors of jail space.

Children love this museum, in part because several exhibits, such as the talking mannequin of the crime-fighting, trenchcoat–wearing dog McGruff, are designed just for them. They can spend a few minutes behind the bars of an old city jail cell or pretend they're riding along on a Harley-Davidson police motorcycle complete with sidecar, flashing lights, and crackling police radio.

Kids of all ages will be intrigued by the case of drug paraphernalia and the collection of items left behind by safecrackers, including drills, crowbars, gloves, fuses, blasting caps, and a well-cushioned tiny bottle of nitroglycerin. There's also a small room filled with confiscated weapons, including pistols, shotguns, meat hooks, and a pair of very large and very sharp scissors.

Portland police history is well documented here too, with photos honoring past police chiefs and officers who died in the line of duty as well as an exhibit celebrating some law-enforcement firsts. For example, the first police radio system in the United States was installed in Portland in 1932; and in 1905, when the city hosted the Lewis and Clark Exposition, Portland hired the first policewoman in the nation, Lola G. Baldwin, after learning that many young girls had vanished during previous expositions in the East. Baldwin coordinated volunteers to meet all incoming trains and boats in order to avoid losing young women to Portland's bawdy houses, who sought innocent recruits. She must have done a good job: By 1908 she was superintendent of an entire Women's Protective Division.

*Hours: Mon–Thurs 10am–3pm.*
*Admission free.*
*Directions: The Justice Center is in downtown Portland, near the foot of the Hawthorne Bridge, at SW Second Avenue and SW Madison Street. The museum is on the 16th floor; look for the five-foot-tall neon police badge.*

■ **Stark's Vacuum Cleaner Museum**
107 NE Grand Avenue (inside Stark's Vacuum Cleaner Sales and Service)
Portland, OR 97232
(503)232-4101

They suck—and that's why they're here. In the back corner of this vacuum cleaner store is Stark's Vacuum Cleaner Museum, featuring more than 100 suction-producing cleaning devices.

The earliest models on display are inefficient, hand-pumped contraptions that look sort of like Pogo sticks "or maybe an ice cream cone

Old logo for a Daisy vacuum cleaner

or an early space rocket with handles on it," says the store's Ted Burk. "You'd work hard pumping, but you'd never really pick up any dirt."

Vacuums didn't really get efficient, says Burk, until after 1908. "That's when someone figured out how to attach an electric motor to a hand-operated mechanical model." Later, companies added features such as clutches, headlights, cloth bags, and quick-release dirt traps. To help sell the machines to housewives, vacuums were dubbed with sleek-sounding, sanitizing names such as Silent Air, Cadillac, Cinderella, and Revelation.

As competition revved up, some companies tried to stand out by mixing and matching features. For example, one Filter Queen vacuum on display came with a variety of useful attachments; one's actually a hair dryer that hooks to the exhaust of the vacuum. That same model had attachments that served as a neck vibrator, a clothes dryer, and a de-mother. Another multipurpose model concealed a heavy-duty cleaner inside a footstool, presumably so it would always be handy for those quick cleanup jobs in the den.

In addition to all the vacuums on display, the museum exhibits hand cleaners, vintage carpet sweepers, and electric floor polishers. But most visitors, it seems, are cosmically drawn to the sleek 1960s Halley's Comet Vacuum. This heavy oblong model arrived from the factory spray-painted gold—with a special message for the modern homemaker under the lid that reads: "The age of space, the rocket race, push-button leisure day, be first to clean your jet-set home the Halley's Comet way."

*Hours: Mon and Fri 8am–8pm, Tues–Thurs 8am–6pm, Sat 9am–6pm. Admission free.*
*Directions: From downtown Portland, cross the Burnside Bridge and turn left on NE Grand Avenue. Stark's is on the left.*

### ◼ State of Oregon Sports Hall of Fame
321 SW Salmon Street
Portland, OR 97204
(503)227-7466

Dedicated to Oregon athletes of all sorts, from the folks who created the Pendleton Round-Up in 1910 to modern-day notables in golf, baseball, basketball, auto racing, and other sports, the interactive State of Oregon Sports Hall of Fame features hands-on displays and activities; videos in which inductees discuss sportsmanship, sports ethics, and other issues; and more.

On the Oregon sports timeline, you'll see Terry Baker's Heisman trophy, a football from the 1917 Rose Bowl, a 1939 "bladder" basketball, a 1962 football signed by the Green Bay Packers in the pre–Super Bowl days, an old wooden bowling ball, and lots of trophies, photos, and sports memorabilia. Sports fans can ride on a rodeo saddle, try racing against a wheelchair athlete, or slip on a catcher's mitt in the virtual-reality dugout and feel what it's like to catch a fastball going 90 miles an hour. Other highlights include a life-size statue of Bill Walton wearing his 1977 NBA Championship jersey and a locker room featuring a dozen lockers filled with artifacts and supplies associated with various sports. For example, the skier's locker is filled with skis, boots, and a tube of lip moisturizer, while the swimmer's locker features a swimsuit worn at the 1948 Olympics.

In addition to the permanent exhibits on display, the museum hosts traveling exhibits from sports museums around the country.

*Hours: Tues–Sun 10am–6pm.*
*Admission charged.*
*Directions: The museum is in downtown Portland, on the corner of SW Salmon Street and SW Fourth Avenue.*

## ■ Washington County Museum
Portland Community College (Rock Creek Campus)
17677 NW Springville Road
Portland, OR 97229
(503)645-5353

Exhibits at the Washington County Museum offer a look at life in Washington County from the times of the early Atfalati Indians, through the pioneer settlements of the 1800s, to the county's diverse population today and the recent influx of high-technology companies to the area. "Vintage photographs, artifacts, and our display of clothing from the 1860s to the 1960s tell just part of the story," says curator Barbara Doyle, "so I make sure visitors take a moment to study our *Discovering History* section, which uses photographs, written documents, artifacts, and maps to teach people how to better 'read' history."

In addition to the permanent exhibits, the museum invites local residents to share their own historical collections in the *Our County Collects* display area. "We've had quite a variety," laughs Doyle, "everything from fine china and toys to Red Cross memorabilia and some very rare and expensive light bulbs."

Each May, on the Saturday after Mother's Day, the museum sponsors a draft-horse plowing exhibition. Each August, at the Washington County Fairgrounds, the museum organizes Black Powder Era: 1820–1865, a living-history event during which noted historical figures are remembered and activities from the Native American, fur trade, settlement, and Civil War periods are reenacted. ("Black powder" refers to the powder used to fire early guns.)

*Hours: Mon–Sat 10am–4:30pm.*
*Admission charged.*
*Directions: The museum is on Portland Community College's Rock Creek campus on NW Springville Road, off 185th Avenue, about a mile and a half north of Highway 26 (Sunset Highway).*

## ■ World Forestry Center
4033 SW Canyon Road
Portland, OR 97221
(503)228-1367

If you've forgotten for a moment that trees are the Northwest's and one of the world's most valued natural resource, then have a little chat (in English, French, German, Japanese, or Spanish) with the 70-foot-tall talking Douglas fir in the main exhibit hall at the World Forestry Center. Push a button and this hearty hardwood will explain how to identify a tree's parts and then reveal the secrets of photosynthesis.

Once you've said your farewells to the talking tree, you're ready to explore the many other forest-related exhibits here, including a nice collection of hand-colored antique photographs of various Pacific Northwest trees, displays illustrating logging practices and logging equipment, life-size dioramas documenting the endangered tropical rain forests, and vintage fly-casting rods and other fly-fishing equipment, showing the connection between healthy forests and healthy streams.

Be sure to spend time at the *Forests of Stone* exhibit, which features 54 pieces of petrified wood from Jim Burnett's 600-piece collection. Many of these specimens, weighing from 1.5 ounces to 102 pounds, were found in Oregon and are anywhere from 12 million to 345 million years old. There are some rare finds on display here, most notably the petrified pinecone and the petrified fig branch complete with petrified fruit. In another part of the museum is yet another wooden wonder: a tree trunk that grew around a .22-caliber rifle. Seven inches of the gun's barrel protrude from one side of the 25-inch trunk of this "armed willow," and three inches of the rifle stock stick out the other side.

There's lots more to see inside and much to explore outside too, including the David Douglas Memorial Garden. A Scottish botanist, Douglas visited the Pacific Northwest in 1825 and 1826 in search of new plants for his garden, and all the plants here are species he catalogued on those trips. The Douglas fir, Oregon's state tree, is his namesake.

If you're all fired up about the great outdoors after visiting the World Forestry Center, you may be up for a hike. Just a few steps from the museum are trails leading to the 175-acre Hoyt Arboretum, which offers miles of hiking trails, including the wheelchair-accessible Bristlecone Pine Trail, a hard-surfaced one-mile path.

The center hosts a wide variety of special programs for adults, kids, and families, including guided walks through the center's Magness Memorial Tree Farm (near Wilsonville), shows featuring wood carving and wooden toys, and an annual international Christmas tree festival.

*Web site: www.worldforest.org/~wfc/*
*Hours: Summer: Daily 9am–5pm. Rest of year: Daily 10am–5pm. Open holidays except Christmas.*
*Admission charged.*

*Directions: From downtown Portland, take westbound Highway 26 to the Zoo–Forestry Center exit.*

## PRAIRIE CITY

■ **Dewitt Museum**
Depot Park (PO Box 283)
Prairie City, OR 97869
(541)820-3598 (curator)

From 1891 to 1947, the narrow-gauge Sumpter Valley Railroad hauled logs, gold ore, cattle, passengers, and supplies between Prairie City and Baker City. Now the historic Sumpter Valley railroad depot serves as the home of the Dewitt Museum, featuring 10 rooms filled with memorabilia from Grant County's early days. What sort of things? "From rocks to hatpins, we have it all," boasts curator Babs Brainard. "It's too much to mention. You must tell folks to come see."

Do visit with Brainard, who's lived in these parts a long time and is the person most responsible for making sure the museum is filled with community memories. The collection includes artifacts belonging to early Chinese residents, record-setting deer horns, household items used by pioneers, and tools and other objects relating to the gold rush, ranching, and early Grant County business ventures. Upstairs, in what was once the living quarters for the railroad station agent, are a tack room, a sewing room, and a collection of old washing machines.

*Hours: May 15 to Oct 15: Thurs–Sat 10am–3pm. Closed rest of year. Admission charged.*
*Directions: From Highway 26, turn into Prairie City on S Main Street. Look for the RV PARK AND MUSEUM signs. The museum is in the RV park.*

## PRINEVILLE

■ **A. R. Bowman Memorial Museum**
246 N Main Street
Prineville, OR 97754
(541)447-3715

Built with stone blocks from a local quarry, the former bank that houses the A. R. Bowman Memorial Museum is the only building in Crook County whose interior remains much the same as when it was first constructed. These days the marble counters, bronze teller cages, etched glass, mahogany paneling, and gilt and alabaster chandeliers serve as a classic backdrop for the collection of Native American artifacts, early weapons, gold-mining tools, and railroad memorabilia.

The old bank safe and other original furnishings are part of the exhibits on the first floor, where you'll also find the Hall of History, a chronological walk through Crook County's past. The second floor is filled with a series of re-created rooms, including a dining room, a tack room filled with saddles, an old-time bedroom, a general store, a post office, and a room full of medical tools donated by early area doctors and dentists.

The museum, named for one of Crook County's leading citizens, sponsors a series of history lectures each fall and celebrates Oregon Archaeology Week and Bowman Museum Pioneer Days with special events each September.

*Hours: June to Aug: Mon–Fri 10am–5pm, Sat–Sun 11am–4pm. Sept to Dec, March to May: Tues–Fri 10am–5pm, Sat 11am–4pm. Closed rest of year.*
*Admission by donation.*
*Directions: Follow State Route 26 to Prineville and through town to Main Street. The museum is on the corner of N Main and Third Streets.*

## REDMOND

### ■ Petersen Rock Garden and Museum
7930 SW 77th Street
Redmond, OR 97756
(541)382-5574

More a folk-art wonder than a true museum, the Petersen Rock Garden and Museum is a must-see fairyland for anyone traveling in the area. An indoor museum displays thousands of rock specimens, and it's fun to see the peacocks, ducks, and chickens that strut around the well-manicured grounds. The real draw, however, is Rasmus Petersen's rock sculptures.

Back in 1935, after Petersen established his 300-acre farm, he turned his attention to the yard. First he built a small rockery next to his house and then, as you can surmise from the four acres of whimsical rock sculptures on the property today, his handiwork got, well, totally out of hand.

The farmer-turned-folk artist used rocks to build ornate castles. He made rock ponds and then created rock bridges across them. He assembled miniature rock churches, laid out a rock flag of the United States, and worked with a local sculptor to turn a giant boulder into a replica of the Statue of Liberty. All the petrified wood, agate, jasper, thundereggs, malachite, lava, and obsidian Petersen needed for these projects, he gathered up within an 85-mile radius of his farm. And he never got tired of all the hard work.

Petersen died in 1952, but his family continues to lovingly maintain the museum and gardens.

*Hours: Summer: Daily 9am–6pm (museum), 9am–8pm (grounds). Rest of year: Daily 9am–4:30pm (museum), 9am–dusk (grounds). Open 365 days a year.*

*Admission by donation.*
*Directions: The gardens are seven miles southwest of Highway 97, between Redmond and Bend. Watch for signs along the road.*

## REEDSPORT

### ■ Umpqua Discovery Center
409 Riverfront Way
Reedsport, OR 97467
(541)271-4816

Located in Old Town Reedsport, on the Umpqua River, the Umpqua Discovery Center is actually a great little museum featuring exhibits on local logging history and displays that focus on the land, the water, and the people that shaped the town.

As the phrase "discovery center" implies, almost every changing and visiting exhibit here is kid-friendly and hands-on, from the working weather station to the interpretive displays exploring the area's ocean, beaches, dunes, and forests.

Kids of all ages can use the computer touch-screens to choose among a wide variety of presentations or just scope out the landscape through the periscope. Everyone should try to pick up the 40-pound fabric salmon and imagine what a workday was like for cannery workers who had to handle at least 100 of these on each shift.

> **While You're in Reedsport:**
>
> In downtown Reedsport, on the corner of Third and Water Streets (on the way to the Umpqua Discovery Center), you'll see the giant Smith and Watson Steam Donkey, considered state of the art when it arrived in town back in 1915. Loggers used this steam-driven machine to yard logs from Reedsport's railroad mainline depot to Winchester Creek Canyon. Abandoned in the 1930s, the donkey was used as a shelter by hunters until it was rescued and moved downtown.

Don't be shy about asking the staff to let you choose from the nature videos in the library. While the video's cueing up in the theater, take a good look at the handmade Album Quilt on the wall. Created by the Coast Quilters, the quilt has squares depicting 15 local historic landmarks, including the Umpqua Lighthouse, the sternwheeler *Eva,* and the *Lily,* a sailing vessel built in 1882 that was later bought by MGM for use in *Mutiny on the Bounty.*

*Hours: Summer: Daily 9am–5pm. Rest of year: Daily 10am–4pm.*
*Admission charged.*
*Directions: From Highway 101, turn east on Highway 38. Turn left on Third Street and take the first right, which leads you behind the sea wall to the center.*

■ **Woodville Museum**
First and Oak Streets
Rogue River, OR 97537
(541)582-3088

Located in the stately 1909 Hatch House, the Woodville Museum strives to "depict life as it was." Displays include vintage clothing, old cookware, furniture, glassware, china, historical documents, tools, and Native American artifacts. In among these local memories are two special treasures: a needlepoint portrait of George Washington that's more than 150 years old and a large, ornate Victorian-era hair wreath that is more than 100 years old. The wreath is an intricate tangle of flowers and leaves made from tightly twisted strands of different shades of hair. The frame that holds the wreath is unusual as well. It's made entirely of leather shaped into the forms of leaves and berries.

If you're scheduling a visit to the area, try to arrive in time for the annual Rooster Crow contest, hosted by the museum on the last Saturday in June.

> *Hours: June to Aug: Tues–Sun 10am–4pm. Sept to May: Tues–Sat 10am–4pm.*
> *Admission by donation.*
> *Directions: From I-5, take exit 48 and cross the railroad tracks into town on N Depot Street, which runs into Oak Street. The museum is on the corner of First and Oak.*

ROSEBURG

■ **Douglas County Museum of History and Natural History**
123 Museum Drive
Roseburg, OR 97470
(541)957-7007

With regional and natural history exhibits scattered throughout four wings of a contemporary structure and in the beautifully restored 1882 Dillard, Oregon, and California railroad depot, the Douglas County Museum of History and Natural History offers something for everyone.

Kids might head straight for the Discovery Room, where they can dress up in pioneer clothing, play in the old schoolroom, and eyeball the live king snake and the well-preserved bullfrog.

Upstairs, things are more serious but just as intriguing. The history exhibits display tools used by the Umpqua, Molalla, Cow Creek, and other Native American peoples who first settled the area. Photographs and historical data tell the stories of towns settled by pioneers. You learn, for example, that Oregon Trail pioneer Jesse Applegate named Yoncalla in honor of the Yoncalla Indians. Early artifacts displayed include a rifle used in the Rogue Indian Wars of 1855–56 and a bowl used to carry sourdough starter across the plains in 1852.

The Natural History Gallery is presented as a walk through Douglas County from the Cascades to the ocean, through six ecological and geological areas. Sand dunes, seals, gulls, and shells are featured in coastal dioramas, while a huge Roosevelt elk, bear, owls, and other creatures populate dioramas exploring more wooded areas. You can push buttons in several exhibits to play the sounds of coyotes, owls, and the acorn woodpecker, a bird that gathers acorns and nuts just like a squirrel but stores them in the holes it drills in dead trees or telephone poles.

Elsewhere you'll find a four-horse-team stagecoach and early touring cars, a blacksmith shop, early farming and logging equipment, and a slab of a Douglas fir cut down in 1979 that was almost 20 feet in circumference.

*Web site: www.co.douglas.or.us/museum/*
*Hours: Daily 9am–5pm.*
*Admission charged.*
*Directions: The museum is one mile south of Roseburg. From I-5, take exit 123 and follow the signs to the fairgrounds.*

## SALEM

### ■ A. C. Gilbert's Discovery Village
116 Marion Street NE
Salem, OR 97301
(503)371-3631

Salem native A. C. Gilbert was a world-class athlete and one of the world's greatest toy inventors. Gilbert earned a gold medal for pole vaulting at the 1909 Olympics, earned a doctorate in medicine at Yale University, and received 150 patents for his inventions. He's best known for creating American Flyer trains, Erector sets, Gilbert chemistry sets, and other hands-on educational toys.

During World War I, Congress tried to turn Gilbert's toy factory into a munitions factory. It didn't work. Armed with telescopes, microscopes, and other educational toys, Gilbert appeared before Congress to explain how, without his toys to play with, the country would surely "lose a generation of doctors, engineers, and scientists." His factory was allowed to stay open, and he became known as "the man who saved Christmas."

Today a visit to A. C. Gilbert's Discovery Village is much like a perfect Christmas morning. In a series of five historic houses and a huge outdoor discovery center, kids can immerse themselves in bubbles in the "wet" room or create a racket in the "acoustically outfitted" music room. They can go "spelunking" in a multilevel cave, dig for fossils in a giant sandbox, or set off a chain reaction in a zany Rube Goldberg–inspired contraption.

Outdoor highlights include a giant version of Gilbert's famous American Flyer train, a paddle wheeler, a 50-foot Erector-set tower (the world's largest), kinetic sculptures, a weather station, and a music deck complete with resonating air columns, vibrating plates, and log drums.

Throughout the year, the museum creates a wide variety of special exhibits and offers children's classes and workshops in the sciences, arts, and humanities.

> **While You're in Salem:**
> Several historic homes in Salem are open to the public. Pick up a brochure at the Salem Convention and Visitors Association (1313 Mill Street SE, (800)874-7012) or at the Mission Mill Museum (see listing). The heavily landscaped five-and-a-half-acre Deepwood Estate and the Bush House Museum each have regular daily tours.

The A. C. Gilbert Discovery Village is not only a great place to play with toys but a place that formally honors them. Inaugurated in 1998 with the induction of 11 classic toys, the museum's Toy Hall of Fame recognizes "the creative geniuses of toy makers." So what were the first 11 toys to make it into the Toy Hall of Fame? Gilbert's Erector set was one, of course. Try to guess the other 10. (The answers are printed upside down below.)

*Web site: www.acgilbert.org*
*Hours: March to June: Mon–Sat 10am–5pm, Sun noon–4pm. July to Feb: Tues–Sat 10am–5pm, Sun noon–4pm.*
*Admission charged.*
*Directions: The village is under the Marion and Center Street Bridges in Salem's Riverfront Park. From southbound I-5, take exit 260A (Salem Parkway) and follow the signs to the city center. Turn right on Court Street and follow the HISTORIC SALEM signs to the museum. From northbound I-5, take exit 253 (N Santiam Highway), turn left on Highway 22/Mission Street, and follow Mission to Liberty Street. Turn right on Liberty, turn left on Union, and continue two blocks to the museum parking lot.*

> Barbie, Crayola crayons, Etch-a-Sketch, Legos, Play-Doh, marbles, teddy bear, Frisbee, Monopoly, and Tinker Toys.

- ### Hallie Ford Museum of Art
  Willamette University
  700 State Street
  Salem, OR 97301
  (503)370-6855

With the opening of the Hallie Ford Museum of Art in October 1998, Willamette University created the second-largest art museum in Oregon and the second-largest university-based art museum in the Pacific Northwest. The six galleries showcase items from the sizable collection assembled by the university over the past 100 years: more than 3,000 paintings, prints, drawings, and other works of art, including two important collections of Native American baskets and artifacts. The museum

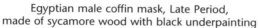

Egyptian male coffin mask, Late Period,
made of sycamore wood with black underpainting

also houses historical photographs of Salem and the Pacific Northwest as well as archival collections of papers and documents on regional artists.

The Carl Hall Gallery of Pacific Northwest and American Art features historical and contemporary art, including work by former faculty members Carl Hall and Constance E. Fowler. The Native American Gallery presents Pacific Northwest and Southwest basketry along with contemporary and traditional Native arts. The General Collections Gallery features European and Asian art and the university's collection of French Barbizon paintings. The Melvin Henderson-Rubio Gallery presents traveling exhibitions, one-person shows by regional artists and current Willamette faculty members, and the annual *World Views* exhibition. Two smaller galleries present works on paper and exhibitions curated by students.

> *Web site: www.willamette.edu/museum_of_art/*
> *Hours: Tues–Sat noon–5pm.*
> *Admission charged. Free Tues.*
> *Directions: The museum is in downtown Salem, one block west of the Willamette University Art Building, across from Willson Park and the Oregon State Capitol.*

## ■ Marion County Historical Museum
260 12th Street SE
Salem, OR 97301
(503)364-2128

Located in Salem's Mission Mill Village, the Marion County Historical Museum includes exhibits about the Kalapuya Indians, boardinghouses, 19th-century health care, the Oregon Trail, and A. C. Gilbert, the Salem-born engineer who invented the Erector set and the American Flyer train (see listing for A. C. Gilbert's Discovery Village).

An exhibit about the lifestyle of the Kalapuya Indians, who lived near the Willamette River in the winter and migrated up and down its tributaries during the rest of the year, features a portion of what is believed to be the only remaining Kalapuya dugout canoe made before 1870.

Since Salem is both Oregon's capital and the home of one of the world's fastest typists, the museum features an exhibit on the typewriter and the changes this machine brought to Salem-area businesses and workplaces. Featured among the vintage typewriters, photographs, and typewriter-related trivia is information about Salem resident Barbara Blackburn. She flunked typing in high school, but at age 62 was listed in the *Guinness Book of World Records* for accurately typing 194 words per minute for 50 minutes on a standard typewriter. She's still using her personal typewriter but promises to donate it to the museum when she's done with it. (Also see next listing for Mission Mill Museum.)

> *Web site: www.open.org/mchs*
> *Hours: Tues–Sat 9:30am–4:30pm.*

*Admission charged.*

*Directions: From I-5, take exit 253 (Highway 22/Mission Street) west and follow the VISITOR INFORMATION signs to 12th and Mill Streets SE. The museum is on the northwest corner of Mission Mill Village.*

■ **Mission Mill Village and Mission Mill Museum**
1313 Mill Street SE
Salem, OR 97301
(503)585-7012

The Mission Mill Village is a bucolic five-acre park housing the Mission Mill Museum, 14 historic structures dating from the days of the earliest non-Native settlers in the Pacific Northwest to the industrial beginnings of Oregon's Willamette Valley.

The historic houses that have been restored and moved to this site include missionary Jason Lee's Methodist parsonage and the Jason Lee House, noteworthy because both were built in 1841, before the first wagon train crossed the Oregon Trail. The Jason Lee House is now the oldest frame house still standing in the Pacific Northwest.

Hand weaving at Mission Mill Village

The Thomas Kay Woolen Mill, founded in 1889 by Thomas Lister Kay, is original to this site and is an example of the many woolen mills that once operated in the Willamette Valley. The mill produced fine woolen blankets and fabrics for more than 70 years and was managed by four generations of the Kay family. Today, descendants of the family own and operate the world-famous Pendleton Woolen Mills.

The mill here is the only woolen-mill museum west of the Missouri River and the only water-powered turbine in the Pacific Northwest that still generates energy from a millrace. The Samson Leffel turbine and a system of pulleys and drive shafts were driven by water power from the Salem millrace and once operated all the mill's machinery. Now the turbine generates electricity for the site and provides a steady rumble to accompany museum visitors as they make their way from the picking and carding stations to the shearing, pressing, and final inspection tables on the fleece-to-fabric mill tour.

At various times throughout the year, costumed interpreters portray pioneers going about their daily tasks throughout the village. A gallery on the second floor of the main mill building features either contemporary textiles or an exhibit on an aspect of pioneer heritage. The museum also hosts an annual speaker series, dances, a full range of textile classes, workshops for all ages and the annual Sheep to Shawl Festival each May. (Also see listing for Marion County Historical Museum.)

*Hours: Museum tours: Tues–Sat 10:30am–3pm. Grounds: Daily 10am–4:30pm.*

*Admission charged for museum tours, but admission to the village is free.*

*Directions: From I-5, take exit 253 (Highway 22/Mission Street) west and follow VISITOR INFORMATION signs to Mission Mill Village at 12th and Mill Streets SE.*

## ■ Prewitt-Allen Archaeological Museum

Western Baptist College Library
5000 Deer Park Drive SE
Salem, OR 97301
(503)581-8600

Robert Allen and curator Dr. J. Frank Prewitt originally created this collection of Egyptian, Greek, Palestinian, and Mesopotamian artifacts as a teaching aid for biblical classes at Western Baptist College. As the Prewitt-Allen Archaeological Museum, it's still great for students but popular with the general public as well, perhaps because of the mummies, biblical-era coins, stones bearing hieroglyphic text, and other items illustrating life and culture in biblical times.

Early writing practices are represented with impressive replicas that include the Rosetta Stone (the monument depicting the famous Code of Hammurabi) and the Black Obelisk of Shalmaneser. There's also an 18th-century Torah and a full-size (24-foot-long) color replica of the Isaiah Scroll from the famous Dead Sea Scrolls.

The items dealing with Egyptian mummification are real, not replicas, and are strangely intriguing. The museum has two genuine Egyptian falcon mummies (circa 1200 B.C.), wrapped in the same manner as the late pharaohs; a falcon-mummy coffin; and an alabaster canopic jar, a vessel designed to hold and protect a deceased person's lungs and other internal organs.

*Hours: Mon–Fri 9am–5pm.*
*Admission free.*
*Directions: From southbound I-5, take exit 253 (Stayton/Detroit Lake). Turn left at the light and drive three-quarters of a mile east to the Lancaster Drive exit. Turn right on Lancaster and follow it for two miles to Deer Park Drive SE. Turn right at the college sign and drive a quarter-mile to the college entrance. The museum is in the library. From northbound I-5, take exit 252 (Kuebler Boulevard), turn right, and follow Kuebler Boulevard three-quarters of a mile to Turner Road. Turn right on Turner, then left on Deer Park Drive SE, and follow it to the college entrance.*

## SEASIDE

### ■ Seaside Museum and Historical Society
570 Necanicum Drive (PO Box 1024)
Seaside, OR 97138
(503)738-7065

In 1806, what is now the Seaside Turnaround was one of the first spots where explorers Meriwether Lewis and William Clark gazed out upon the Pacific Ocean. Clark wrote in his journal that he had "beheld the grandest and most pleasing prospect which my eyes ever surveyed. . . ." These earliest tourists couldn't have imagined that by 1888 the town would already be a major tourist destination, and that later it would sprout game arcades and concessions hawking corn dogs and saltwater taffy.

Lewis and Clark weren't the first to discover this choice spot. The Seaside Museum and Historical Society displays artifacts discovered in a Smithsonian Institution dig that have been dated to 230 A.D. as well as a wide variety of items used by the Clatsop Indians, who lived here long before any explorers or settlers showed up.

From the turn of the century until the mid-1950s, Seaside was a classic beach resort. The museum celebrates old Seaside with pictures from the area's grand old hotels and displays the door from the Seasider Hotel suite John F. Kennedy stayed in on August 3, 1959, just a few years before he became president.

The museum also pays homage to the Daddy Train, the nickname given to the summertime runs of the Astoria and Columbia River Railway. Hordes of dads who worked weekdays in Portland took the train to Seaside on Friday night to spend the weekend with wives and children staying at cottages rented by the season; on Sunday evenings, the dads returned to the city via train. Meeting the Friday night Daddy Train and seeing it off again Sunday night was a summertime tradition. Railroad ridership plummeted after 1937, when the Sunset Highway between Portland and the coast was completed. The last train to Seaside ran in 1952.

The restored Butterfield Cottage, an example of the sort of cottages that were everywhere in Seaside at the turn of the century, is part of the Seaside Museum. The cottage contains a wonderful folk-art treasure: a seashell tower (on a seashell-encrusted table) that features glass windows of different shapes and colors, a hinged door, and little cows, people, sheep, horses, and dogs glued along the ledges. The tower exemplifies the type of handiwork with which wives occupied themselves until the weekend came and their husbands arrived on the Daddy Train.

*Hours: Daily 10:30am–4:40pm.*
*Admission by donation.*
*Directions: From Highway 101, watch for the CONVENTION CENTER*
*sign and turn west on First Avenue. Necanicum Drive will be on your*
*right as you cross the river. Follow the signs to the museum.*

## SILVERTON

### ■ Silverton Country Museum
428 S Water Street
Silverton, OR 97381
(503)873-4766

The Silverton Country Museum is made up of two buildings: a 1908 house and a 1906 Southern Pacific Company train depot, both of which were moved to the banks of Silver Creek to serve as museum structures. The train depot houses a variety of railroad memorabilia, while the house is used to display well-loved community artifacts ranging from souvenir church plates to the first gas pump used in Silverton (around 1910). Exhibits feature classic furniture and period rooms, historical photographs, an early spinning wheel, collections of dolls, marbles, and award-winning wood carvings, and numerous items that came out west via the Oregon Trail. Look for the 1916 Maxwell logging truck, an exhibit honoring the champion Silverton Red Sox baseball team from the 1930s, 1940s, and 1950s, and, out in the gazebo, the stump of the old oak tree that once served as a gathering spot in the center of town.

Each May the town puts on a pet parade and, in the first full weekend in August, hosts Homer Davenport Days, with davenport races and other activities in honor of Silverton political cartoonist and Arabian horse breeder Homer Davenport. Look for his work in the museum.

*Hours: Thurs and Sun 1pm–4pm.*
*Admission by donation.*
*Directions: The museum is next to Old Mill Park, on the banks of Silver Creek, just down the way from the visitors center.*

SPRINGFIELD

■ **Springfield Museum**
590 Main Street
Springfield, OR 97477
(541)726-3677

The Springfield Museum is housed in the town's tallest building: the handsome three-story brick Oregon Power Company substation, built in 1911 and listed on the National Register of Historic Places as a symbol of the industrial age's arrival in a pioneer community.

The building serves as both a museum and a cultural center for the city: the lower Main Street Gallery hosts up to nine art and antiques exhibits each year as well as an annual puppet festival, while upstairs the Historic Springfield Interpretive Center focuses on the history of the area's timber industry, the railroad, the Kalapuya people (the first to call the valley home), early agricultural activities, and historic events in old-time Springfield. There's a hands-on area for kids, a video on the rivers surrounding Springfield, and a CD-ROM about Springfield's history, produced by the local high schools. If you visit on a Friday or Saturday, you'll likely encounter museum greeter Wanda Mountjoy, who'll be happy to show you her favorite part of the museum: the photographs her husband contributed to the exhibit on the hop industry, which flourished around Springfield from 1887 to 1937.

After visiting the museum, be sure to stop at Springfield City Hall, right next door, to see the mosaic replica of the Springfield city seal made of more than 4,200 items former city worker Russell Ziolkowski found in 1972, when he helped jet-clean the city's sanitary sewer system. Included in this wondrous three-foot-wide, 70-pound piece of folk art are a gold nugget, a diamond pin, a tiny revolver, false teeth, a jackknife, coins, clay marbles, and a 1942 dog tag.

*Hours: Wed–Fri 10am–4pm, Sat noon–4pm.*
*Admission by donation.*
*Directions: From I-5, take exit 194A. Head east on Highway 126/I-105 to the City Center exit. Turn right on Pioneer Parkway W and follow the CITY CENTER signs to A Street. Turn left on A Street, right on Sixth Street, and right on Main.*

## STAYTON

■ **Santiam Historical Society Museum**
260 N Second Avenue (PO Box 574)
Stayton, OR 97383
(503)769-1406

The Santiam Historical Society Museum is housed in a 1928 building that was originally the clubhouse of the Stayton Women's Club and later the Stayton Public Library. Now the building welcomes visitors with a large collection of photographs and memorabilia from the towns of Stayton and Sublimity and the Santiam Valley, including a considerable agglomeration of railroad lanterns as well as glassware, toys, tools, medical equipment, and vintage office equipment.

*Hours: Fri–Sat 1pm–4pm.*
*Admission free.*
*Directions: From I-5 (in Salem), take eastbound State Route 22 to*
    *Stayton. Once in town, look for signs pointing to the museum.*

## ST. HELENS

■ **Columbia County Historical Society Museum (St. Helens)**
On First Street, in the Old County Courthouse
St. Helens, OR 97051
(503)397-3868

Housed in the 1906 county courthouse, the Columbia County Historical Society Museum at St. Helens features maritime and logging exhibits, a collection of antique firearms, pioneer artifacts, and a military display.

Among the maritime-related artifacts, look for tools, nails, spikes, and other shipbuilding materials, a sternwheeler wheel, and a huge rudder dredged up from the floor of the Columbia River. The logging exhibit features logging tools, of course, but also hard hats, boots, machinery used in logging operations, and a wide variety of historical photographs.

> **While You're in St. Helens:**
> On summer weekends, be sure to ask at the Columbia County Historical Society Museum for a walking-tour brochure that will lead you through the waterfront historic district. Along the way, you'll encounter volunteers from St. Helens dressed as characters from local history.

The museum also displays a collection of 10 sets of horseshoes in among the saddle and harness exhibit, a wide variety of vintage typewriters and adding machines, 15 lovely crocheted lace throws, a small collection of tea sets, dolls, and other Japanese artifacts, and seven antique long rifles from the late 1800s.

*Hours: Thurs–Sat noon–4pm, Sun 1pm–4pm.*
*Admission by donation.*
*Directions: The museum is on Highway 30, about 30 miles north of Port-*
*land. At St. Helens, turn east off Highway 30 and follow the signs for*
*the historic district, driving about a mile and a half east toward the*
*river. The museum is on the second floor of the old Columbia County*
*courthouse, off First Street in "Olde Towne" St. Helens.*

## SUNNY VALLEY

### ■ Applegate Trail Interpretive Center
500 Sunny Valley Loop
Sunny Valley, OR 97497
(888)411-1846

Known as the southern route of the Oregon Trail, the Applegate Trail was promoted as a safer alternative for early westward-bound pioneers who wanted to avoid the perils of the Columbia River. The earliest settlers to take this route arrived in this area in 1846, and their journey west is portrayed in the Applegate Trail Interpretive Center's exhibits, which feature everything from synchronized sounds, stuffed oxen, and large-format murals to a multiscreen movie starring many local residents.

Museum displays detail the area's growth: from the days before trappers, trackers, and wagon trains arrived, through the changes brought about by the arrival of trains and commerce, and on to other modern developments. Other exhibits depict an early train station and huge oxen pulling wagons over the steep summit of Mount Sexton. The local hotel room in which President Rutherford B. Hayes spent a night is re-created here, along with the Pettingill Store, which served as a newspaper office, post office, printing shop, and general mercantile center.

*Hours: May to Oct: Daily 10am–6pm. Nov to April: Tues–Sun*
*11am–5pm.*
*Admission charged.*
*Directions: The museum is just off I-5, at the Sunny Valley exit (exit 71),*
*about 14 miles north of Grants Pass.*

## THE DALLES

### ■ Columbia Gorge Discovery Center and the Wasco County Historical Museum
5000 Discovery Drive
The Dalles, OR 97058
(541)296-8600

While they're a mouthful to say, the Columbia Gorge Discovery Center and the Wasco County Historical Museum are truly two separate museums in one. As the official interpretive center for the Columbia River Gorge National Scenic Area, the Discovery Center tells the stories of the Native Americans who first lived here, explorers Meriwether Lewis and William Clark, early pioneers, and the development of travel and industry. Other exhibits explore the gorge's geology, wildlife, and foliage. The Wasco County Historical Museum, on the other hand, presents the colorful history of a county that was once the largest in the nation, stretching east all the way to the Rockies. Together these facilities offer a fun (and educational) stop for both kids and adults. There are buttons to push, drawers to pull, knobs to turn, original film footage and photographs to see, and lots of history to experience "firsthand."

In the museum, visitors can create their own cannery labels, board the sidewheeler *Oneonta,* learn how to change a wagon wheel, and discover what life was like for early settlers. For example, while many pioneers risked their lives traveling by raft down the Columbia River, others decided to drive their wagons over the rough Barlow Road and Mount Hood. Visitors can weigh the risks of each route for themselves and decide which route they'd have chosen. In the interactive model of an early 19th-century town, you can listen to news and music "of the day" in the lobby of the Umatilla House or visit the railroad depot and try pumping an antique handcar. Then you can see what the Columbia River looked like when Lewis and Clark stopped here—and what it looks like now. With water and hidden jets, Celilo Falls, Five-Mile Rapids, and the Long Narrows all come to life in a 33-foot-long model of the river from the Deschutes River to The Dalles.

There's plenty to do in the Discovery Center too: A Claymation video takes visitors through 40 million years of geological history, a thunderstorm greets visitors in the pine-oak woods of the natural history exhibit, and Baldy Eagle, the center's mascot, shows up along the way with activities to engage children. An exhibit featuring Native American baskets, trade goods, and tools also offers recorded interviews that acquaint visitors with the cultures of the local Indians. And after trying on hats, goggles, and dusters to experience what travel in the gorge was like in the 1920s, when automobiles first arrived, visitors can try the area's newest form of transportation: windsurfing. A simulator lets visitors stay perfectly dry while seeing what they'd look like skimming across the swells of the Columbia River.

The Discovery Center and the museum are high on a bluff overlooking the Columbia, so don't forget to go outside and walk along the paths that wind through the Oregon Trail Living History Park, where you're likely to meet Oregon Trail emigrants, pioneer settlers, members of the Lewis and Clark expedition, or Native Americans, all going about their daily business.

In addition to all these permanent exhibits, there are films and lectures every day and special programs throughout the year.

*Web site address: www.gorgediscovery.org*

*Hours: Daily 10am–6pm.*
*Admission charged.*
*Directions: From I-84, take exit 82, get on Highway 30, and follow the*
  *signs to the museum.*

■  **Fort Dalles Museum**
   500 W 15th Street
   The Dalles, OR 97058
   (541)296-4547

The Fort Dalles Museum is housed in the last remaining officer's house
of the Fort Dalles military complex, an army post established in 1850 as
Fort Drum. The look of the fort became more Prairie Gothic than Army
in 1856, when new fort buildings were constructed according to plans
adapted from A. J. Downing's 1850 book *The Architecture of Country
Houses.*

Although the only buildings still standing are the gardener's cottage
and the surgeon's quarters (the smallest and least expensive of the four
officer's houses), you'll see evidence of the unusual handiwork that went
into this frontier outpost in the museum's furniture, front-hall cupboard,
and inlaid kitchen cabinet. In the surgeon's quarters, you'll also see
Native American artifacts, Oregon Trail relics, military guns, saddles, early
tools and household items, and photographs of people and places important to the area's history.

The museum grounds include two buildings filled with early automobiles and horse-drawn vehicles as well as three late-1800s buildings
from the Anderson homestead, including a granary, a barn, and the
Swedish-style home built with logs cut by Mr. Anderson and hauled by
horse team to the homestead by his wife. The two-story house is furnished with many original Anderson family heirlooms, including an early
Singer sewing machine, a spinning wheel, and a cream separator.

*Hours: April to Sept: Daily 10am–5pm. Oct to March: Thurs–Mon*
  *10am–4pm.*
*Admission charged.*
*Directions: From I-84, take exit 85 (City Center) onto Second Street. Turn*
  *left onto Union Street and right onto W 15th Street. The museum is*
  *on the corner of W 15th and Garrison Streets.*

TILLAMOOK

■  **Tillamook Naval Air Station Museum**
   6030 Hangar Road
   Tillamook, OR 97141
   (503)842-1130

Housed in an old navy blimp hangar in the middle of Oregon dairyland,
the Tillamook Naval Air Station Museum displays at least one blimp and

more than two dozen privately owned vintage airplanes from around the world, including everything from a 1917 Spad to World War II Warbirds and jets. They aren't just grounded, beat-up old display items, either; most still fly, so it's possible that one or more of them may be roaring overhead during your visit.

The building that houses the museum is perhaps even rarer than any of the planes on display. During World War II, the U.S. Navy built two huge wooden hangars in Tillamook to house eight 250-foot-long blimps assigned to Squadron ZP-33. With a range of 2,000 miles and the ability to stay aloft for up to three days, these "K-ships" patrolled for enemy submarines along the Pacific coast from northern California up to the Strait of Juan de Fuca, escorted convoys in Puget Sound, and trailed targets for fighter-plane practice. According to the museum, the navy was conscientious about maintaining good relations with the community and made quick reparations when a "cow was accidentally 'sandbagged' or a barn cupola damaged by a low-flying blimp."

The two blimp hangars ("A" and "B") were oriented at different angles to accommodate for varying wind conditions, and since steel was in high demand elsewhere during the war, the 1,072-foot-long, 15-story hangars were made of salt-treated, fire-resistant lumber. Unfortunately, Hangar A was destroyed in a 1992 fire, but Hangar B is still listed in the *Guinness Book of World Records* as the largest clear-span wooden structure in the world.

In addition to the P-38 Lightning, the P-51 Mustang, and other vintage aircraft on display, there are photos of the hangars' construction and the blimps that were stationed here as well as uniforms and artifacts from World War II. The museum's theater shows laserdisc videos and documentaries featuring Warbirds and stories from aviation history.

Web site: *www.tillamookair.com*
Hours: *Memorial Day to Labor Day: Daily 9am–6pm. Rest of year: 10am–5pm.*
Admission charged.
Directions: *The museum is two miles south of Tillamook on Highway 101.*

### ■ Tillamook County Pioneer Museum
2106 Second Street
Tillamook, OR 97141
(503)842-4553

The more than 35,000 items belonging to the Tillamook County Pioneer Museum fill three floors and several storage units around town. Plans are under way to secure funds to build a new facility on a five-acre plot outside of town, but for now, the museum's collection is delightfully displayed the old-fashioned way: in just about every nook, cranny, and vault space of an old courthouse building.

Six rooms on the first floor display objects ranging from Tillamook Indian basketry and pioneer clothing to fancy washbasins, glassware, dolls, portraits, and a purple, green, and blue carnival-glass tumbler labeled "Elmer Snook's most prized possession."

Next to the well-stocked pioneer workshop, visitors can peer into a replica of the "stump house" of Joseph Champion, Tillamook's first white settler. When Champion arrived in 1851, he moved into the stump of a big hollow spruce tree he called his "castle." To get an idea of just how big Champion's castle really was, look closely at the picture of the real stump. In the photo, three women stand in the stump's "doorway" with their outstretched hands fingertip to fingertip across the opening.

On the second floor, in the old courtroom, is Alex Walker's wonderful natural history collection. The museum's first curator, Walker had a personal specimen collection of more than 3,200 birds and 1,100 mammals. Taxidermied swans, beavers, wolves, bears, penguins, and even a moose and a bald eagle are given plenty of room. Many of the animals are "posed" in dioramas that show their relationship—as predator or dinner—to others in the animal kingdom. A box displays 46 species of bird eggs, and an exhibit titled *Colors in Nature* gives examples of nature's use of the colors red, blue, yellow, and green, and even the combination of black and white. The "yellow box" contains a Tillamook canary, a yellow Florida sulphur butterfly, a yellow Cuban tropical tree snail, and, from Nevada, a piece of yellow sulphur ore.

Some of the more charming local treasures are down in the basement. One look at the stagecoach used in the North Yamhill and Tillamook Stage Line, which ran from 1906 through 1911 and was advertised as "the cheapest, shortest, quickest, and best" way to travel, and you'll understand why "comfortable" isn't a feature on the list. Moving along, you'll meet a talking Smokey the Bear and see a lumberjack sitting down to a hearty breakfast in "Grandma's Kitchen." There's roomful of washtubs and a display of ocean finds that includes a grass ball created on the ocean floor and a piece of driftwood found on a nearby beach that looks exactly like a two-headed baby dinosaur.

*Hours: March 16 to Sept 30: Mon–Sat 8am–5pm, Sun noon–5pm. Oct 1*
    *to March 15: Tues–Sat 8am–5pm, Sun noon–5pm.*
*Admission charged.*
*Directions: The museum is at the junction of Highway 101 and State*
    *Route 6. It's the large building with the logging donkey out front.*

## Trail

■ **Trail Creek Tavern Museum**
Old Highway 62 (PO Box 144)
Trail, OR 97541
(541)878-2932 (Upper Rogue Historical Society)

Housed in an old tavern, the Trail Creek Tavern Museum features historical photographs, household items, tools, furniture, and clothing that once
belonged to folks in the Upper Rogue Valley. Household items on display
include mangles, washboards, and an intriguing rocking washing
machine. Other exhibits feature pioneer furniture and clothing, a case of
axes and logging tools, shake-cutting equipment, cameras, a door from
one of the area's original homes, guns, fishing poles, and a variety of personal care items.

> *Hours: Memorial Day to Oct: Fri–Sun 10am–4pm. Closed rest of year.*
> *Admission by donation.*
> *Directions: Trail is about 20 miles north of Medford. Heading north on*
>     *State Route 62 from Medford, drive through Shady Cove and look for*
>     *the* Trail *signs. The museum is easy to find in this tiny town; it's*
>     *next to the post office.*

## Union

■ **Union County Museum**
333 S Main Street
Union, OR 97883
(541)562-6003

Maybe you stopped by the *Cowboys Then and Now* exhibit when it was
over in Portland and wondered where Zack and his cowpoke buddies
had wandered off to. Well, it seems they packed up their saddlebags, their
horses, and their chuck wagon and made tracks for Union, a town a bit
more cowboy- and cattle-oriented than bustling Portland.

Put together by the Oregon Beef Industry Council, the *Cowboys
Then and Now* exhibit at the Union County Museum presents a colorful
and accurate journey through the evolution of the American cowboy
and the North American cattle industry. A cowboy timeline accompanies
the exhibit, which features early branding irons, barbed wire, and a tack
room that encourages kids to sit tall in a saddle, ring a cowbell, try on a
few Stetsons, and run their hands through a pair of Angora riding chaps.
Zack's chuck wagon is here too, and Zack (a talking mannequin) is
mighty anxious to tell you how important food was to cowboys, so be
sure to ask to be formally "introduced."

Working cowboys are one thing, but city folks will want to test their
knowledge of box-office buckaroos and scan souvenirs from area rodeos,

A cowboy's dining room

especially the long-running Pendleton Round-Up. And don't forget the cowgirls: Longtime Union resident Ollie Osborn rode the rodeo circuit in the early 1900s, and the museum displays the leather gauntlets she wore as part of her costume.

Other exhibits feature Native American and pioneer artifacts, natural history dioramas, toys, musical instruments, and a series of furnished period rooms, including a turn-of-the-century kitchen, parlor, and bathroom, and an ice cream shop. Logging and agricultural exhibits are outside.

*Hours: Mon–Sat 10am–4:30pm.*
*Admission charged.*
*Directions: From the north, take eastbound I-84 to La Grande, then take southbound State Route 203 to Union. From the south, take northbound I-84 to North Powder, then take State Route 237 to Union.*

## VERNONIA

### ■ Columbia County Historical Society Museum
511 E Bridge Street
Vernonia, OR 97064
(503)429-3713

This is the heart of Oregon logging country, so it's fitting that the county museum is housed in the former mill office of the Oregon American Logging Company. Things at the Columbia County Historical Society Museum are jam-packed but homey, and everything is watched over by a taxidermied moose head, several elk, and a raccoon. Exhibits include a nice rock and fossil collection, Native American artifacts, vintage clothing, historical photographs, and a wide variety of tools used at one time or another on area farms and out in the woods.

Highlights include a chain-saw collection and a wonderful hair wreath made around 1890 from hair donated by Lucy Woods and her friends and relatives.

Be sure to inspect the large 6-by-12-foot scale model of a 1940s logging yard made by Bernard Dowling back in 1957. He spent two years and countless hours making sure everything was just right, even figuring out a way to incorporate gears salvaged from old sewing machines. The model includes two hand-carved log trucks, a six-foot-tall fully rigged spar tree, and tiny carved loggers depicting a whistlepunk, choker setters, hook tenders, splicers, and a little saw filer in the saw-filer's shack. "At one time the model worked," says curator Robb Wilson. "Dowling made the model with a little stream that ran into the river and figured out how to use those sewing machine gears so folks could actually 'yard' and load logs."

> *Hours: Summer: Thurs–Sun noon–4pm. Rest of year: Fri–Sun noon–4pm.*
> *Admission free.*
> *Directions: From Portland, take Highway 26 to northbound State Route 47 and follow it for 14 miles to the center of Vernonia. The museum is near the fire station.*

## WALDPORT

■ **Waldport Heritage Museum**
320 NE Grant Street
Waldport, OR 97394
(541)563-7092

Housed in a former barracks built by the Civilian Conservation Corps in 1941, the Waldport Heritage Museum displays a small but interesting collection of fishing gear, logging equipment, schoolhouse memorabilia, vintage clothing, and kitchenware. Of special interest are the artifacts from the Alsea community (the Native Americans who originally lived along Alsea Bay) and the "tramp art"–style picture frame and thread holder among the items honoring town founder David Ruble. The logging exhibit, appropriately titled *Working Up a Sweat,* includes a drag saw, a crosscut saw, climbing gear, a springboard, an oxen yoke, and a logger's lunch pail.

> *Hours: Sat–Sun 10am–4pm.*
> *Admission free.*
> *Directions: From the stoplight in downtown Waldport on Highway 101, turn east on Highway 34. Drive about four blocks and turn left on*

Broadway, between the market and the hardware store. The museum is three blocks north, on the right, on the corner of Broadway and NE Grant Street.

WARM SPRINGS

■ **The Museum at Warm Springs**
On State Route 26 (PO Box C)
Warm Springs, OR 97761
(541)553-3331

Everything about the Museum at Warm Springs, from the placement and design of the building to the personal stories associated with each item in the collection, is a reflection of the history and traditions of the Confederated Tribes of Oregon's Warm Springs reservation.

Native American saddle and riding accoutrements

Designed to resemble a traditional encampment along Shitike Creek, the building incorporates symbols meaningful to the tribes, such as the drum, dance costume bustles, and patterns from Klickitat baskets. A natural stream leads to the circular stone drum that serves as the museum's entrance, and a curving "stream" of polished slate creates an inviting path to the permanent exhibition.

Spend a few moments watching the introductory video, *According to the Earth,* before starting your museum tour. The film presents a brief history of the different tribes and their lifestyles and introduces tribal elders who speak about the importance of remembering and preserving the tribes' languages and traditions.

Audiotapes of elders telling traditional stories are featured in one pictograph-adorned exhibit area, a 20-minute videotape in the Song Chamber introduces visitors to ceremonial dances and songs, and a word game teaches simple phrases in the dialects of the Warm Springs band, the Wascos, and the Northern Paiutes.

You can't miss the large-scale re-creations of traditional tribal dwellings, including a Paiute wickiup, a Wasco cedar-plank house, and a Warm Springs tepee, each furnished with appropriate tools, food, clothing, and other artifacts. Look closely at the diorama depicting a Wasco wedding scene. The exchange of gifts among the families includes large quantities of food, clothing, cornhusk bags, jewelry, and a horse decked out in fine beaded regalia.

Prize heirlooms, some kept by tribal families for many generations and some reclaimed from private collections, are displayed in a variety of cases throughout the museum. The history of the Confederated Tribes following the arrival of white settlers is illustrated through photographs, handwritten accounts, historical documents, and the remains of the Treaty Oak, the tree that witnessed the signing of the Treaty of 1855 between the tribes and U.S. government.

In addition to the permanent exhibits, the museum features a wide variety of changing shows and hosts annual exhibitions of art by tribe members and by children. Each weekend from Memorial Day through Labor Day, the museum presents live demonstrations ranging from drumming and dancing to hide tanning. Lectures and classes throughout the year explore everything from dancing and storytelling to basket-making and traditional knot tying; there's also a small gift shop.

*Web site: www.tmaws.org*
*Hours: Daily 10am–5pm.*
*Admission charged.*
*Directions: The museum is on State Route 26 in the town of*
  *Warm Springs.*

British Columbia

## ■ B.C. Museum of Mining
(PO Box 188)
Britannia Beach, BC V0N 1J0
(604)896-2233 or (604)688-8735

In the 1920s the Britannia Mines was the largest copper producer in the British empire. By the time it shut down, in 1974, a multiracial work-force of more than 60,000 had produced more than 50 million tons of copper ore. The B.C. Museum of Mining, on Howe Sound at Britannia Beach, presents a down-under tour of the Britannia Mines and a look at mining history in British Columbia.

You enter the museum through one of the restored mine service buildings, view a video presentation on Britannia's history, then don hard hats and follow guides dressed as miners on an extensive tour through the industrial yard and three levels of the mining house—filled with histor-ical exhibits, rare photographs, maps, drawings, rock and mineral displays, and a wide variety of other artifacts—before boarding a train and heading 1,200 feet underground for a look at the mine tunnel. Down there you'll witness a demonstration of old and new methods of drilling, blasting, mucking, slushing, and rock stabilization.

Tour highlights aboveground include the enormous gravity-fed con-centrator building, the giant 235 Super Mine Truck, the geology collec-

Mine site in Britannia Beach

tion housed in a restored assay lab, and—for an added fee—the chance to try the "gold recovery" process firsthand.

> *Hours: May to June, Sept to mid-Oct: Wed–Sun 10am–4:30pm. July to Aug: Daily 10am–4:30pm. Closed rest of year.*
> *Admission charged.*
> *Directions: The museum is on Britannia Beach, on Highway 99 about 32 miles north of Vancouver.*

## BURNABY

### ■ Burnaby Village Museum
6501 Deer Lake Avenue
Burnaby, BC V5G 3T6
(604)293-6500

In 1971, when British Columbia was celebrating its centennial, the Burnaby Centennial Committee decided to build a place where families could come to see what life in BC's Lower Mainland was like in the early 1900s.

Now the 34 buildings in the Burnaby Village Museum offer a "living history" experience: two streets full of replica buildings, historic structures moved here from other locations, and costumed town "residents" eager to chat about days gone by. Stop by the Seaforth School for a lesson in penmanship, chat with the shopkeepers along the main road, find out what the druggist or the Chinese herbalist might have prescribed for that cough, and see what's showing at the movie theater.

Highlights for kids include sundaes at the ice cream parlor and a ride on the restored vintage 1912 C.W. Parker carousel (the "Carry-Us-All"). This carousel (No. 119) was built in Leavenworth, Kansas, and entertained kids of all ages in Vancouver's Hastings Park beginning in 1936. Saved from demolition and the auction block, No. 119 moved to the Burnaby Village Museum in 1993.

Special programs include a Victoria Day weekend to honor Queen Victoria's May birthday, and celebrations to honor Canada Day, BC Day, and Labour Day. Following a tradition begun by the Victorian Order of Nurses more than 60 years ago, each September the museum hosts a "Best Baby in Burnaby" contest.

> *Hours: May 2 to Sept 20, Nov 29 to Dec 23: Daily 11am–4:30pm.*
> *Dec 26 to Dec 29: Daily 5pm–9pm. Closed rest of year.*
> *Admission charged.*
> *Directions: From Highway 1, take exit 33S (Kensington Avenue to Canada Way). Turn right on Sperling Avenue. The museum borders Deer Lake Park.*

## LANGLEY

### ■ Canadian Museum of Flight
216th Street, Unit 200
Langley, BC V2Y 2N3
(604)532-0035

Appropriately located at the Langley airport, south of Vancouver, the Canadian Museum of Flight dedicates itself to collecting, restoring, and preserving aircraft and aviation artifacts, including uniforms, instrument gauges, historical photographs, and assorted parts ranging from propellers to pontoon floats. Among the 23 aircraft on display are a DH82c Tiger Moth, a Bowlus Bumblebee BB1, a Sopwith Camel replica, a Benson Gyrocopter, and something called a Canadian Quickie. Whenever you visit, you'll be able to see planes undergoing reconstruction, but if you're lucky, you'll be on hand when some of the restored aircraft in flying condition get taken out for a whirl.

> *Web site: www.canadianflight.org*
> *Hours: Daily 10am–4pm.*
> *Admission charged.*
> *Directions: From northbound I-5, enter Canada at the Peace Arch and continue as I-5 becomes Highway 99. Turn right on 8th Avenue, then left on 200th Street. At 16th Avenue, turn right, then left on 216th Street. The airport is on your left, just past Fraser Highway. The museum is in Hangar 3.*

## VANCOUVER

### ■ B.C. Sports Hall of Fame and Museum
B.C. Place Stadium
777 Pacific Boulevard S
Vancouver, BC V6B 4Y8
(604)687-5520

When you visit the B.C. Sports Hall of Fame and Museum in B.C. Place Stadium, dress comfortably and be prepared to row a boat, ride a bicycle, and learn a great deal about the history of sports and recreation in this Canadian province.

In the Hall of Champions, photographs, videos, and a bank of touch-screen computers introduce each of the museum's Hall of Famers. Much-heralded disabled British Columbia athletes Terry Fox and Rick Hansen each have a dedicated gallery describing their heroic accomplishments. The History Gallery's *Time Tunnel* offers an entertaining audio and artifact-filled journey through Canadian sports history, from early lacrosse games and rowing clubs to the accomplishments of modern-day athletes in hockey, track and field, and a wide variety of other sports. Video clips from the latest sporting events as well as historical highlights are shown on a giant screen in the Stardome Theater.

Once you've seen the artifacts, learned the history, and watched the athletes in action, you might be ready to join the game. In the Participation Gallery, you can climb a rock wall, work on your fastball, or race against the clock.

Kids will enjoy this museum anytime, but for extra fun call ahead to find out about any scheduled celebrity autograph signings, trophy displays, or special school-break programs.

*Hours: Daily 10am—5pm.*
*Admission charged.*
*Directions: The museum is at Gate A of B.C. Place Stadium, in downtown Vancouver at the east end of Robson Street.*

## ■ British Columbia Golf House Museum
2545 Blanca Street
Vancouver, BC V6R 4N1
(604)222-4653

Located in the original clubhouse on the grounds of the University Golf Club, the British Columbia Golf House Museum celebrates provincial golf history, from the formation of the Jericho Golf Club in 1892 to the advent of golf tournaments broadcast on television.

The museum has an extensive library and six galleries that include an 1895 pro shop, a club room highlighting noted British Columbia golfers and golf tournaments, and a hands-on display where visitors can try out a wide variety of vintage clubs. Other exhibits display golf trophies and golf clothing, detail the development of the wound golf ball and the steel-shafted club, and show videos of Ben Hogan at the 1967 Masters Tournament. "Of special interest," says museum director Dorothy Brown, "is the turn-of-the-century parlor scene we've filled with golf-related items, including a sewing kit with a measuring tape in a container shaped like a little caddy."

*Web site: www.bcgolfguide.com/golfmuseum/index.html*
*Hours: Tues—Sun noon—4pm.*
*Admission by donation.*
*Directions: The museum is at the intersection of W 10th Avenue and Blanca Street, at the University of British Columbia gates, a few miles southeast of downtown Vancouver.*

## ■ Canadian Craft Museum
Cathedral Place Courtyard
639 Hornby Street
Vancouver, BC V6C 2G3
(604)687-8266

Located just beyond the serene downtown courtyard of Cathedral Place is the Canadian Craft Museum, the country's first national museum devoted to crafts. It celebrates Canadian and international craftsmanship and design with at least six major exhibits a year in the Main Gallery and an equal number of smaller exhibits on the Mezzanine Gallery.

While the exhibits focus mainly on contemporary crafts—everything from award-winning pottery, fiber arts, glasswork, and jewelry to basketry, sculpture, and hand-carved wooden furniture made by living craftspeople—the museum will often juxtapose a historical piece from its permanent collection with a newer work to illustrate the long-held traditions that influence contemporary artists.

The museum presents workshops, demonstrations, lectures, and studio visits throughout the year. Gingerbread houses built by Vancouver architects are the highlight of the annual winter holiday craft exhibit and sale.

> *Hours: June to Aug: Mon–Wed, Fri–Sat 10am–5pm, Thurs 10am–9pm, Sun and holidays noon–5pm. Sept to May: Same as summer except closed Tues.*
>
> *Admission charged. Thurs 5pm–9pm by donation.*
>
> *Directions: The museum is in the heart of downtown Vancouver, in the Cathedral Place courtyard, at the corner of W Georgia Street and Hornby Street, just across from the Hotel Vancouver and kitty-corner from the Vancouver Art Gallery.*

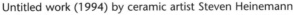

Untitled work (1994) by ceramic artist Steven Heinemann

# ■ Granville Island Sport Fishing and Model Ships Museums
1502 Duranleau Street
Granville Island, Vancouver, BC V6H 3S4
(604)683-1939

Located in the Maritime Market on Vancouver's Granville Island, these two museums celebrate the history of sportfishing and the maritime industry in the Pacific Northwest.

The Sport Fishing Museum contains more than 300 classic and antique reels, including many rare Hardy Silex models; an extensive array of flies, lures, hoochies, and hooks; and fishing-related artwork. The exhibit includes a display of Rufus Gibb's manufactured lures, antique fishing nets, and baskets as well as a mounted 97-pound salmon, the largest salmon caught on a rod and reel. If what you see inspires you, try your luck with large game fish on the fish-fighting simulator.

Over in the Model Ships Museum, you'll find extremely detailed large-scale models of early-1900s ships, including military vessels, sailing ships, coastal working vessels, fishing boats, and international submarines. The museum is especially proud of its 13-foot, 700-pound model of the HMS *Hood*, built over a period of 18 years by Rodney Henriksen.

*Web site: www.sportfishingmuseum.bc.ca*
*Hours: Tues—Sun 10am—5:30pm.*
*Admission charged. One admission fee grants you access to both museums.*
*Directions: Granville Island is at the south end of the Granville Street*
*Bridge, which connects downtown Vancouver with Kitsilano and the*
*Granville South district. From northbound Highway 99, turn left on*
*Broadway, then turn right at Hemlock Street, the next major intersec-*
*tion. Stay to the left beside the bridge on-ramp, and follow the signs to*
*Granville Island.*

Wooden fishing tackle box

## ■ Museum of Anthropology
University of British Columbia
6393 NW Marine Drive
Vancouver, BC V6T 1Z2
(604)822-3825 (recorded message)
(604)822-5087 (tours)

Housed in a spectacular award-winning building overlooking the mountains and the sea, the Museum of Anthropology at the University of British Columbia houses more than 30,000 cultural objects and 200,000 archaeological specimens from cultures throughout the world.

While boasting a fine 600-piece collection of 15th- to 19th-century European ceramics in the Koerner Ceramics Gallery, the museum is best known for its collection of totem poles, boxes, sculptures, and other objects created by the aboriginal peoples of coastal British Columbia. While epidemics of smallpox devastated the population, livelihood, and culture of the Northwest First Nations in the late 19th century, more than 170,000 First Nations people now live in urban areas and on government-established Reserve communities within ancestral territories. These First Peoples maintain a complex social and ceremonial life, and the artistic traditions on display are still relevant to their culture.

> ### While You're on the UBC Campus:
> The M. Y. Williams Geological Museum, on the first floor of UBC's Geological Sciences Center (6339 Stores Road; (604)822-2449), features spectacular displays of thousands of rocks, minerals, and fossils. Of special interest to kids and dinosaur fans is the 80-million-year-old Lambeosaurus, mounted on the wall just inside the door.
>
> *Hours: Mon–Fri, 8:30am–4:30pm. Admission free. Directions: Same as the Museum of Anthropology.*

You'll want to start your visit in the Great Hall, which features cedar-plank boxes, huge bowls and dishes used in feasts or potlatches, and impressive groupings of large pole sculptures from the Central Coast Salish, Kwakwaka'wakw (Kwagiutl), Haida, and other tribes. Many of these sculptures, emblazoned with frogs, bears, beavers, and humanlike figures, once formed parts of cedar-plank homes occupied by First Nations families. While some pieces served as posts supporting roof beams, others were purely decorative. The specific meanings of many of the figures are not known today, but the images on the sculptures generally represent family ancestors and powerful beings associated with a home's residents.

Just beyond the Great Hall, you'll find masks and temporary exhibits in the Theater Gallery and, in the Masterpiece Gallery, delicate smaller carvings of creatures depicted on larger sculptures elsewhere in the museum. While some of these objects are contemporary creations, most

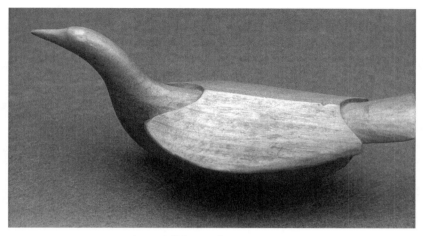

Coast Salish wooden mat creaser

Haida and Tsimshian red cedar totem poles in the museum's Great Hall

date from the 19th century and use bone, ivory, horn, and fine metals in addition to wood.

The Rotunda Gallery features work by acclaimed Haida artist Bill Reid, most notably his large carved yellow-cedar work, *The Raven and the First Men*. This piece portrays the moment in Haida history when the wise and mischievous Raven found the first humans in a clamshell on the beach and coaxed them into venturing out.

Speaking of venturing out, you'll definitely want to step outside the museum to explore the grounds, which include several carved totem poles, an outdoor sculpture garden, and a Haida House complex showing you the types of structures that would have been present in a 19th-century Haida village. (Whether or not you enter the museum, you can enjoy the totem poles and the breathtaking views from here.)

Don't leave the museum, however, without spending some time in the unusual Visible Storage area. Most museums can't display everything in their collections and end up storing thousands of objects in inaccessible areas like basements. But the Museum of Anthropology stores more than 14,000 objects in a way that's accessible to visitors—in cabinet after cabinet full of glass-topped drawers. Objects are grouped by cultural origin, but every drawer holds a delightful surprise.

The museum makes good use of its Great Hall, with its abundant natural light and 50-foot glass walls, for concerts, theater and dance performances, lectures, and other special programs.

> Web site: www.moa.ubc.ca/
> Hours: Mid-May to Aug: Tues 10am–9pm, Wed–Mon 11am–5pm. Sept to mid-May: Tues 10am–9pm, Wed–Sun 11am–5pm.
> Admission charged. Free Tues 5pm–9pm.
> Directions: The museum is on the University of British Columbia campus, a few miles southeast of downtown Vancouver.

### ■ Pacific Space Centre
1100 Chestnut Street
Vancouver, BC V6J 3J9
(604)738- 7827

Got a craving for the cosmos? Thinking about sending the kids "straight to the moon"? Then pack up the shuttle and blast off for the Pacific Space Centre. This fun-filled "space attraction" offers multimedia theater presentations about Mars and beyond, talks on space exploration and astronomy, and loads of hands-on exhibits, space artifacts, videos, and, of course, out-of-this-world interactive computer games.

Highlights include a full-motion flight simulator, which takes brave voyagers on a lifesaving mission to Mars, and Ground Station Canada, where experts not only let you see and hear the latest from space but also explain what it all means. Flight suits and other personal items used by astronauts in the Apollo program are displayed along with an actual moon rock in the Cosmic Courtyard, where computer games let you morph yourself into an alien, dock the shuttle on the international space station, and plan a voyage to Mars.

After you've unraveled some of the mysteries of the universe, you can go next door to the Gordon MacMillan Southam Observatory and, if the weather is clear, take a free look at the sky through the telescope. Or you can make an appointment to visit with the folks who work at the Canadian Space Resource Centre, the regional office of the Canadian Space Agency.

Many of the center's programs and presentations are offered at regular times during the day. Ask about special evening lectures and the schedule of the evening laser shows, set to rock music.

*Web site: pacific-space-centre.bc.ca*
*Hours: Tues—Sun 10am—5pm.*
*Admission charged.*
*Directions: From downtown Vancouver, cross the Burrard Street Bridge. The museum is in Vanier Park on Chestnut Street.*

## ■ Vancouver Art Gallery
750 Hornby Street
Vancouver, BC V6Z 2H7
(604)662-4719 (recorded message)
(604)662-4700

The Vancouver Art Gallery (VAG) occupies an imposing turn-of-the-century building that once served as a provincial courthouse. Designed in 1907 by architect Francis Rattenbury, who also designed the landmark Empress Hotel in Victoria, the building features impressive Greek columns, two stone-cut lions, and a central interior rotunda topped by a copper-sheathed dome.

*Indian House Interior with Totems* (1912) by Emily Carr

The VAG mounts an ambitious program of more than 20 changing exhibitions each year, but it's best known for its collection of the work of Emily Carr (1871–1945), a native of Vancouver Island and British Columbia's best-known artist. She traveled throughout northern British Columbia documenting First Nations totem poles, the lives of Native peoples, and the lush coastal rain forests. The gallery owns the world's most extensive collection of Carr's paintings and drawings, and space on the third floor is devoted permanently to an exhibition of work by Carr, her contemporaries, and artists influenced by her.

The VAG, which has one of the largest acquisition budgets in Canada, also has a growing permanent collection of contemporary art by local and Canadian artists, as well as a collection of European and North American masters, including works by Pablo Picasso and Canada's Group of Seven. The permanent collection also includes modern British painting, 17th-century Dutch painting, American art of the 1960s, and modern Quebec painting.

Throughout the year the VAG offers lectures, gallery talks, workshops, open studios, concerts, and monthly family-oriented "SuperSuns" featuring workshops, classes, and performances. The museum also has a lovely cafe and a large gift shop.

*Web site: www.vanartgallery.bc.ca/info/info.htm*
*Hours: Mon–Wed and Fri 10am–6pm, Thurs 10am–10pm, Sat*
*    10am–5pm, Sun noon–5pm.*
*Admission charged.*
*Directions: The museum is in downtown Vancouver, between Georgia and*
*    Robson Streets.*

■ **Vancouver Maritime Museum**
1905 Ogden Avenue
Vancouver, BC V6J 1A3
(604)257-8300

Located in Vanier Park (also the home of the Vancouver Museum and the Pacific Space Centre, see listings), the Vancouver Maritime Museum features programs and exhibits highlighting maritime history, art, culture, and technology that will appeal to both landlubbers and old salts.

Visitors can board and explore the restored *St. Roch*, a schooner built in 1928 as a supply ship for the isolated Arctic detachments of the Royal Canadian Mounted Police. In 1944 the *St. Roch* traveled the northerly route of the Northwest Passage from east to west, and became the first ship to do so in both directions. In 1950, after the vessel was retired, it was sent to Halifax by way of the Panama Canal. This voyage made the *St. Roch* the first ship to circumnavigate North America.

Too small to board, but just as intriguing, are the ships in the extensive model ship collection, which includes lead cast models used in World War II training, a replica of the *Bluenose,* a toy submarine built by an eight-year-old boy, and a Chinese barge carved from ivory. The *Model-mania* exhibit also includes a model made from pork and beef bones by prisoners of war at Porchester Castle in England in 1798.

Sailors can't get far without charts, and more than 200 years ago Captain George Vancouver and the crews of the *Chatham* and *Discovery* took on the task of charting Canada's Pacific coast. An exhibit paying tribute to the captain's work includes 18th-century navigational and survey equipment such as sextants, telescopes, compasses, and replicas of the detailed charts.

By popular demand from kids and their parents, the museum has reinstalled portions of the highly successful *Pirates!* exhibit, including the pirate ship *Shark,* a treasure chest, pirate weapons, pirate costumes, and pictures that tell the story of pirates around the world. Kids will also enjoy the Maritime Discovery Center, which offers young sailors a chance to pilot a full-scale tugboat replica, observe port activity through high-powered telescopes, visit a model maker at work, and dress up in fishermen's workday oilskins.

For an up-close look at a variety of heritage vessels in their natural habitat, visit the museum's Heritage Harbour. Notable vessels displayed or

1798 bone model of *Le Vengeur du Peuple,* built from pork and beef bones by prisoners of war

berthed in the harbor have included the schooner *Maple Leaf,* a crash rescue boat, and the historic seiner *BCP 45,* once featured on Canada's $5 bill.

In addition to the changing fine art and other exhibits in the Finning Gallery, the museum hosts workshops, lectures, festivals, and programs to celebrate such events as Canada Day and Oceans Day.

> *Web site: www.vmm.bc.ca*
> *Hours: Victoria Day (third Monday of May) to Labour Day (first Monday in Sept): Daily 10am–5pm. After Labour Day to day before Victoria Day: Tues–Sun 10am–5pm.*
> *Admission charged. Seniors free Tues.*
> *Directions: From downtown Vancouver, cross the Burrard Street Bridge. The museum is in Vanier Park at the north end of Chestnut Street, where False Creek opens to English Bay.*

### ■ Vancouver Museum
1100 Chestnut Street
Vancouver, BC V6J 3J9
(604)736-4431

Located in Vanier Park, at the south end of the Burrard Bridge, the Vancouver Museum chronicles the cultural diversity and history of Vancouver and the Lower Mainland.

Start your visit in the Orientation Gallery, with its grand view of the city—and display cases in the shape of mountain formations that mirror the city's natural environment. Then follow one (or all) of the three historical pathways on the Timeline Wall. The *World Timeline* features an extinct passenger pigeon and objects from around the world, while the *City Timeline* traces Vancouver's history with photos and objects that include relics from the great fire of 1886 and souvenirs from Expo '86 (1986, that is). The whimsical *Toy Timeline* covers 100 years of playthings and includes dolls, a multistoried playhouse, a turn-of-the-century magic lantern projector, and other fun stuff. An exhibit on the city's settlement features a replica of a ship's passenger berth, a trading post, and a re-created Edwardian parlor.

The museum was founded in 1894 and records show that the first donation it received was a stuffed trumpeter swan. Now it has extensive collections in natural history, archaeology, ethnology, and Asian arts, including a Chinese compass from the 4th century B.C., 750,000 shells, and an Egyptian mummy acquired in 1922 and only recently put back on display.

The museum is part of the planetarium complex and features a cone-shaped roof reminiscent of the hats worn by Coast Salish people. The *Crab Fountain* out front, by George Norris, is a futuristic vision of the creature the First Nations people believed to be the keeper of the harbor behind the museum.

*Web site: www.vanmuseum.bc.ca*
*Hours: Tues–Sun 10am–5pm.*
*Admission charged.*
*Directions: From downtown Vancouver, cross the Burrard Street Bridge. The*
   *museum is in Vanier Park on Chestnut Street.*

## ■ Vancouver Police Centennial Museum
240 E Cordova Street
Vancouver, BC V6A 1L3
(604)665-3346

Some of this museum's exhibits might be a bit grisly for very young kids, but most everyone else will likely find this museum—dare we say it?—very arresting.

Founded in celebration of Expo '86, the museum has a large collection of department-issued firearms and unusual weapons seized from crooks. Other exhibits feature counterfeit currency and evidence from actual crime scenes. Visitors can learn about infamous crimes, such as the case of the man who tried to murder his wife by putting arsenic in her chocolate milk shakes, and see exhibits that re-create more "successful" crimes. The museum also has a large collection of police artifacts, historical photographs, and a coroner's forensic exhibit.

*Web site: www.city.vancouver.bc.ca/police/museum*
*Hours: May to Aug: Sun–Fri 9am–3pm, Sat 10am–3pm. Sept to April:*
   *Sun–Fri 9am–3pm.*
*Admission charged.*
*Directions: The museum is on the corner of Main and E Cordova Streets*
   *in downtown Vancouver, near the Main Street police station.*

## VANCOUVER ISLAND (SIDNEY)

## ■ British Columbia Aviation Museum
Victoria International Airport
1910 Norseman Road
Sidney, BC V8L 5V5
(250)655-3300

The British Columbia Aviation Museum is dedicated to the history of aviation in Canada, with a special emphasis on British Columbia history. On display you'll find aircraft, engines, airplane models, aviation artifacts, and, in the Memorial Room, items from the wars in which Canadians fought, as members of either the Royal Canadian Air Force, the Royal Flying Corps, or the Royal Air Force.

Aircraft on display include a Gibson Twin Plane, a replica of the first aircraft designed and flown in Canada back in 1910; an Eastman Sea Rover, used for gold mining and exploration in the 1930s; and a Bristol

Bolingbroke MK IV, a front-line combat aircraft and training plane during World War II.

*Web site: www3.bc.sympatico.ca/bcam/index.htm*
*Hours: April to Oct: Daily 10am–4pm. Nov to March: Daily 11am–3pm.*
*Admission charged.*
*Directions: From Victoria or Sidney, take Highway 17 to the airport exit on*
    *McTavish Road. Follow the signs to the museum entrance, on your left*
    *off Canora Road.*

## Vancouver Island (Victoria)

### ■ Art Gallery of Greater Victoria
1040 Moss Street
Victoria, BC V8V 4P1
(250)384-4101

Housed in an 1889 mansion tucked into Victoria's historic Rockland district, the Art Gallery of Greater Victoria features six exhibition halls filled with works by North American and European artists, contemporary Canadian artists, and traditional and contemporary Asian artists.

Drawing on touring shows and on its permanent collection of more than 15,000 works of art, the museum presents more than 30 exhibitions a year. On permanent exhibition are works by Emily Carr, a king-size dollhouse, the only authentic Shinto shrine outside of

Right: 14th-century Chinese stone Buddha head. Below: *Above the Gravel Pit* (1936) by Emily Carr

Japan, a 14th-century Buddha head, and the city of Victoria's Ming dynasty bell, weighing in at almost a ton.

Special programs include films, tours, art classes, and lectures by artists and curators.

*Web site: carver.pinc.com/aggv/*
*Hours: Mon–Wed, Fri–Sat 10am–5pm, Thurs 10am–9pm, Sun 1–5pm. Admission charged.*
*Directions: From Government Street in downtown Victoria, take Fort Street east to Moss Street and turn right.*

## ■ Craigdarroch Castle
1050 Joan Crescent
Victoria, BC V8S 3L5
(250)592-5323

Robert Dunsmuir was a Scottish immigrant who made a vast fortune from Vancouver Island coal. Of course, the richest man in British Columbia needed a grand place to live, so in 1887, Dunsmuir commissioned a mansion to be built on a hill overlooking Victoria. The majestic 39-room Craigdarroch Castle (it means "rocky oak place" in Gaelic) took three years to finish; only the finest woods are used on the interior and the highest-quality granite, marble, and sandstone on the exterior. The castle has a huge dance hall, rare wood-paneling and parquet-flooring designs, and one of North America's finest collections of residential art nouveau stained- and leaded-glass windows.

Obviously, only the best was good enough for Dunsmuir. The irony is that Dunsmuir never got to live in the castle—he died shortly before construction was completed. But his wife, Joan, did move in and lived there until her death in 1908.

Since then, the castle has had quite a life. In 1909 it was sold to an accountant who subdivided the 28-acre estate into residential lots and then raffled off the castle among the folks who purchased the lots. Afterward, the castle served as a military hospital, a college, and a music conservatory before being refurbished in 1979 as a historic house museum.

As you tour the home, note that the stained-glass window in the smoking room on the first floor sports the image of Sir Walter Raleigh, the man who introduced tobacco to Europe. On the second floor, a guest bedroom has been turned into a mini-museum for Victoria College, which used the castle as its campus from 1921 to 1946.

During December the castle is dressed in its holiday finest and special programs are offered, including music, dance, theater, and storytelling.

*Web site: www.vicsurf.com/attracti/castle.htm*
*Hours: June 15 to Labour Day: Daily 9am–7pm. After Labour Day to June 14: Daily 10am–4:30pm.*
*Admission charged. If you arrive by taxi, show your receipt for a discount.*

*Directions: From Victoria's Inner Harbour downtown, take Government Street south to Fort Street, and follow Fort to Joan Crescent.*

## ■ Maltwood Art Museum and Gallery
University of Victoria
(PO Box 3025)
Victoria, BC V8W 2Y2
(604)721-8298

Located on the University of Victoria campus, the Maltwood Art Museum and Gallery has a vast collection of objects, images, and texts. Artwork is scattered around the campus and featured in two main exhibition spaces.

The University Centre Gallery has several changing shows each year and one long-running exhibit featuring items from the permanent collection arranged by theme. For example, an Olive Oyl doll is one of the items displayed in the Arts and Leisure section, while early Iranian bronze swords are part of Arts and War.

Many of the exhibits draw from the university's Katherine Emma Maltwood collection, which ranges from Oriental ceramics, costumes, and rugs to 17th-century English furniture, Canadian paintings, and Mrs. Maltwood's own sculptures. The museum also owns a variety of items illustrating the growth and development of the international Arts and Crafts movement.

Exhibitions featuring work by local artists, students, and faculty are featured in the McPherson Library Gallery and change every four to six weeks.

*Web site: www.maltwood.uvic.ca*
*Hours: University Centre Gallery: Mon–Fri 10am–4pm, Sun noon–4pm. McPherson Library Gallery: Open whenever the library is open; call (604)721-8228 for a recorded message of current library hours.*
*Admission free.*
*Directions: From downtown Victoria, follow Johnson Street north as it becomes Begbie Street and then Shelborne Street. Turn right on McKenzie Avenue, which leads to the university. The University Centre Gallery is in the University Centre building.*

## ■ Maritime Museum of British Columbia
28 Bastion Square
Victoria, BC V8W 1H9
(250)385-4222

First, a couple of nonmaritime details about the grand 1889 provincial courthouse that houses the Maritime Museum of British Columbia: The building is allegedly haunted, and it's serviced by the oldest continually operating open-cage elevator in North America.

1918 photo of the *Princess Sophia* stranded on Vanderbilt Reef
(she later sank here)

Of course, the real attraction here is the colorful story of British Columbia's maritime history, told in galleries whose themes range from early exploration to Captain Cook, Canadian Pacific steamships, and the Royal Navy.

On the first floor, learn about European exploration, the "Age of Sail," fishing, whaling, and the daring adventures undertaken by a variety of yachtsmen and navigators. On display is the *Trekka,* the 20-foot yawl John Guzzwell used in 1955 to sail around the world in just over four years, as well as the more primitive *Tilikum,* the carved dugout canoe in which Captain John Voss set out from Victoria in 1901 in his quest to circumnavigate the globe.

On the second floor are exhibits about tugboats and barges, displays on the British naval presence in the Pacific Northwest, and models that provide a glimpse back to the elegant era of passenger steam liners. This floor also has a section honoring Captain Cook, the explorer who began charting British Columbia's waters while searching for the elusive

Northwest Passage. Look for the two rare antique globes in this exhibit, which map what was known of the world after Cook's voyage.

The museum hosts lectures, children's programs, workshops, and films in the restored vice admiralty courtroom.

*Web site: mmbc.bc.ca*
*Hours: July and Aug: Daily 9:30am–7:30pm. Sept to June: Daily*
  *9:30am–4:30pm.*
*Admission charged. The Web site has a two-for-one coupon.*
*Directions: The museum is in the center of downtown Victoria, four blocks*
  *north of the Empress Hotel. Drive north on Government Street, past*
  *Fort Street, to Bastion Square.*

### ■ Royal British Columbia Museum
675 Belleville Street (PO Box 9815 Stn Prov Govt)
Victoria, BC V8W 9W2
(800)661-5411 or (250)387-3701

Founded in 1886, the Royal British Columbia Museum promotes itself as "one of the best museums in the world!" Could be. For sure, it's one of the best in North America, offering three huge galleries that showcase the human and natural history of British Columbia.

The Natural History Gallery takes visitors from the last ice age into the coasts, forests, and marine environments of today. Here you'll find a variety of animals, including a huge woolly mammoth, a grizzly bear, a blue heron, a cave lion, and a musk ox. This floor also features the *Open Ocean* exhibit, which takes you on an imaginary 30-minute underwater voyage with films based on the dives Otis Barton and William Beebe made in the Atlantic Ocean in 1930. You can also visit a live tidal pool and get up close and personal with sea anemones, starfish, and other creatures of the sea.

On the third floor, the impressive First Peoples Gallery includes the ceremonial Jonathan Hunt House, named for the late Chief Kwakwabalasami of Fort Rupert and built by members of his family, who maintain the rights to ceremonial use of the house. The house, totem poles, masks, and a remarkable collection of artifacts combine to relate the diverse stories and experiences of British Columbia's First Nations.

The Modern History Gallery follows the growth of British Columbia from the 1700s through the 1970s. Here you'll find a replica of the stern section of Captain George Vancouver's ship, the HMS *Discovery* (1792–94), as it may have looked during its stay in Nootka Sound. You'll also see a water wheel used in a gold mine to pump water and hoist ore buckets (and miners) to the surface, a pioneer family homestead, a saloon, a railroad depot, and the sort of shops, services, and household appliances that became commonplace with the rise of British Columbia's industrial society.

Model of Native American totem pole and village

In addition to the permanent exhibits, the museum features special touring exhibits and the National Geographic Theater, with an IMAX movie screen six stories high.

*Web site: rbcm1.rbcm.gov.bc.ca*
*Hours: Daily 9am–5pm.*
*Admission charged.*
*Directions: The museum is at the corner of Belleville and Douglas Streets, close to both the Parliament Buildings and the Empress Hotel in downtown Victoria.*

## ■ Royal London Wax Museum
470 Belleville Street
Victoria, BC V8V 1W9
(250)388-4461

Where would kings, queens, princes, wizards, and dukes all be hanging out these days? Only at a place like the Royal London Wax Museum, where King George III, Queen Victoria, Prince Charles, the Wizard of Oz, John Wayne, and Elvis keep company with more than 300 life-size wax figures displayed in theatrical settings.

If you feel a bit uneasy here, it may be because the museum uses human hair, medical glass eyes, and a secret formula of chemical compounds and beeswax to make the figures seem almost alive. Or it may be because the art of wax sculpture was perfected during medieval times, when wax was used to create the death masks of monarchs and other important figures for display on funeral tombs and crypts. Or because, before she opened her popular Parisian "wax salon" and London wax museum, Madame Tussaud had the job of making death masks from the heads of French aristocracy as they rolled from the guillotine.

Keeping with Victoria's "little bit of old England" theme, the Royal London Wax Museum imports wax figures from London and offers visitors a whirlwind tour of history, fantasy, horror, and ideology that ranges from the educational to the downright creepy. Gallery exhibits range from *Royalty Row,* with sculptures of Queen Elizabeth, Prince Charles, and Princess Diana, to *Storybook Land,* featuring Gepetto's toy shop, the Mad Hatter's tea party, and a sleeping—and breathing!—Snow White. In the *Galaxy of Stars,* you can visit with Charlie Chaplin, Marilyn Monroe, Superman, Elvis, and the *Gunsmoke* cast. But think twice before venturing into the *Chamber of Horrors,* home of the guillotine, "the rope," and the rack.

*Web site: www.waxworld.com*
*Hours: May 11 to Sept 2: Daily 9am–7:30pm. Sept 3 to Dec 31: Daily*
*    9:30am–6pm. Jan 1 to May 10: Daily 9:30am–5pm.*
*Admission charged.*
*Directions: The museum is on downtown Victoria's Inner Harbour, across*
*    from the Parliament Buildings.*

## WHITE ROCK

## ■ White Rock Museum and Archives
14970 Marine Drive
White Rock, BC V4B 1C4
(604)541-2222

The city of White Rock gets its name from a large white rock down on the beach. According to local legend, a sea god's son fell in love with a Cowichan Indian maiden, but both fathers disapproved of the match.

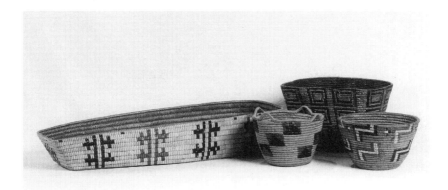

Four Native American baskets from the museum's collection

The sea god's son picked up the big white rock and threw it across Georgia Strait; then he and the Cowichan princess followed the rock to begin a new life and a new tribe.

The White Rock Museum and Archives, housed in a 1912 Great Northern Railway station, doesn't have any firsthand accounts of that early rock-throwing event, but the museum's archives and collection of artifacts do a fine job of documenting the early lifestyles of the area's First Nations people and the history of the city's pioneer settlers. Most of the exhibits feature artifacts, photographs, and other items taken from the museum's own eclectic collection. "For example," museum director Kathleen Tsang says, "we have a great collection of Salish baskets, a wonderful photograph collection, and a small wooden writing desk with glass inkwells and a velvet top that calls to mind the era when people would travel by train and actually write letters home. We also have an early metal prosthetic leg that came from the collection of an early White Rock doctor."

*Hours: Daily 10am–4pm.*
*Admission free.*
*Directions: From Highway 99, take the White Rock exit and head west along Marine Drive.*

# Index